Do You Love Your Mo...

- Art: Meicha
- Original St...
- Character Design: Iida Pochi.

This book is a work of fiction. Names, characters, places, and incidents are the product of the author's imagination or are used fictitiously. Any resemblance to actual events, locales, or persons, living or dead, is coincidental.

- Translation: Andrew Cunningham
- Lettering: Phil Christie

TSUJYOU KOUGEKI GA ZENTAI KOUGEKI DE NIKAI KOUGEKI NO OKASAN WA SUKI DESUKA? Vol. 2
©Meicha 2019 ©Dachima Inaka 2019 ©Iida Pochi. 2019
First published in Japan in 2019 by KADOKAWA CORPORATION, Tokyo.
English translation rights arranged with KADOKAWA CORPORATION, Tokyo through TUTTLE-MORI AGENCY, INC., Tokyo.

English translation © 2019 by Yen Press, LLC

Yen Press, LLC supports the right to free expression and the value of copyright. The purpose of copyright is to encourage writers and artists to produce the creative works that enrich our culture.

The scanning, uploading, and distribution of this book without permission is a theft of the author's intellectual property. If you would like permission to use material from the book (other than for review purposes), please contact the publisher. Thank you for your support of the author's rights.

First Yen Press Edition: December 2019

Yen Press is an imprint of Yen Press, LLC.
The Yen Press name and logo are trademarks of Yen Press, LLC.

The publisher is not responsible for websites (or their content) that are not owned by the publisher.

- Yen Press
  150 West 30th Street, 19th Floor
  New York, NY 10001

- Visit us at yenpress.com
  facebook.com/yenpress
  twitter.com/yenpress
  yenpress.tumblr.com
  instagram.com/yenpress

Library of Congress Control Number: 2019941096

ISBNs: 978-1-9753-8745-7 (paperback)
978-1-9753-8656-6 (ebook)

10 9 8 7 6 5 4 3 2 1

WOR

Printed in the United States of America

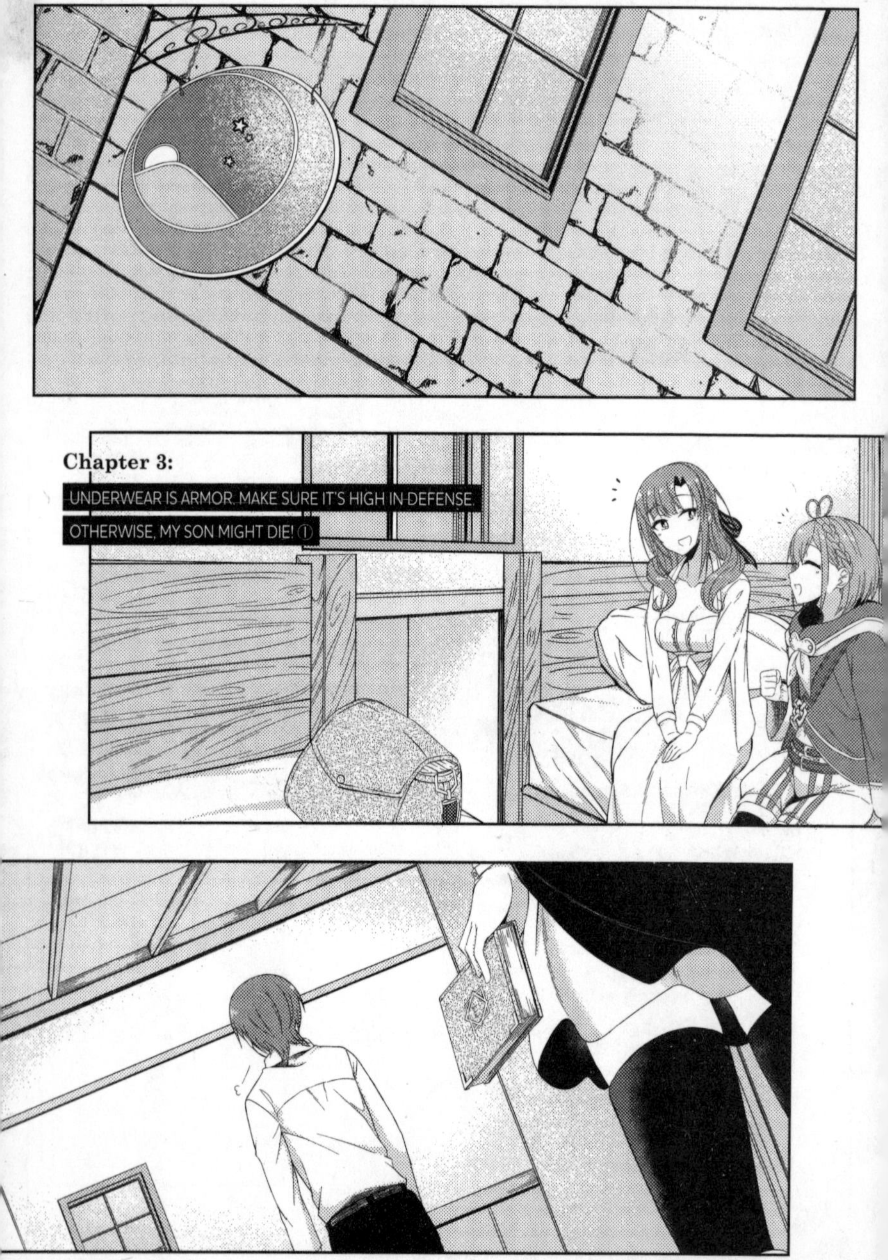
Chapter 3:
UNDERWEAR IS ARMOR. MAKE SURE IT'S HIGH IN DEFENSE.
OTHERWISE, MY SON MIGHT DIE! ①

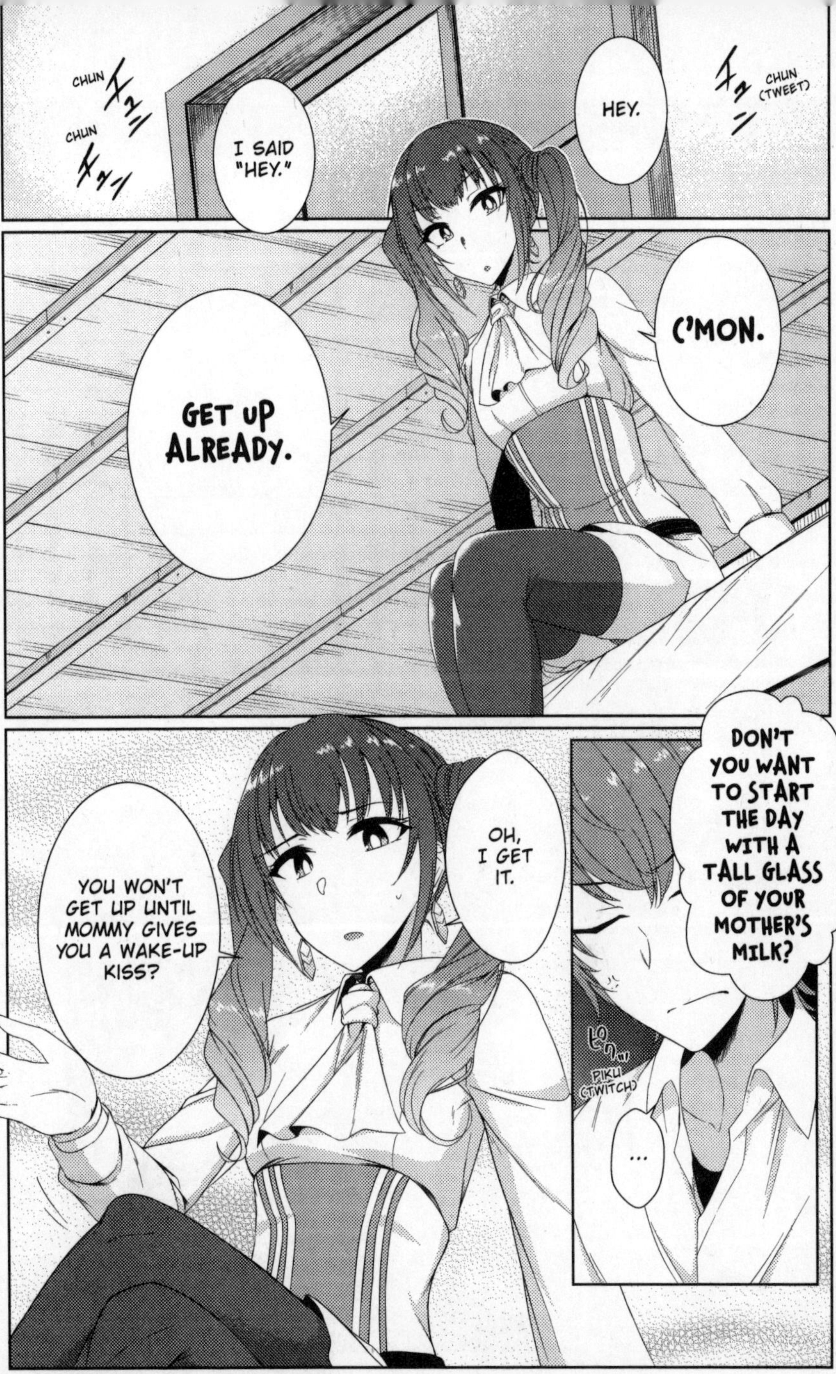
CHUN (TWEET)
HEY.
I SAID "HEY."
CHUN
CHUN
C'MON.
GET UP ALREADY.
DON'T YOU WANT TO START THE DAY WITH A TALL GLASS OF YOUR MOTHER'S MILK?
PIKU (TWITCH)
...
OH, I GET IT.
YOU WON'T GET UP UNTIL MOMMY GIVES YOU A WAKE-UP KISS?

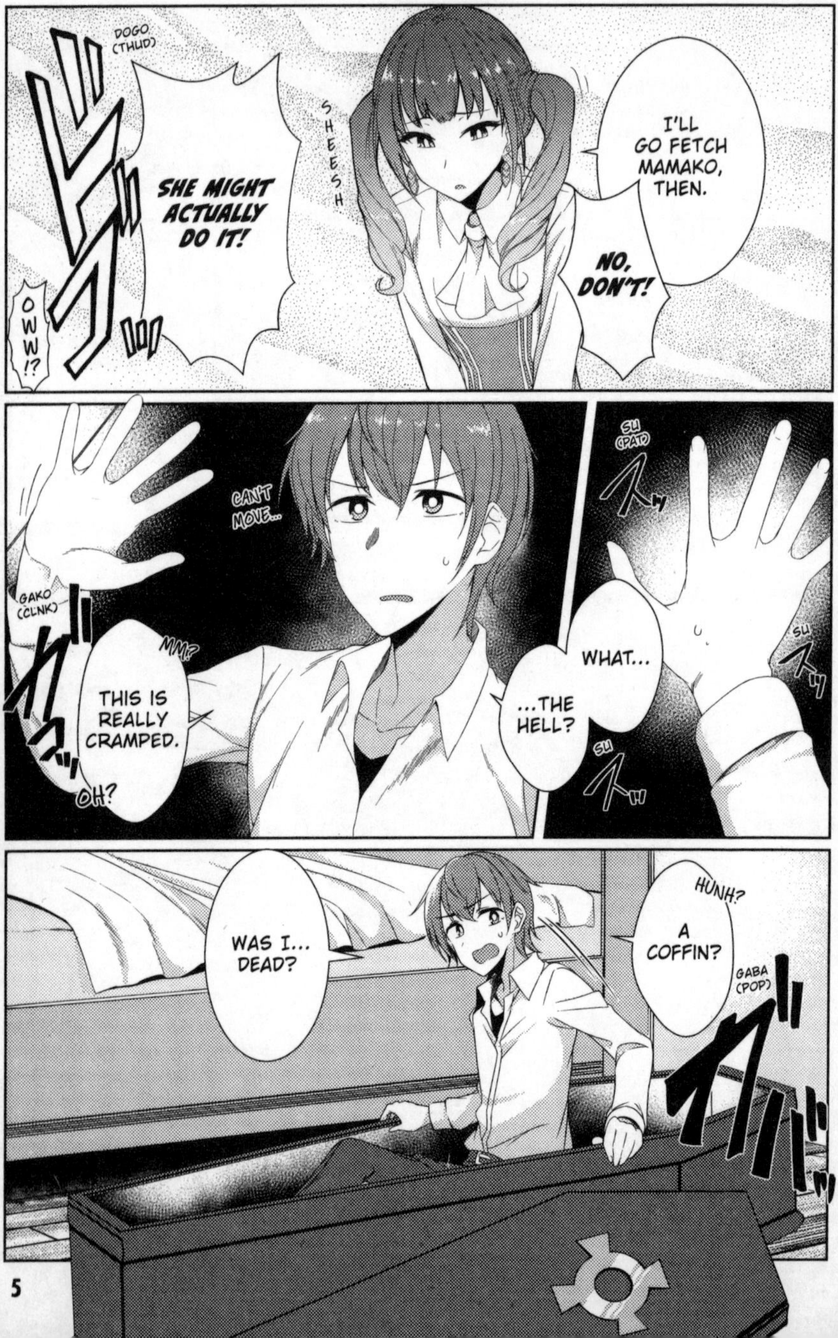
I'LL GO FETCH MAMAKO, THEN.
NO, DON'T!
SHEESH
SHE MIGHT ACTUALLY DO IT!
DOGO (THUD)
OWW!?
SU (PAT)
WHAT...
...THE HELL?
SU
SU
CAN'T MOVE...
MM?
THIS IS REALLY CRAMPED.
GAKO (CLNK)
OH?
HUNH?
A COFFIN?
GABA (POP)
WAS I... DEAD?

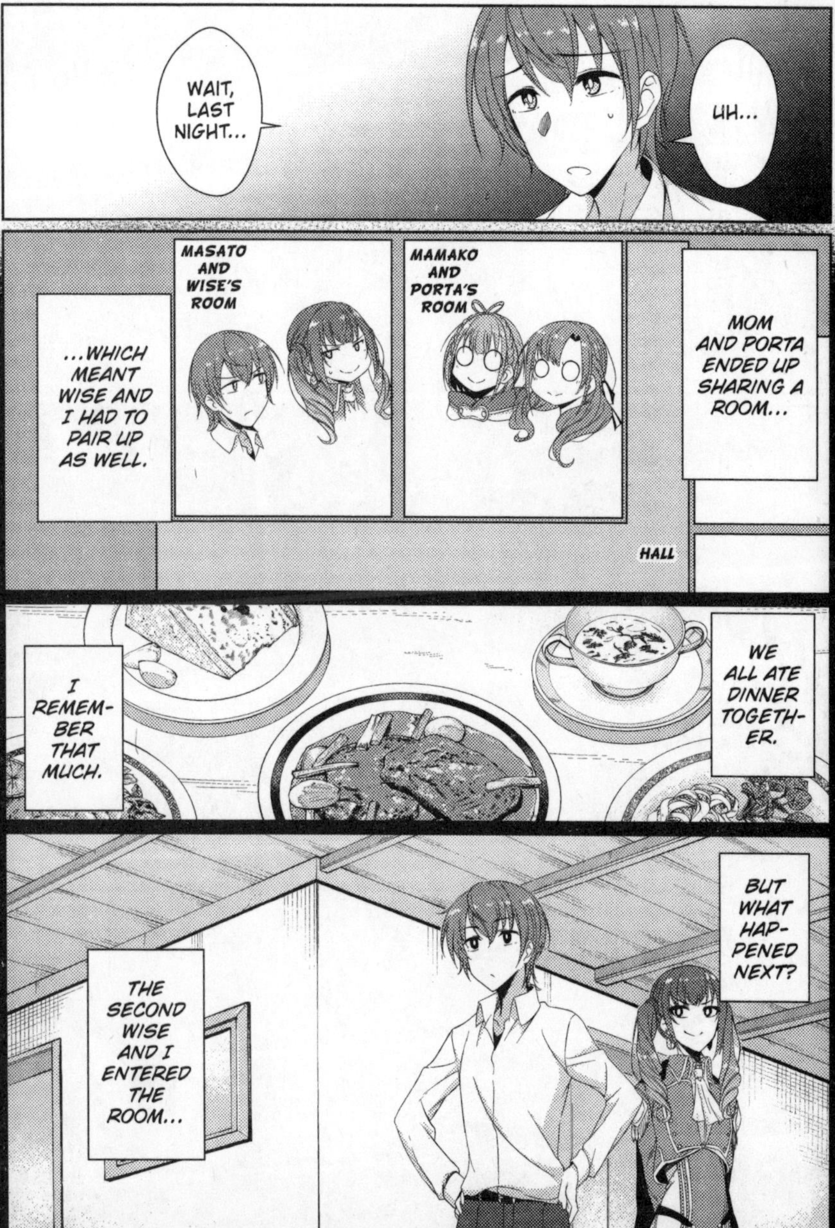
UH...
WAIT, LAST NIGHT...
MOM AND PORTA ENDED UP SHARING A ROOM...
MAMAKO AND PORTA'S ROOM
MASATO AND WISE'S ROOM
...WHICH MEANT WISE AND I HAD TO PAIR UP AS WELL.
HALL
WE ALL ATE DINNER TOGETHER.
I REMEMBER THAT MUCH.
BUT WHAT HAPPENED NEXT?
THE SECOND WISE AND I ENTERED THE ROOM...

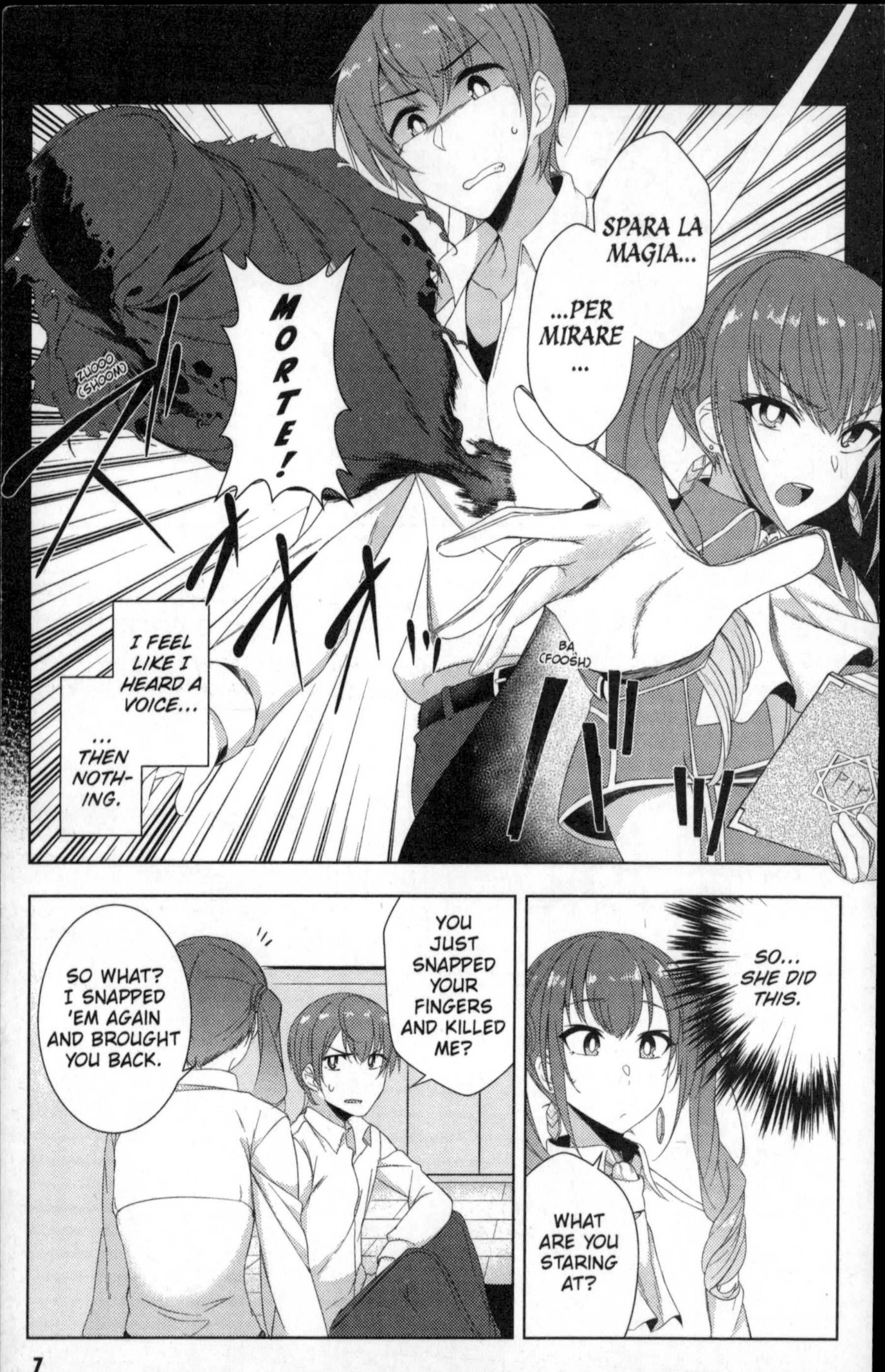
SPARA LA MAGIA...
...PER MIRARE ...
MORTE!
ZUOOO (WHOOSH)
I FEEL LIKE I HEARD A VOICE...
... THEN NOTHING.
BA (FOOSH)
SO... SHE DID THIS.
WHAT ARE YOU STARING AT?
YOU JUST SNAPPED YOUR FINGERS AND KILLED ME?
SO WHAT? I SNAPPED 'EM AGAIN AND BROUGHT YOU BACK.

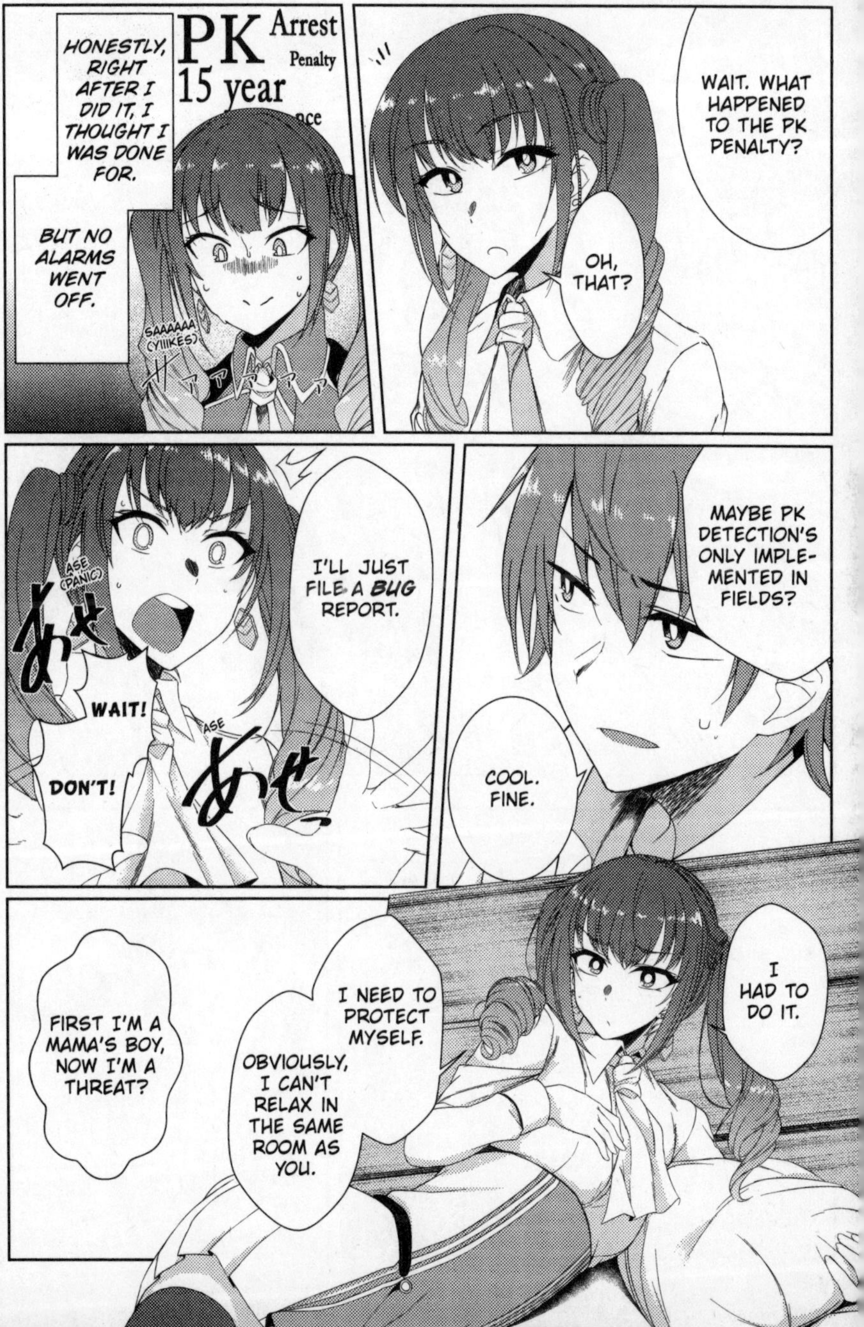

WAIT. WHAT HAPPENED TO THE PK PENALTY?
OH, THAT?
PK
Arrest
Penalty
15 year
HONESTLY, RIGHT AFTER I DID IT, I THOUGHT I WAS DONE FOR.
BUT NO ALARMS WENT OFF.
SAAAAAA (YIIIKES)
MAYBE PK DETECTION'S ONLY IMPLE-MENTED IN FIELDS?
COOL. FINE.
I'LL JUST FILE A BUG REPORT.
ASE (PANIC)
あせ
WAIT! DON'T!
ASE
あせっ
I HAD TO DO IT.
I NEED TO PROTECT MYSELF.
OBVIOUSLY, I CAN'T RELAX IN THE SAME ROOM AS YOU.
FIRST I'M A MAMA'S BOY, NOW I'M A THREAT?

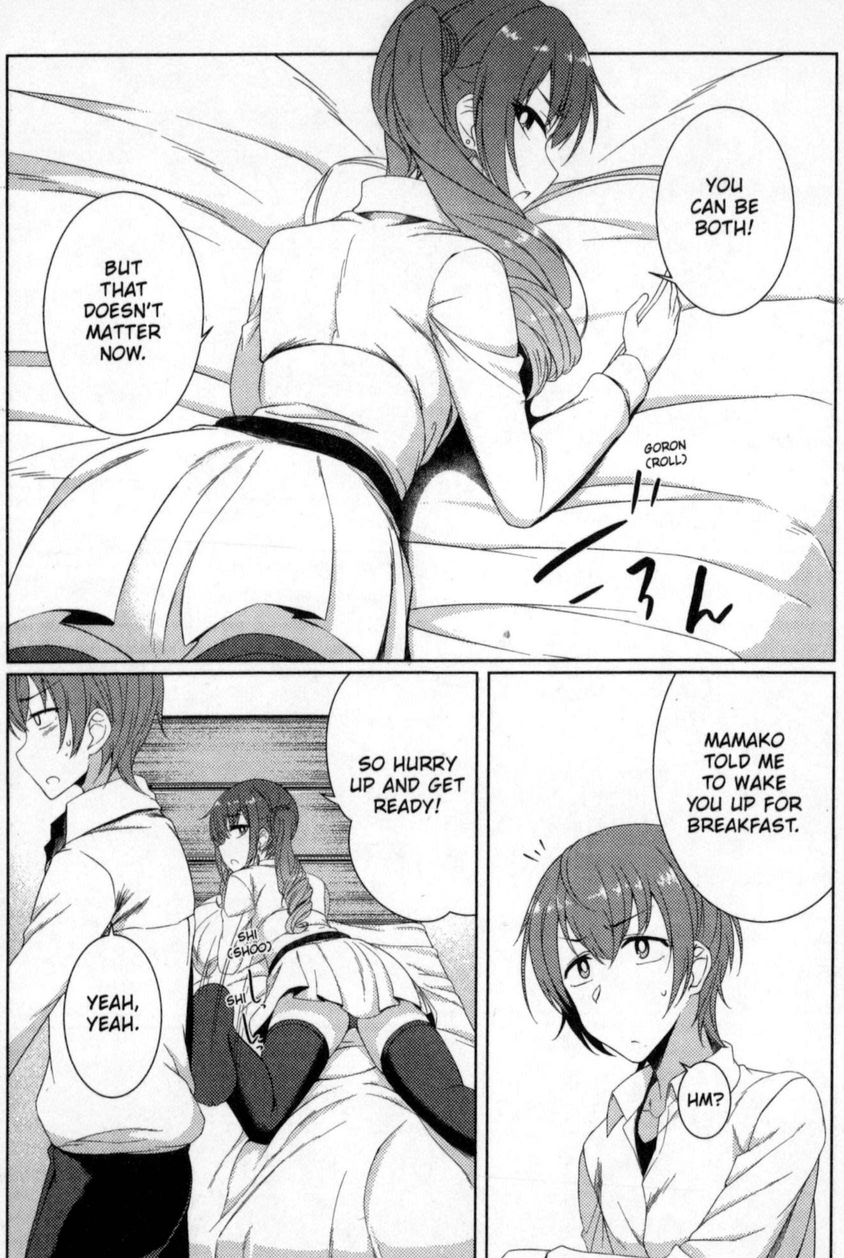
YOU CAN BE BOTH!
BUT THAT DOESN'T MATTER NOW.
GORON (ROLL)
ごろん
MAMAKO TOLD ME TO WAKE YOU UP FOR BREAKFAST.
HM?
SO HURRY UP AND GET READY!
SHI (SHOO)
SHI
YEAH, YEAH.

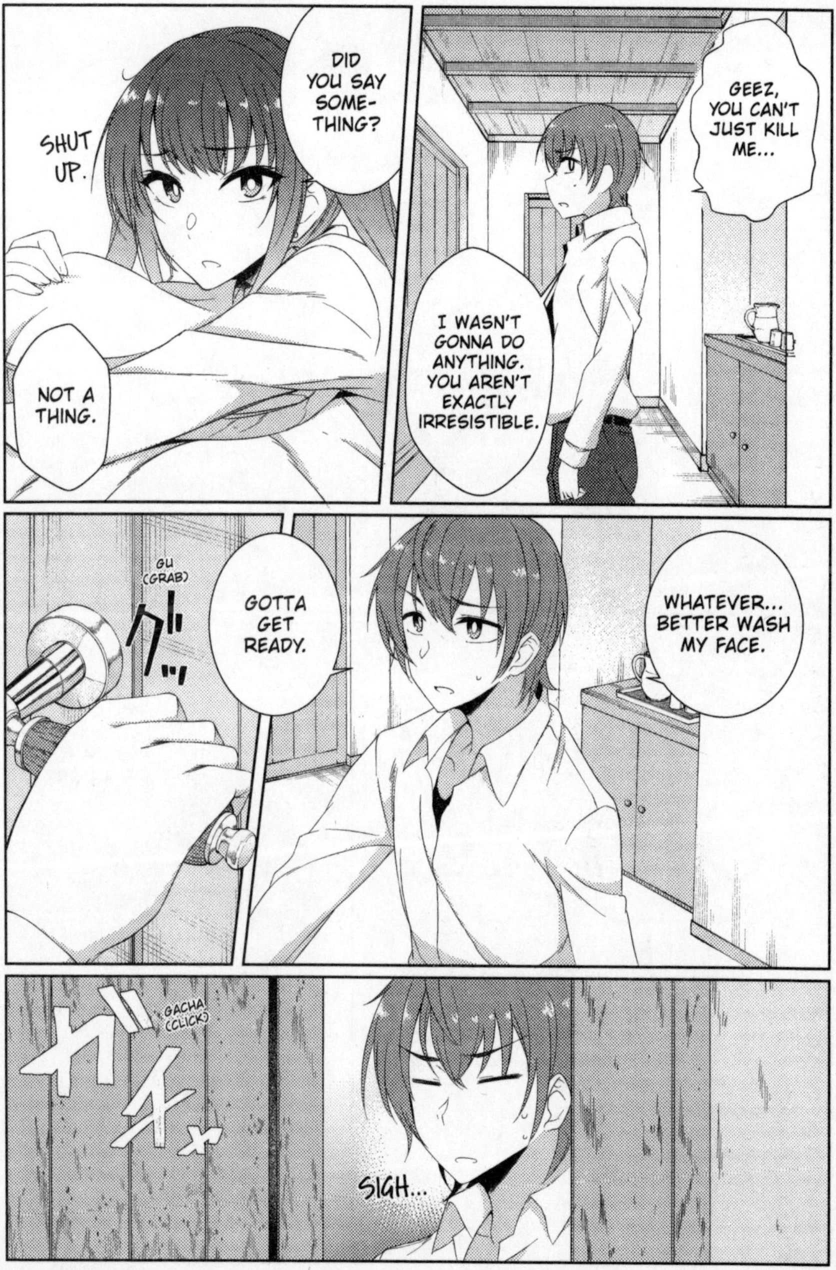
GEEZ, YOU CAN'T JUST KILL ME...
I WASN'T GONNA DO ANYTHING. YOU AREN'T EXACTLY IRRESISTIBLE.
DID YOU SAY SOME-THING?
SHUT UP.
NOT A THING.
WHATEVER... BETTER WASH MY FACE.
GOTTA GET READY.
GU (GRAB)
SIGH...
GACHA (CLICK)

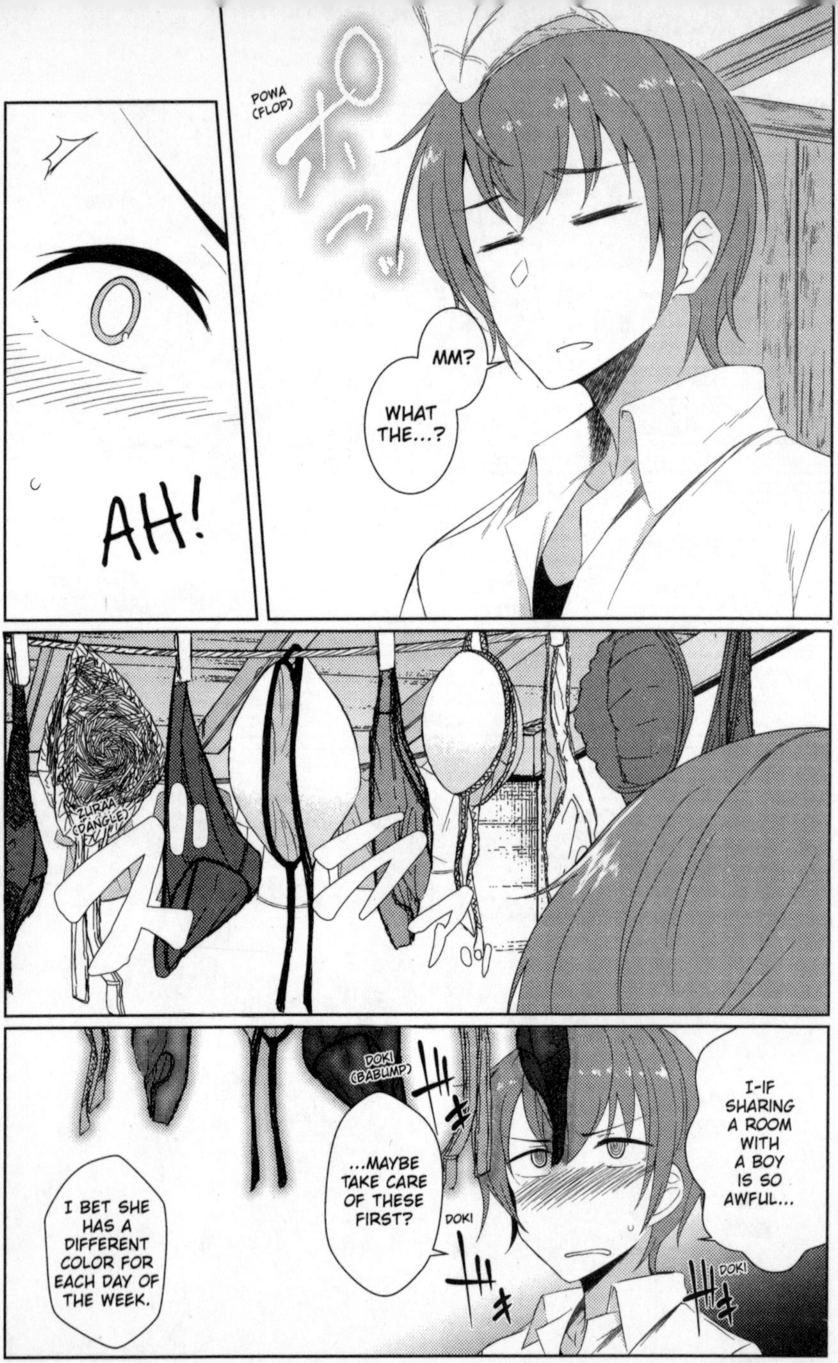
POWA (FLOP)
MM?
WHAT THE...?
AH!
ZURAA (DANGLE)
I-IF SHARING A ROOM WITH A BOY IS SO AWFUL...
DOKI
...MAYBE TAKE CARE OF THESE FIRST?
DOKI (BABUMP)
DOKI
I BET SHE HAS A DIFFERENT COLOR FOR EACH DAY OF THE WEEK.

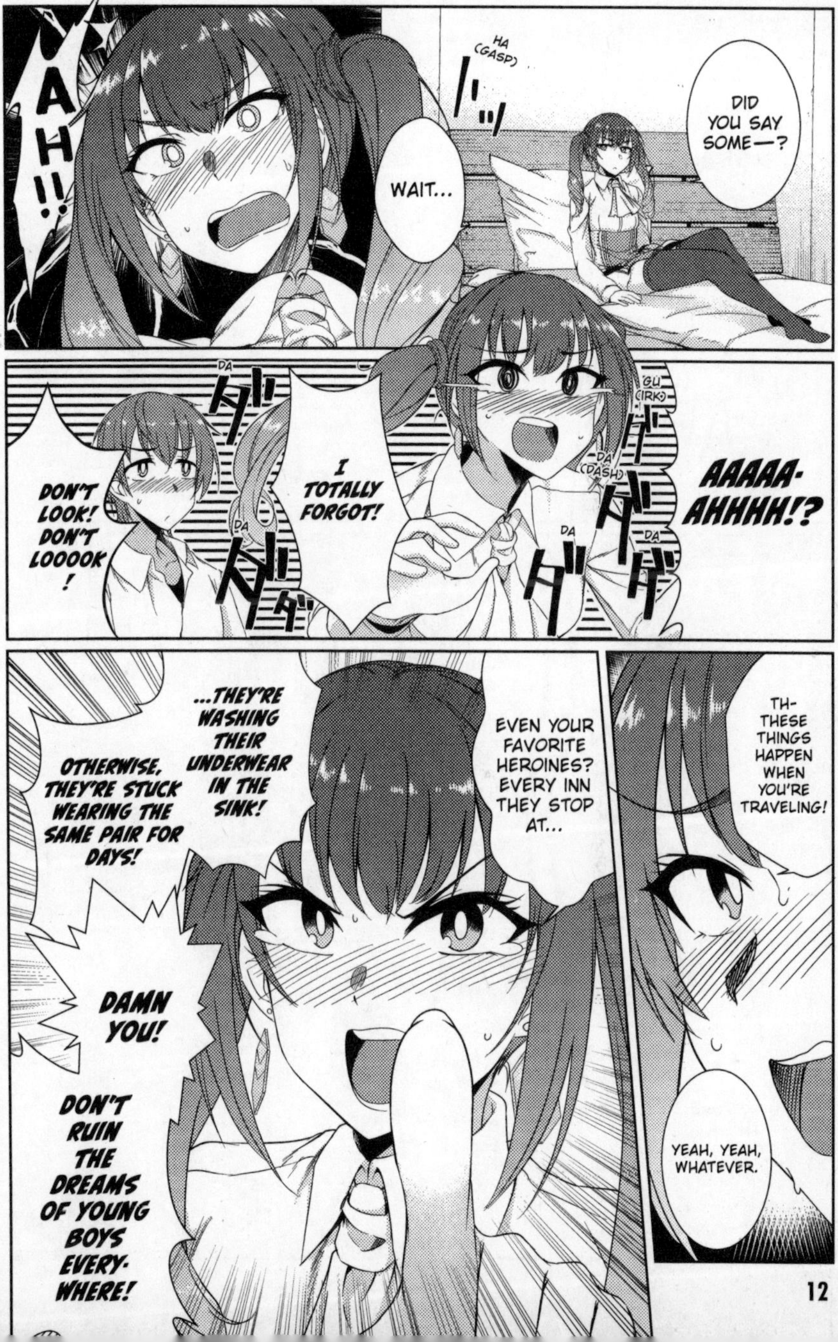
DID YOU SAY SOME—?
HA (GASP)
WAIT...
AH!!
AAAAA-AHHHH!?
GU (IRK)
DA (DASH)
DA
DA
I TOTALLY FORGOT!
DA
DA
DON'T LOOK! DON'T LOOOOK!
TH-THESE THINGS HAPPEN WHEN YOU'RE TRAVELING!
YEAH, YEAH, WHATEVER.
EVEN YOUR FAVORITE HEROINES? EVERY INN THEY STOP AT...
...THEY'RE WASHING THEIR UNDERWEAR IN THE SINK!
OTHERWISE, THEY'RE STUCK WEARING THE SAME PAIR FOR DAYS!
DAMN YOU!
DON'T RUIN THE DREAMS OF YOUNG BOYS EVERY-WHERE!

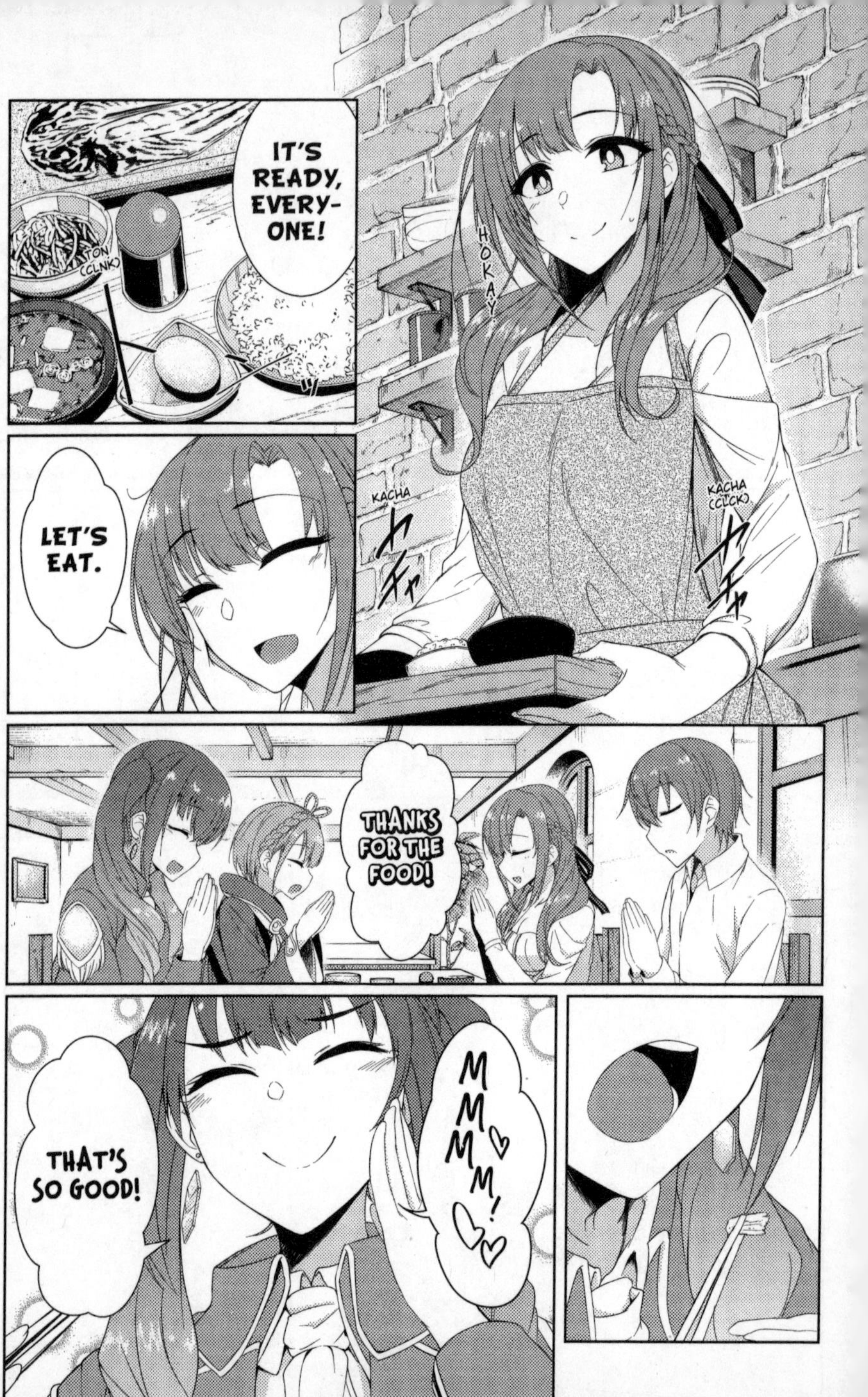
HOKAY
KACHA (CLICK)
カチャ
KACHA
カチャ
TON (CLNK)
IT'S READY, EVERY-ONE!
LET'S EAT.
THANKS FOR THE FOOD!
MMMM! ♡♡♡
THAT'S SO GOOD!

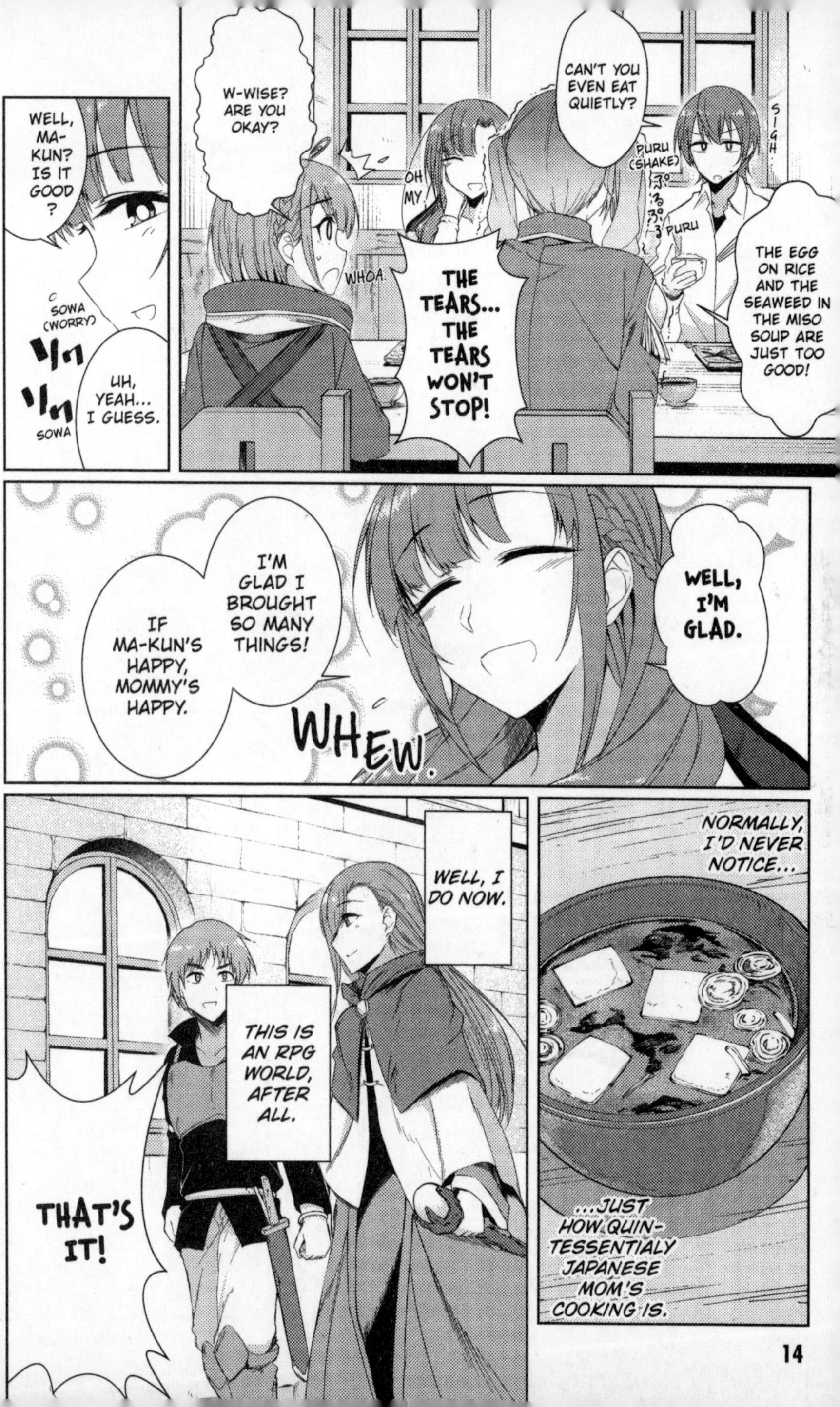
SIGH
CAN'T YOU EVEN EAT QUIETLY?
PURU (SHAKE)
PURU
THE EGG ON RICE AND THE SEAWEED IN THE MISO SOUP ARE JUST TOO GOOD!
W-WISE? ARE YOU OKAY?
OH MY
THE TEARS... THE TEARS WON'T STOP!
WHOA.
WELL, MA-KUN? IS IT GOOD?
SOWA (WORRY)
SOWA
UH, YEAH... I GUESS.
WELL, I'M GLAD.
I'M GLAD I BROUGHT SO MANY THINGS!
IF MA-KUN'S HAPPY, MOMMY'S HAPPY.
WHEW.
NORMALLY, I'D NEVER NOTICE...
...JUST HOW QUIN-TESSENTIALY JAPANESE MOM'S COOKING IS.
WELL, I DO NOW.
THIS IS AN RPG WORLD, AFTER ALL.
THAT'S IT!

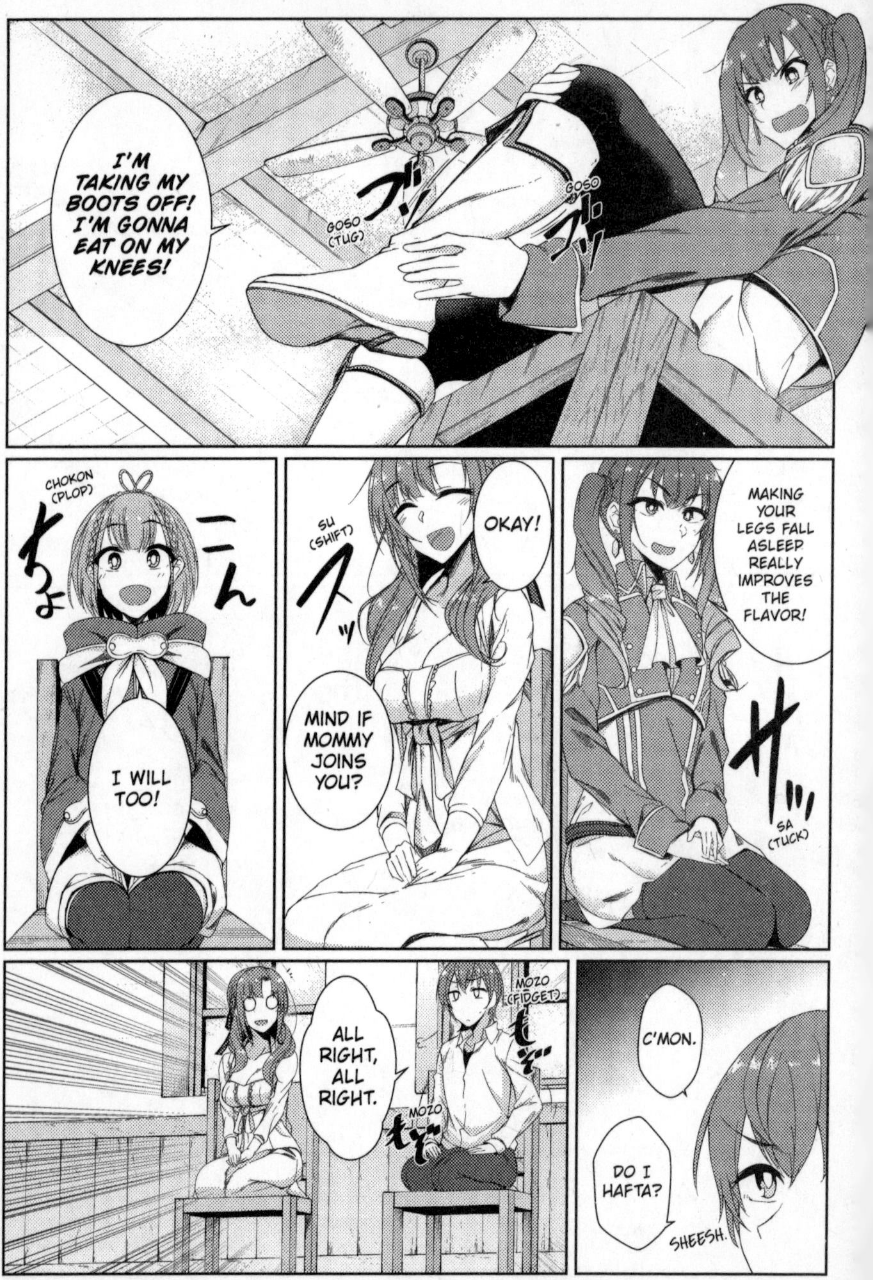
GOSO
GOSO (TUG)
I'M TAKING MY BOOTS OFF! I'M GONNA EAT ON MY KNEES!
MAKING YOUR LEGS FALL ASLEEP REALLY IMPROVES THE FLAVOR!
SA (TUCK)
OKAY!
SU (SHIFT)
MIND IF MOMMY JOINS YOU?
CHOKON (PLOP)
I WILL TOO!
C'MON.
DO I HAFTA?
SHEESH.
MOZO (FIDGET)
ALL RIGHT, ALL RIGHT.
MOZO

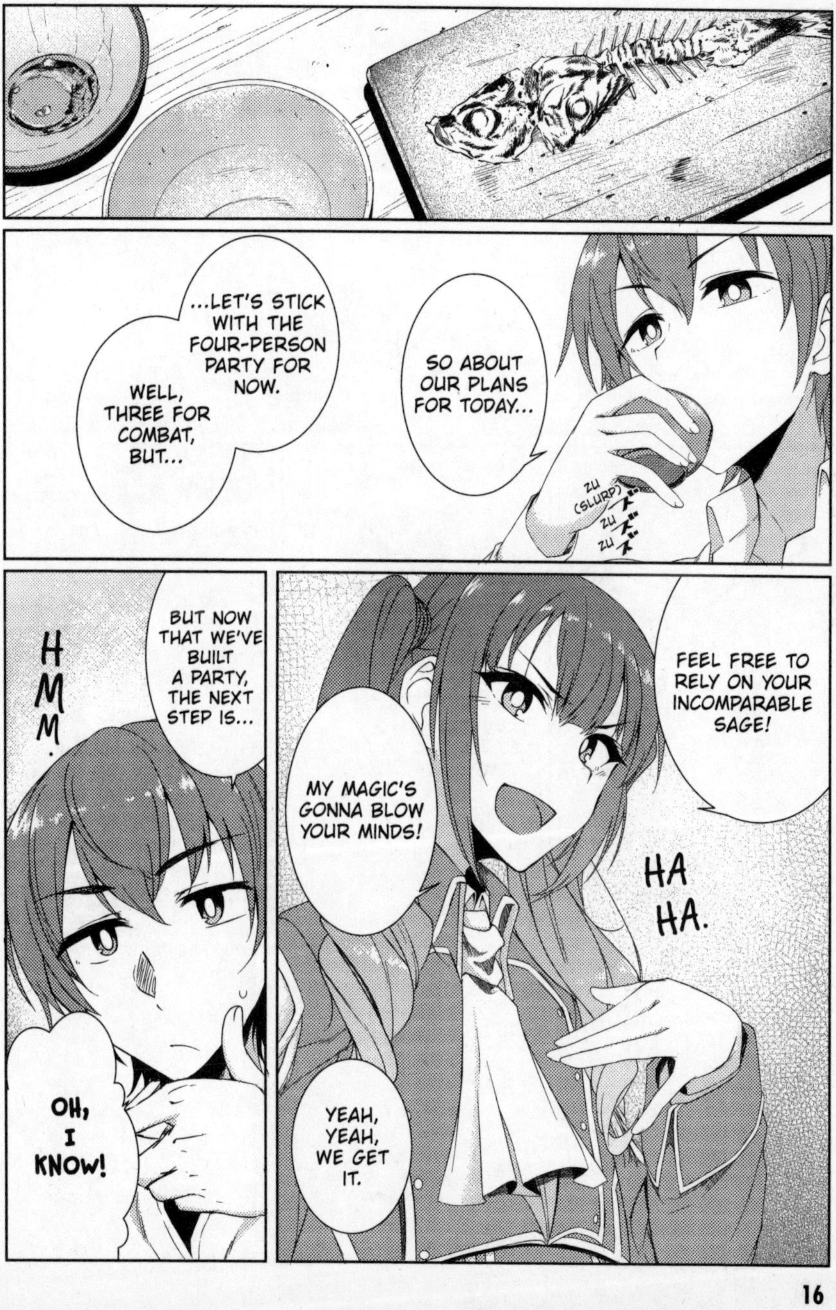
SO ABOUT OUR PLANS FOR TODAY...
ZU (SLURP) ZU ZU
...LET'S STICK WITH THE FOUR-PERSON PARTY FOR NOW.
WELL, THREE FOR COMBAT, BUT...
FEEL FREE TO RELY ON YOUR INCOMPARABLE SAGE!
MY MAGIC'S GONNA BLOW YOUR MINDS!
HA HA.
YEAH, YEAH, WE GET IT.
BUT NOW THAT WE'VE BUILT A PARTY, THE NEXT STEP IS...
HMM.
OH, I KNOW!

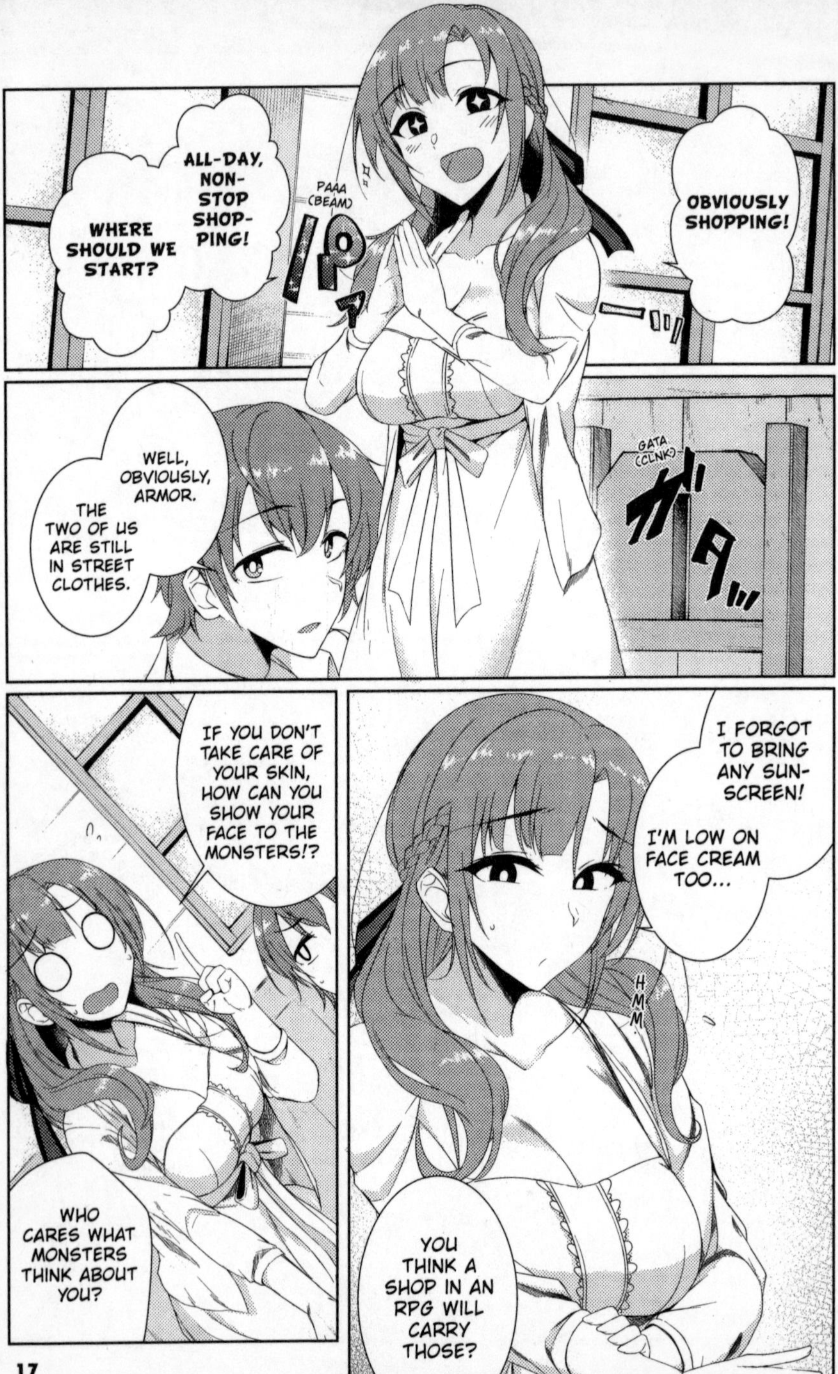
OBVIOUSLY SHOPPING!
PAAA (BEAM)
ALL-DAY, NON-STOP SHOP-PING!
WHERE SHOULD WE START?
GATA (CLNK)
WELL, OBVIOUSLY, ARMOR.
THE TWO OF US ARE STILL IN STREET CLOTHES.
I FORGOT TO BRING ANY SUN-SCREEN!
I'M LOW ON FACE CREAM TOO...
HMM.
YOU THINK A SHOP IN AN RPG WILL CARRY THOSE?
IF YOU DON'T TAKE CARE OF YOUR SKIN, HOW CAN YOU SHOW YOUR FACE TO THE MONSTERS!?
WHO CARES WHAT MONSTERS THINK ABOUT YOU?

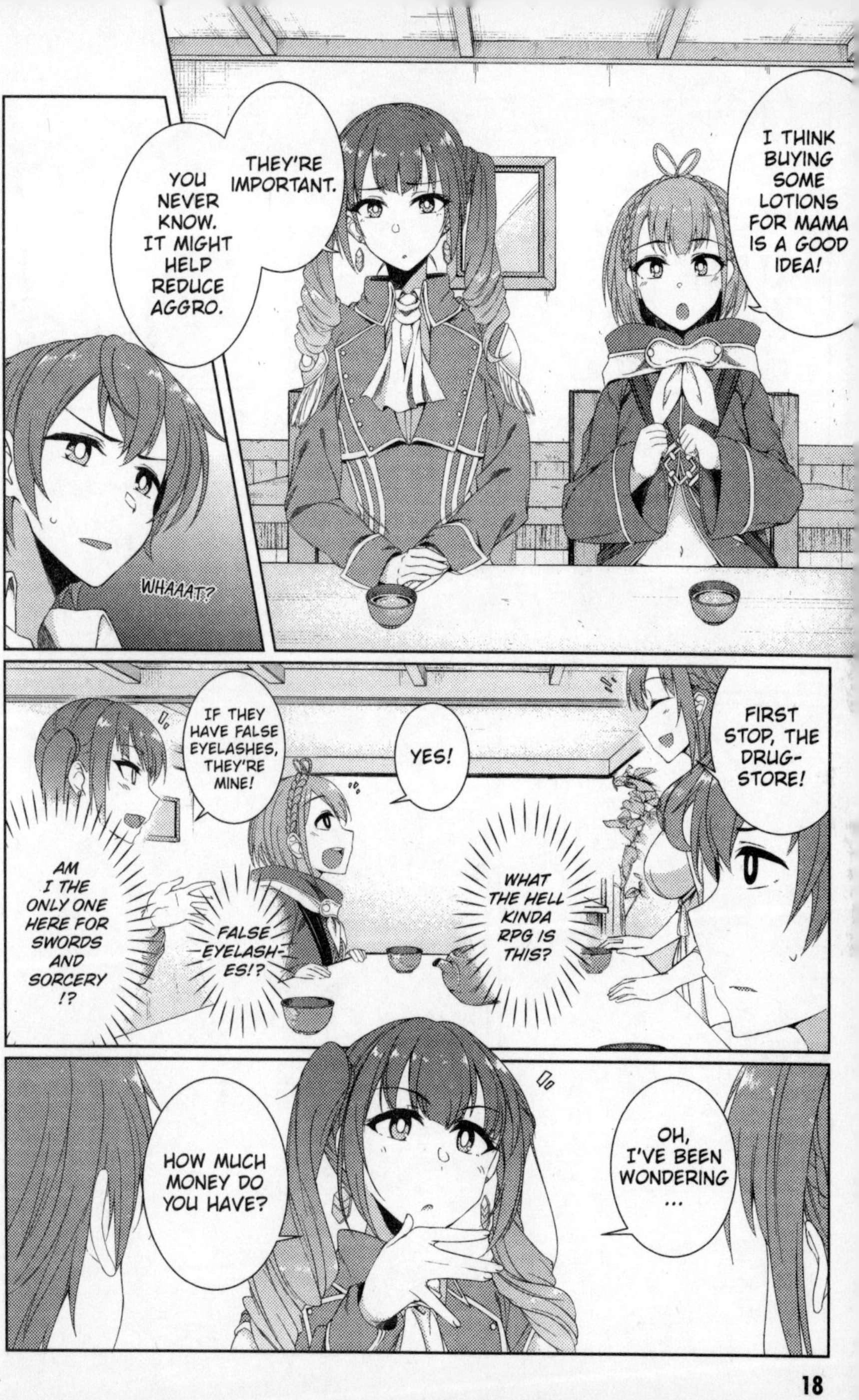
I THINK BUYING SOME LOTIONS FOR MAMA IS A GOOD IDEA!
THEY'RE IMPORTANT.
YOU NEVER KNOW. IT MIGHT HELP REDUCE AGGRO.
WHAAAT?
FIRST STOP, THE DRUG-STORE!
YES!
IF THEY HAVE FALSE EYELASHES, THEY'RE MINE!
WHAT THE HELL KINDA RPG IS THIS?
FALSE EYELASH-ES!?
AM I THE ONLY ONE HERE FOR SWORDS AND SORCERY!?
OH, I'VE BEEN WONDERING...
HOW MUCH MONEY DO YOU HAVE?

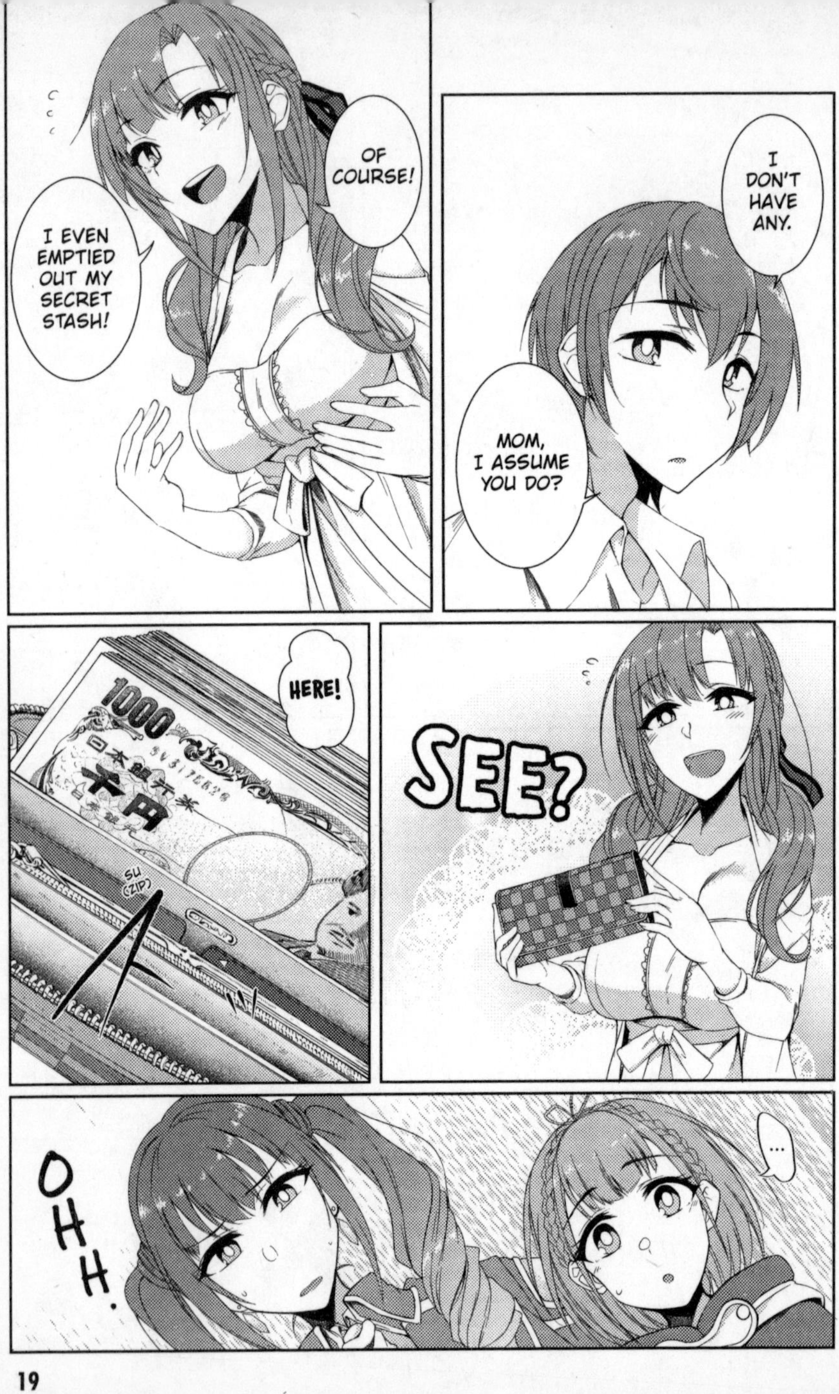
I DON'T HAVE ANY.
MOM, I ASSUME YOU DO?
OF COURSE!
I EVEN EMPTIED OUT MY SECRET STASH!
SEE?
HERE!
1000
千円
SU (ZIP)
...
OHH.

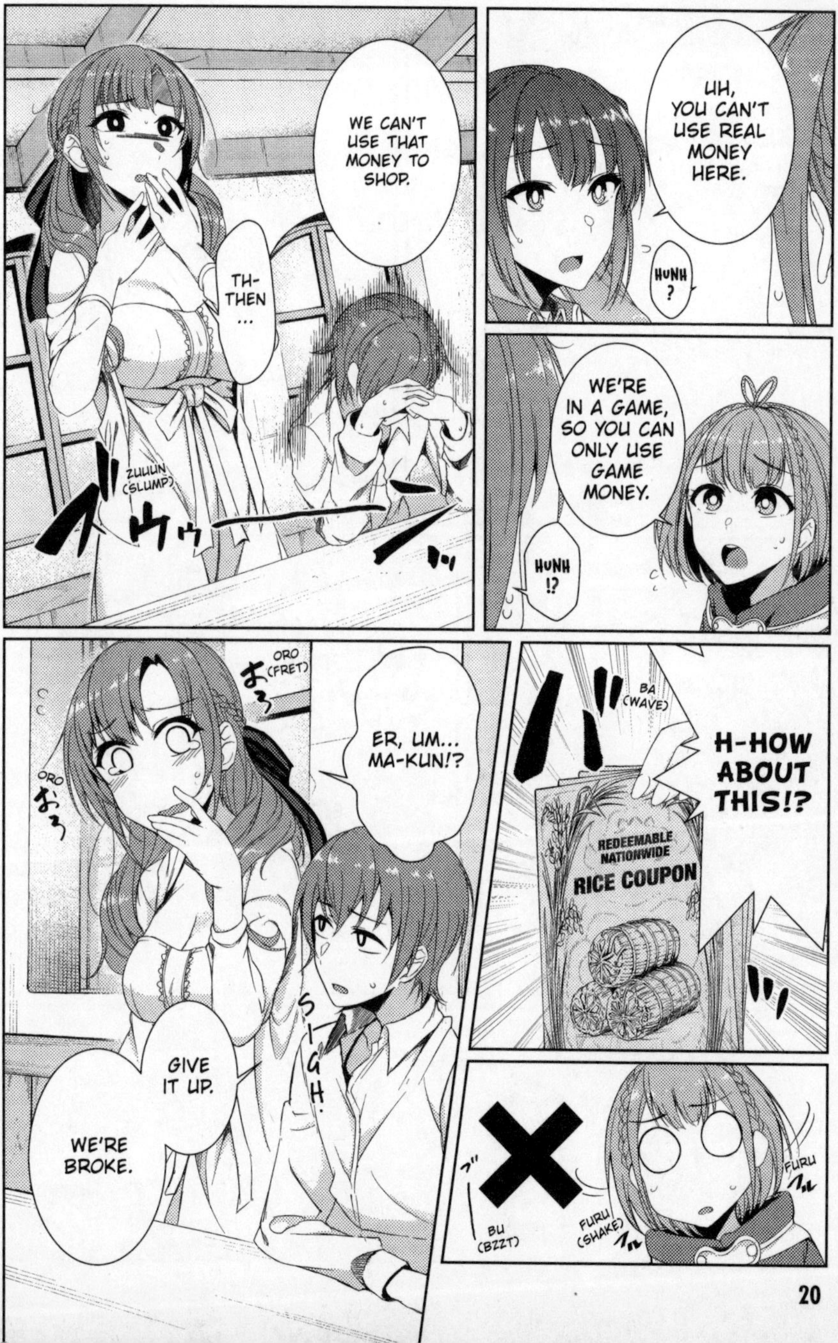

UH, YOU CAN'T USE REAL MONEY HERE.
HUNH?
WE'RE IN A GAME, SO YOU CAN ONLY USE GAME MONEY.
HUNH!?
WE CAN'T USE THAT MONEY TO SHOP.
TH-THEN...
ZUUUN (SLUMP)
BA (WAVE)
H-HOW ABOUT THIS!?
REDEEMABLE NATIONWIDE
RICE COUPON
FURU
FURU (SHAKE)
BU (BZZT)
ORO (FRET)
ORO
ER, UM... MA-KUN!?
SIGH.
GIVE IT UP.
WE'RE BROKE.

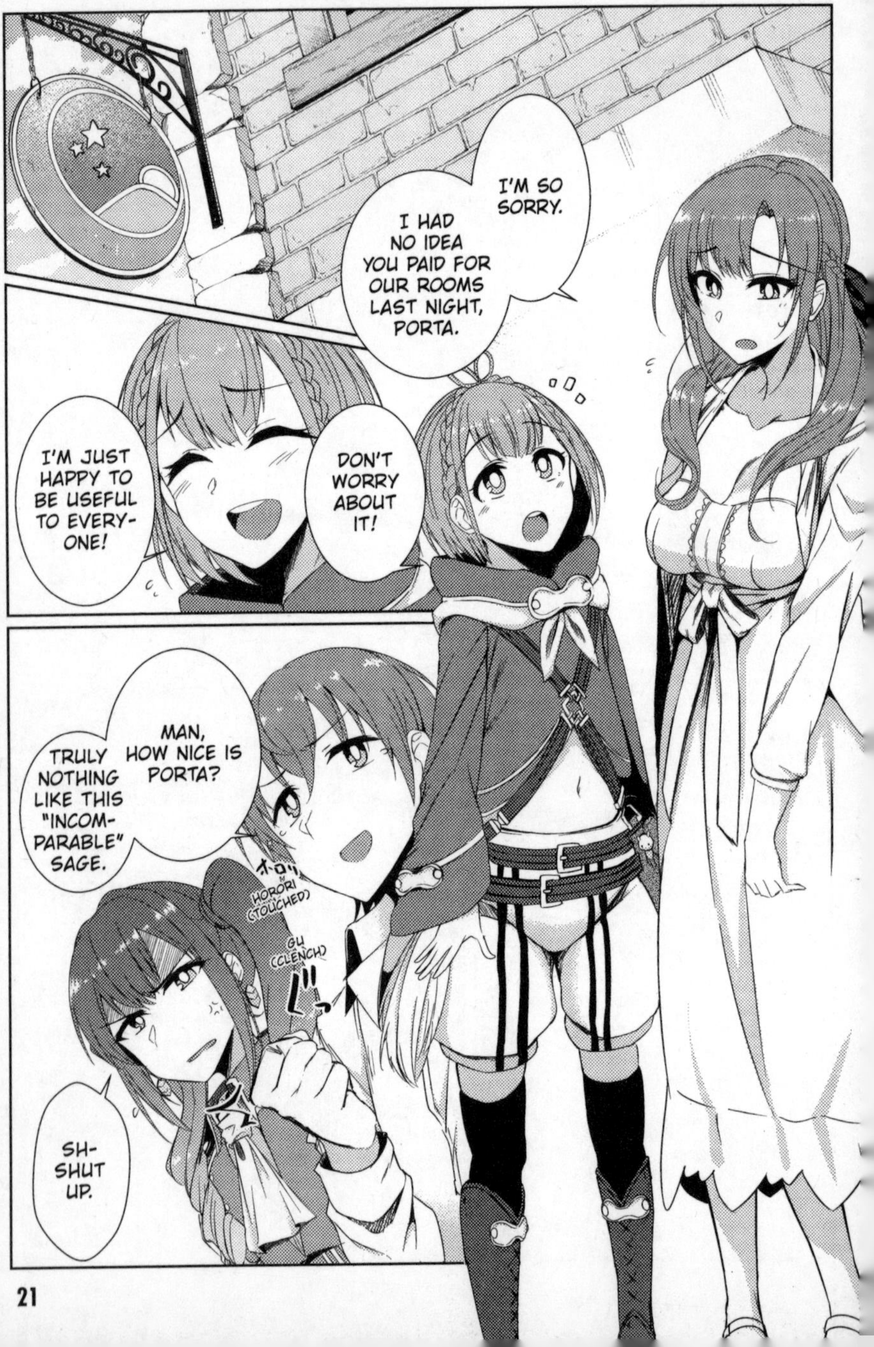
I'M SO SORRY.
I HAD NO IDEA YOU PAID FOR OUR ROOMS LAST NIGHT, PORTA.
DON'T WORRY ABOUT IT!
I'M JUST HAPPY TO BE USEFUL TO EVERY-ONE!
MAN, HOW NICE IS PORTA?
TRULY NOTHING LIKE THIS "INCOM-PARABLE" SAGE.
HORORI (TOUCHED)
GU (CLENCH)
SH-SHUT UP.

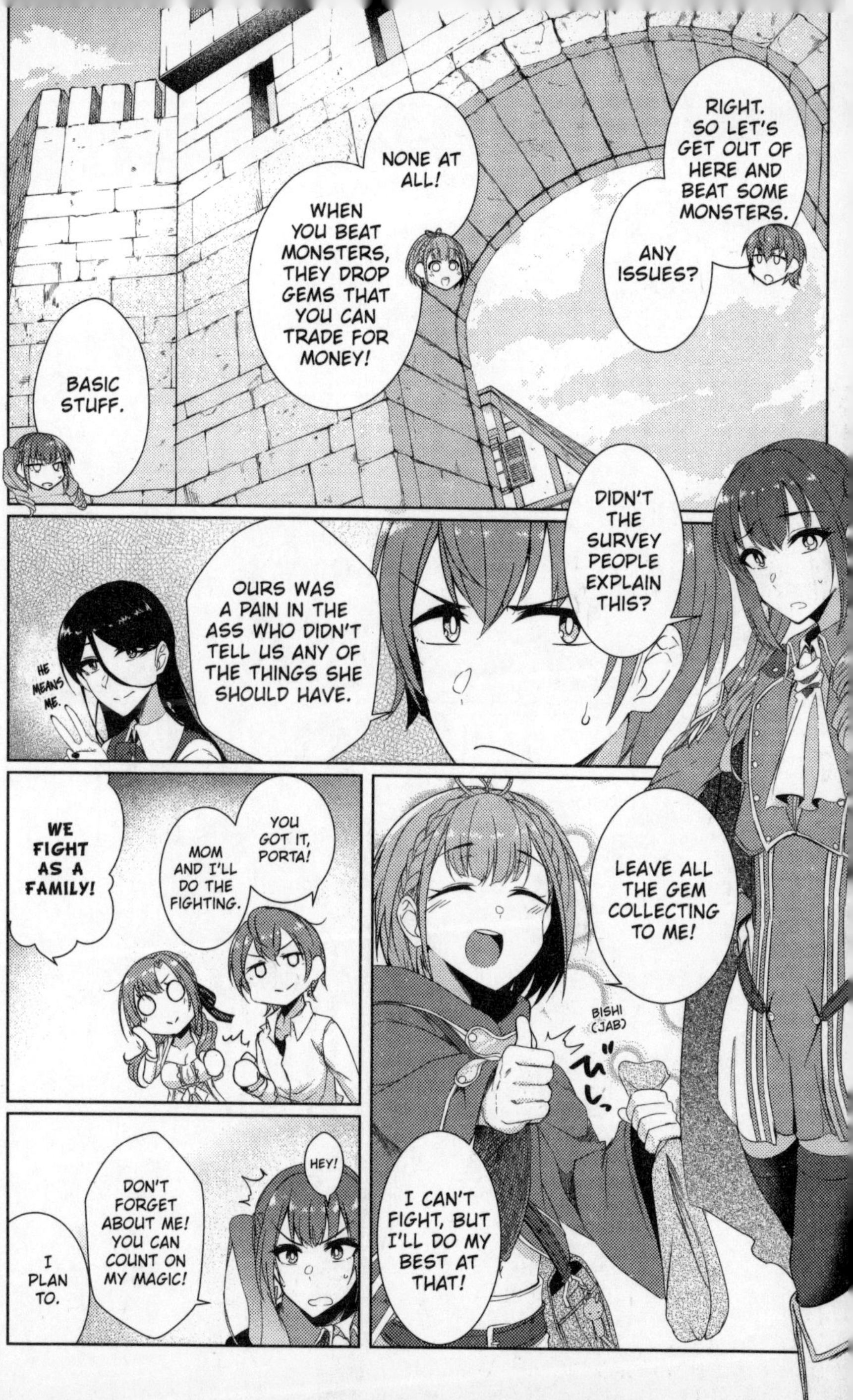
RIGHT. SO LET'S GET OUT OF HERE AND BEAT SOME MONSTERS.
ANY ISSUES?
NONE AT ALL!
WHEN YOU BEAT MONSTERS, THEY DROP GEMS THAT YOU CAN TRADE FOR MONEY!
BASIC STUFF.
DIDN'T THE SURVEY PEOPLE EXPLAIN THIS?
OURS WAS A PAIN IN THE ASS WHO DIDN'T TELL US ANY OF THE THINGS SHE SHOULD HAVE.
HE MEANS ME.
LEAVE ALL THE GEM COLLECTING TO ME!
BISHI (JAB)
I CAN'T FIGHT, BUT I'LL DO MY BEST AT THAT!
YOU GOT IT, PORTA!
MOM AND I'LL DO THE FIGHTING.
WE FIGHT AS A FAMILY!
HEY!
DON'T FORGET ABOUT ME! YOU CAN COUNT ON MY MAGIC!
I PLAN TO.

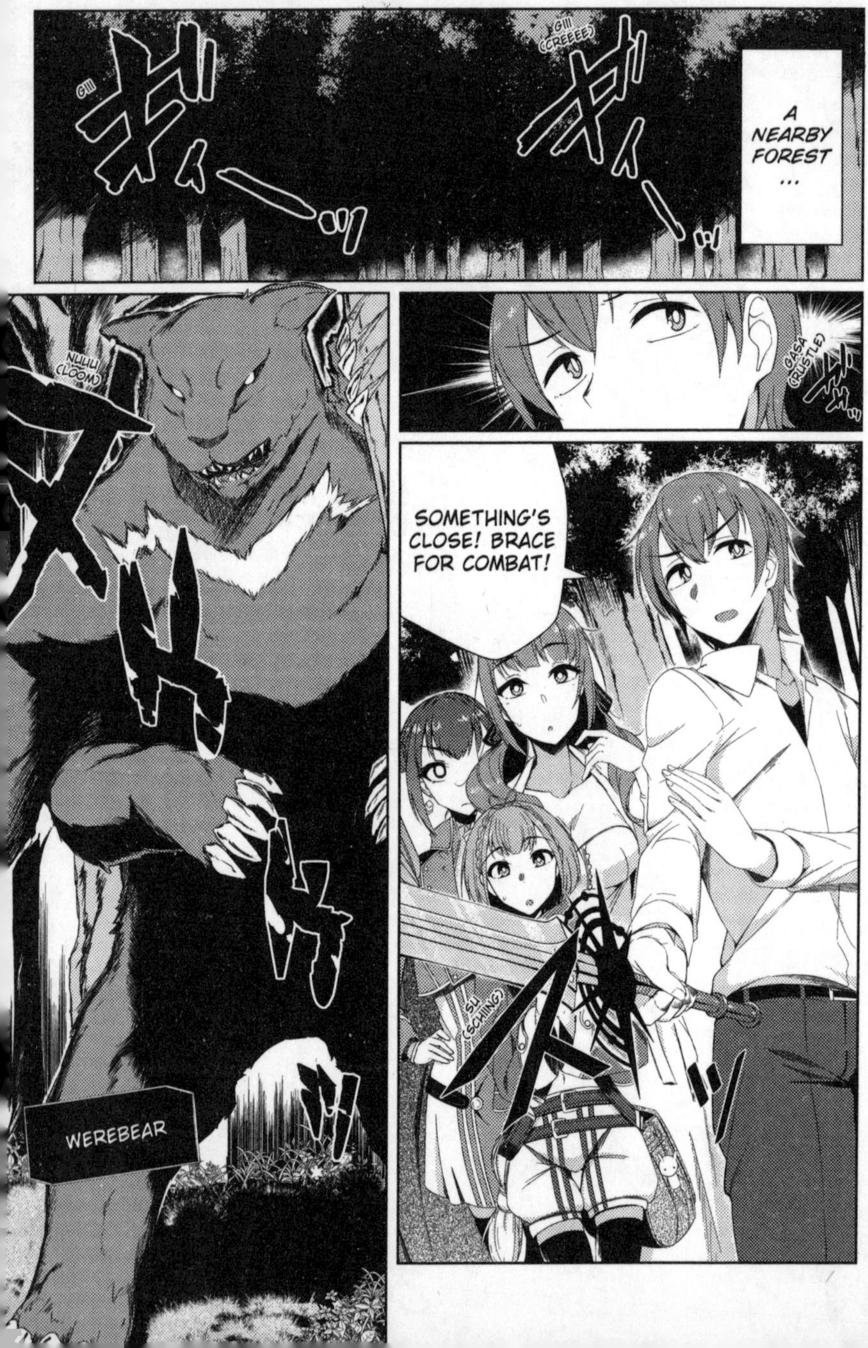
A NEARBY FOREST...
GIII (CREEEE)
GIII
GASA (RUSTLE)
SOMETHING'S CLOSE! BRACE FOR COMBAT!
SU (SCHIING)
NUUUN (LOOM)
WEREBEAR

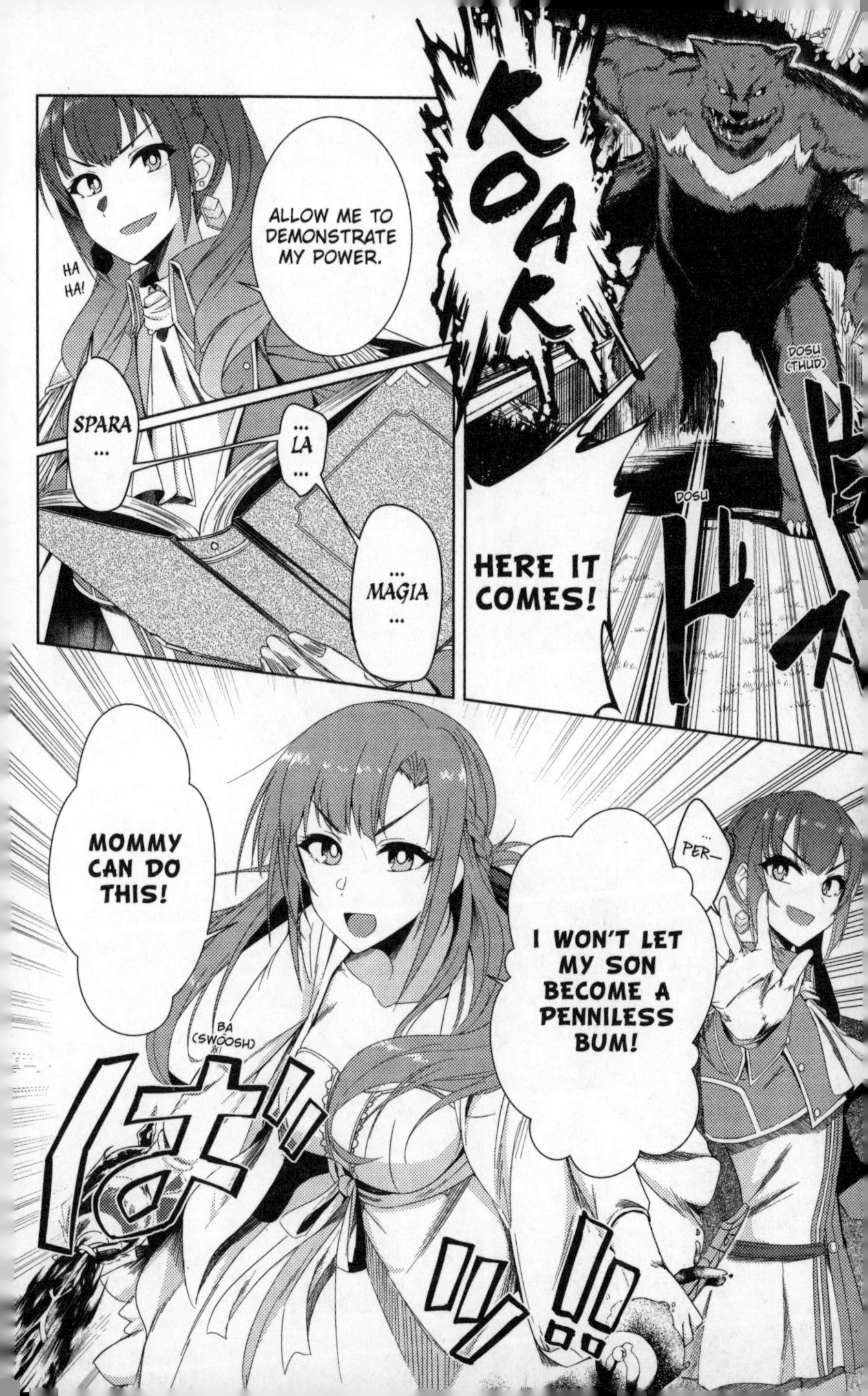
KOAR
DOSU (THUD)
DOSU
HERE IT COMES!
ALLOW ME TO DEMONSTRATE MY POWER.
HA HA!
SPARA ...
... LA ...
... MAGIA ...
... PER—
I WON'T LET MY SON BECOME A PENNILESS BUM!
MOMMY CAN DO THIS!
BA (SWOOSH)

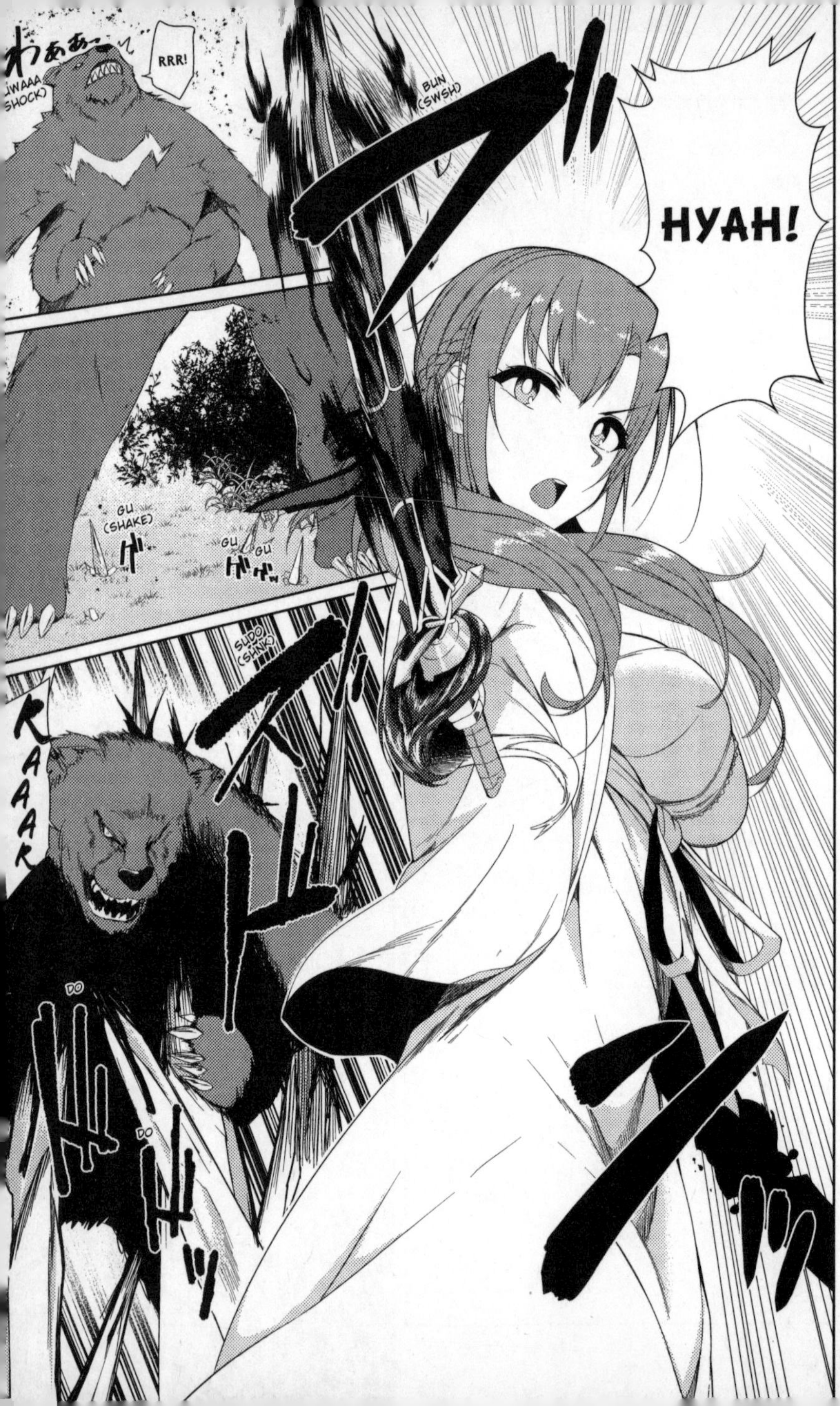

HYAH!
BUN (SWSH)
RRR!
わぁあっ
UWAAA (SHOCK)
GU (SHAKE)
GU GU
SUDO (SHNK)
RAAAAR
DO
DO

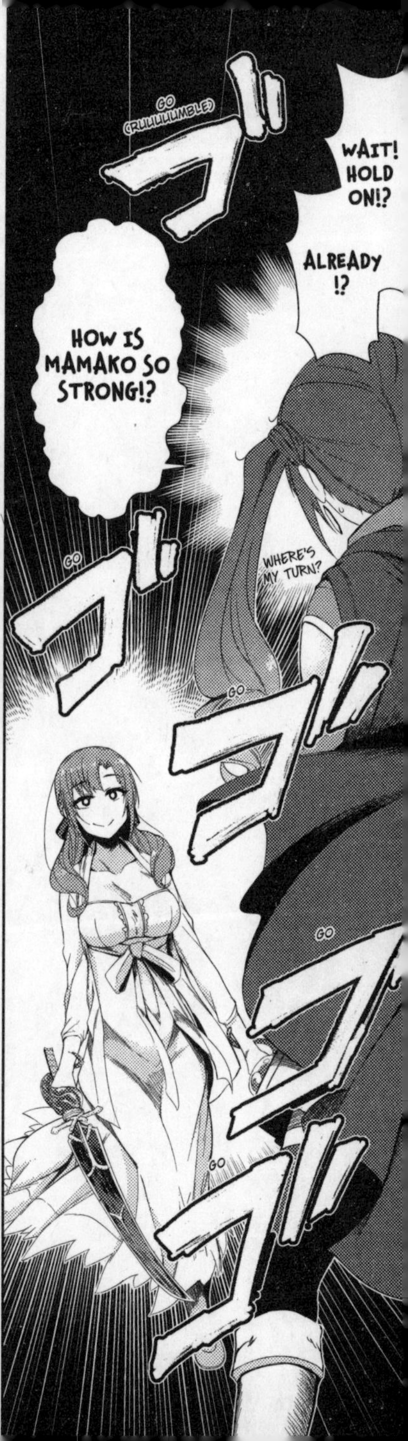
WAIT! HOLD ON!?
ALREADY!?
GO (RUUUUUUMBLE)
HOW IS MAMAKO SO STRONG!?
WHERE'S MY TURN?
GO
GO
GO
GO

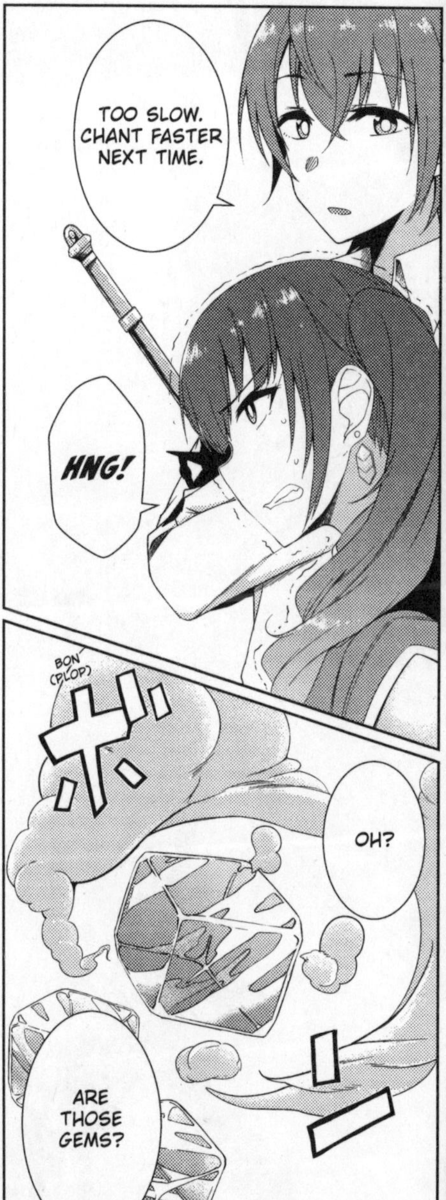
TOO SLOW. CHANT FASTER NEXT TIME.
HNG!
OH?
BON (PLOP)
ARE THOSE GEMS?

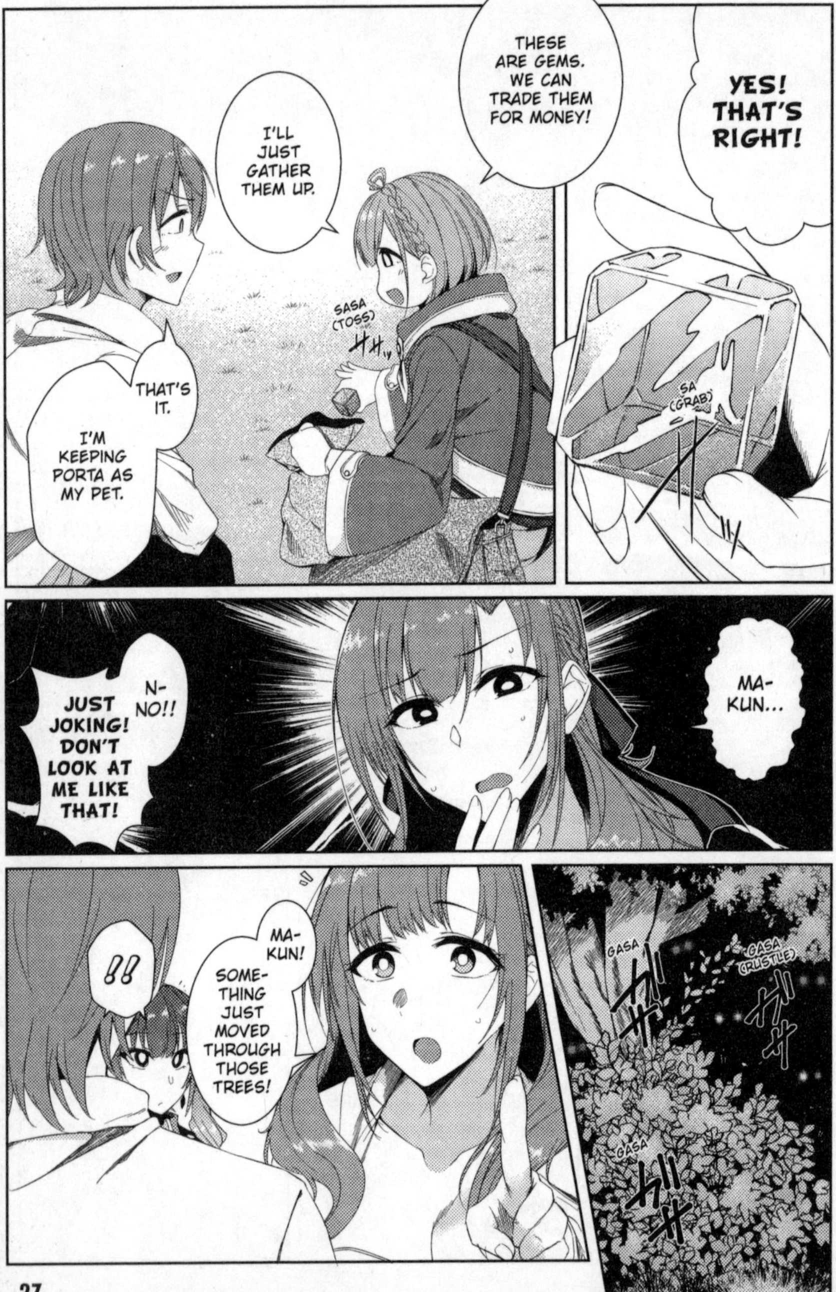
YES! THAT'S RIGHT!
SA (GRAB)
THESE ARE GEMS. WE CAN TRADE THEM FOR MONEY!
I'LL JUST GATHER THEM UP.
SASA (TOSS)
THAT'S IT.
I'M KEEPING PORTA AS MY PET.
MA-KUN...
N-NO!!
JUST JOKING! DON'T LOOK AT ME LIKE THAT!
GASA (RUSTLE)
GASA
GASA
MA-KUN! SOMETHING JUST MOVED THROUGH THOSE TREES!
!!

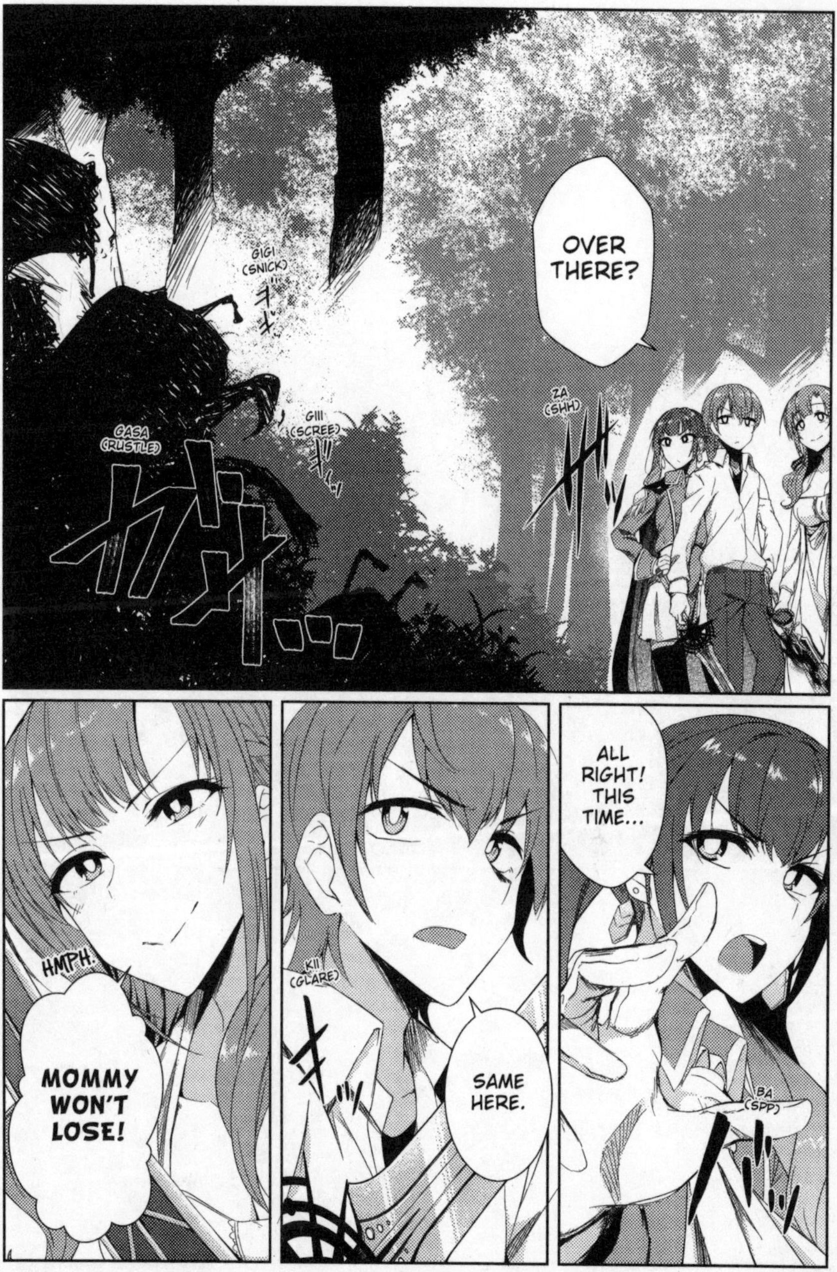
OVER THERE?
ZA (SHH)
GIGI (SNICK)
GIII (SCREE)
GASA (RUSTLE)
ALL RIGHT! THIS TIME...
BA (SPP)
KII (GLARE)
SAME HERE.
HMPH.
MOMMY WON'T LOSE!

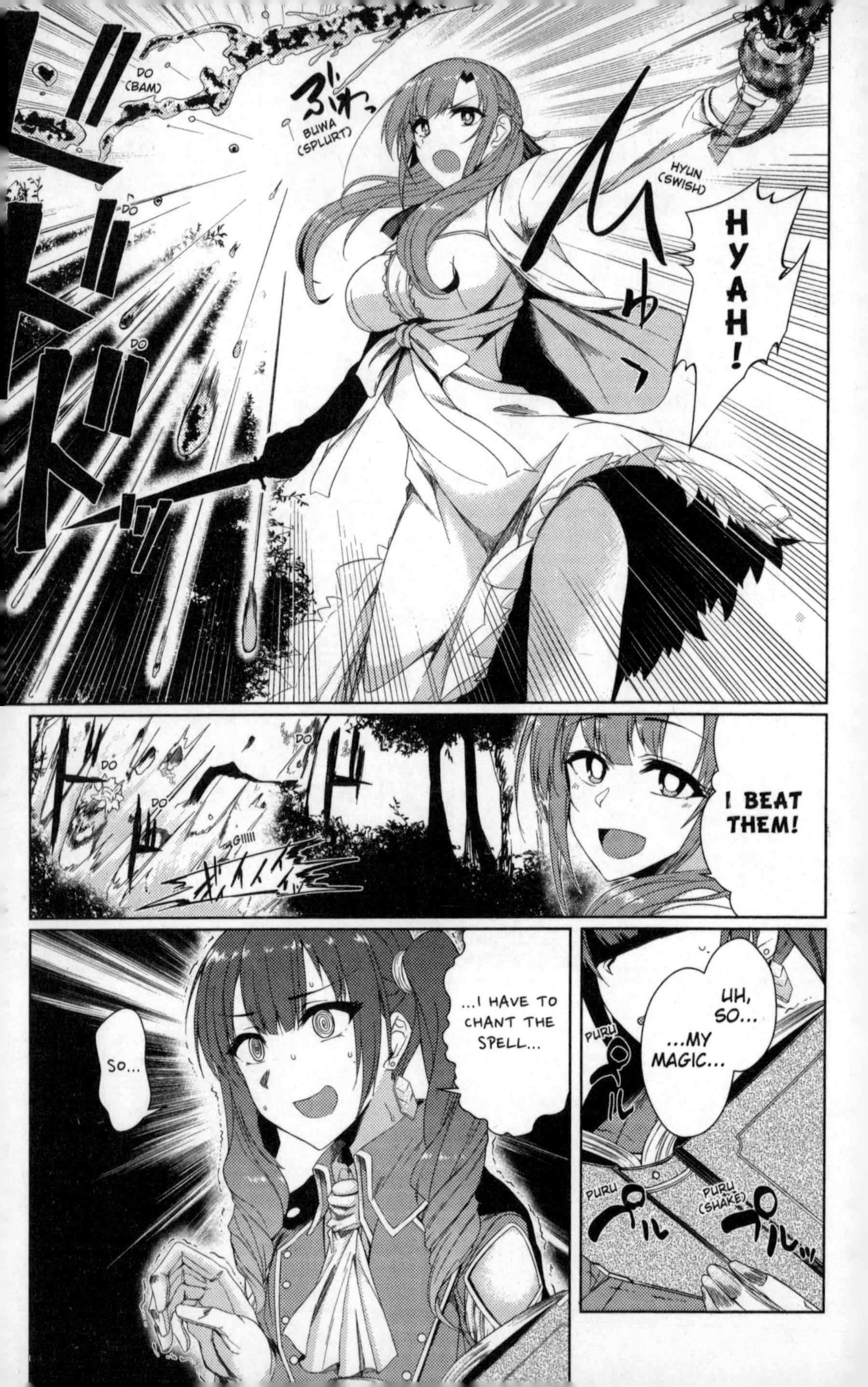

HYUN (SWISH)
ひゅっ
HYAH!
ぶわっ
BUWA (SPLURT)
DO (BAM)
DO
DO
I BEAT THEM!
DO
DO
DO
GIIIII
UH, SO... ...MY MAGIC...
PURU
PURU (SHAKE)
PURU
...I HAVE TO CHANT THE SPELL...
SO...

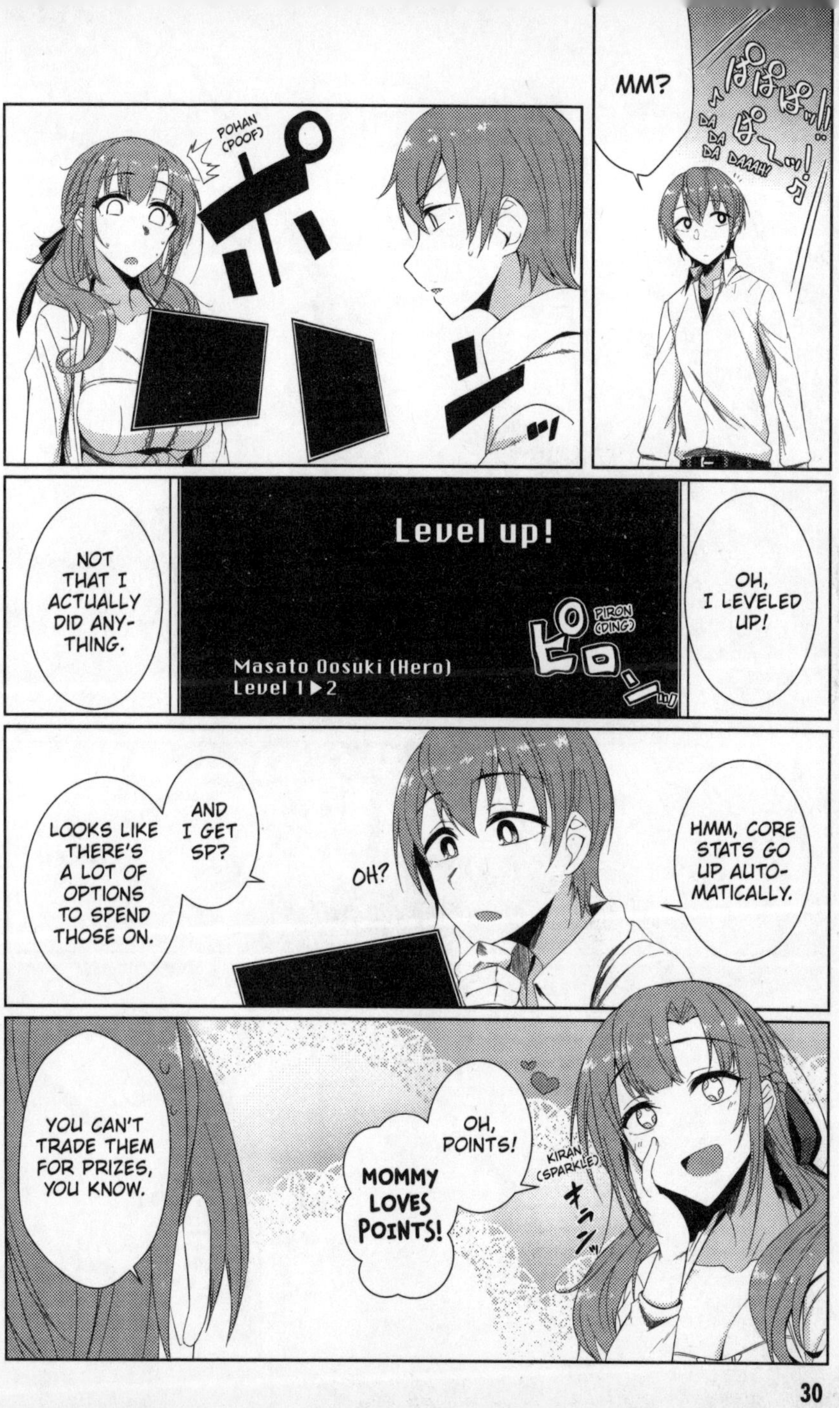
MM?
DA DA DA DAAAH!
POHAN (POOF)
OH, I LEVELED UP!
PIRON (DING)
Level up!
Masato Oosuki (Hero)
Level 1▶2
NOT THAT I ACTUALLY DID ANY-THING.
HMM, CORE STATS GO UP AUTO-MATICALLY.
OH?
AND I GET SP?
LOOKS LIKE THERE'S A LOT OF OPTIONS TO SPEND THOSE ON.
OH, POINTS!
MOMMY LOVES POINTS!
KIRAN (SPARKLE)
YOU CAN'T TRADE THEM FOR PRIZES, YOU KNOW.

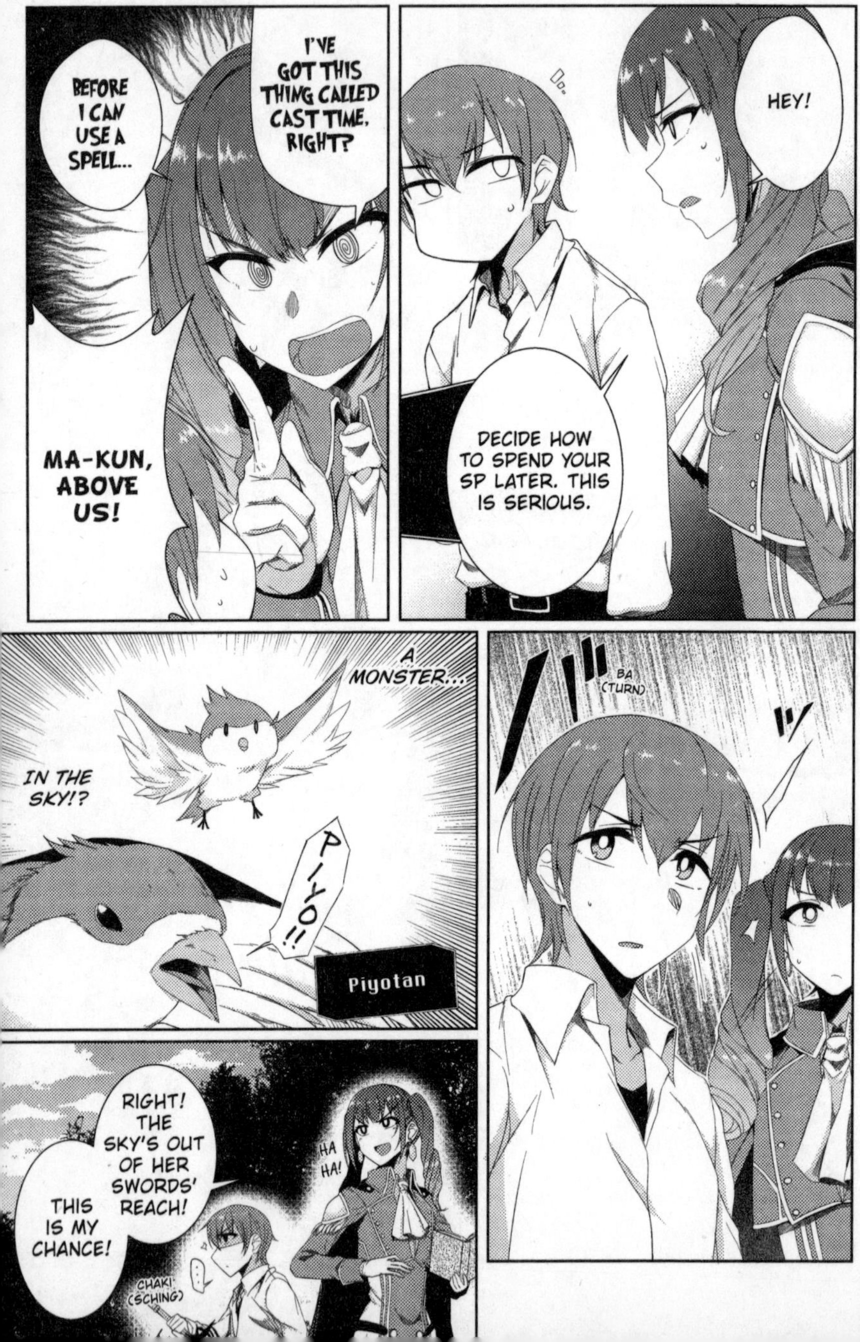
HEY!
DECIDE HOW TO SPEND YOUR SP LATER. THIS IS SERIOUS.
I'VE GOT THIS THING CALLED CAST TIME, RIGHT?
BEFORE I CAN USE A SPELL...
MA-KUN, ABOVE US!
BA (TURN)
A MONSTER...
IN THE SKY!?
PIYO!!
Piyotan
RIGHT! THE SKY'S OUT OF HER SWORDS' REACH!
HA HA!
THIS IS MY CHANCE!
CHAKI (SCHING)

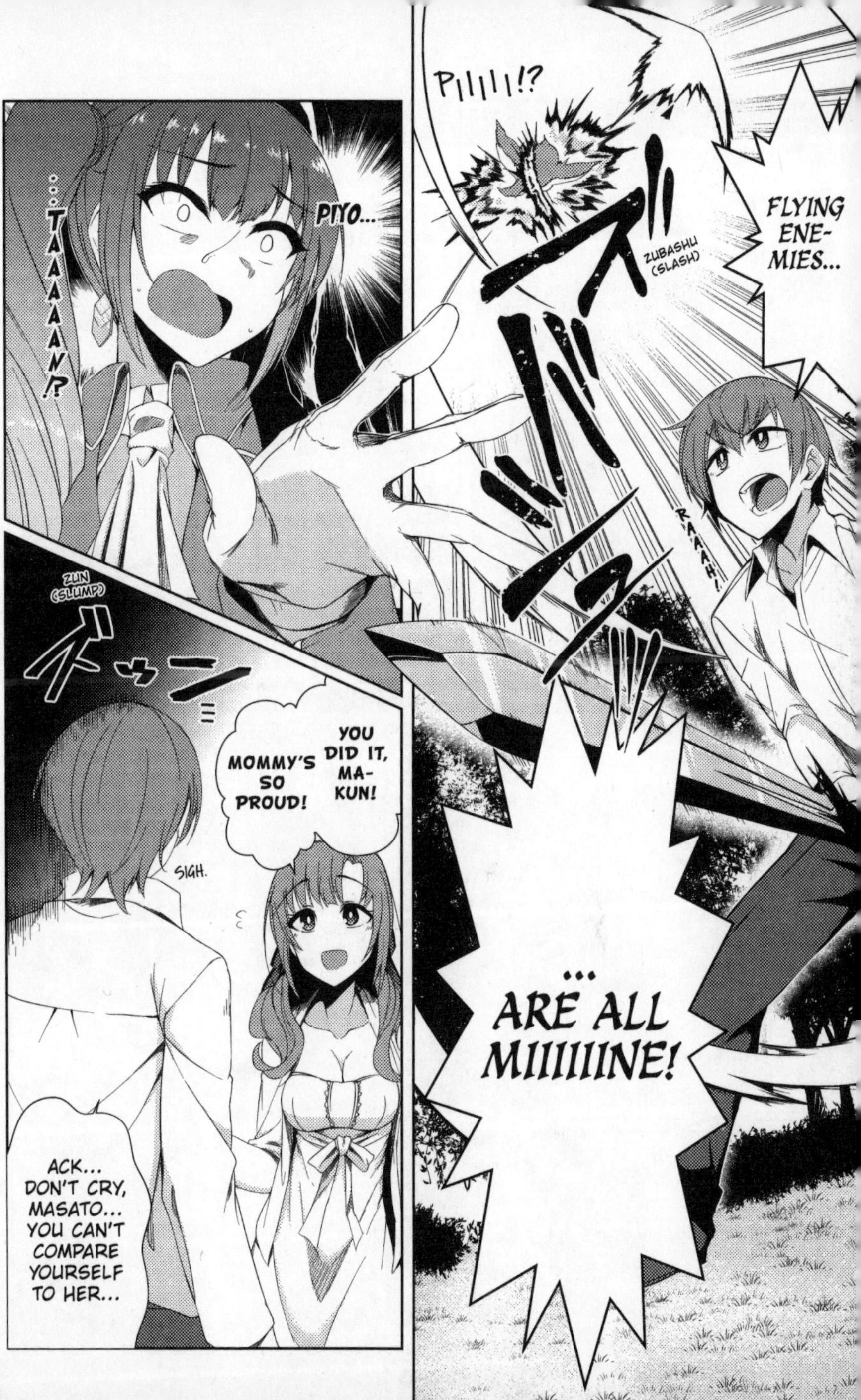
PIIIII!?
FLYING ENE-MIES...
ZUBASHU (SLASH)
RAAAH!
... ARE ALL MIIIIIINE!
PIYO...
...TAAAAAAN!?
ZUN (SLUMP)
YOU DID IT, MA-KUN!
MOMMY'S SO PROUD!
SIGH.
ACK... DON'T CRY, MASATO... YOU CAN'T COMPARE YOURSELF TO HER...

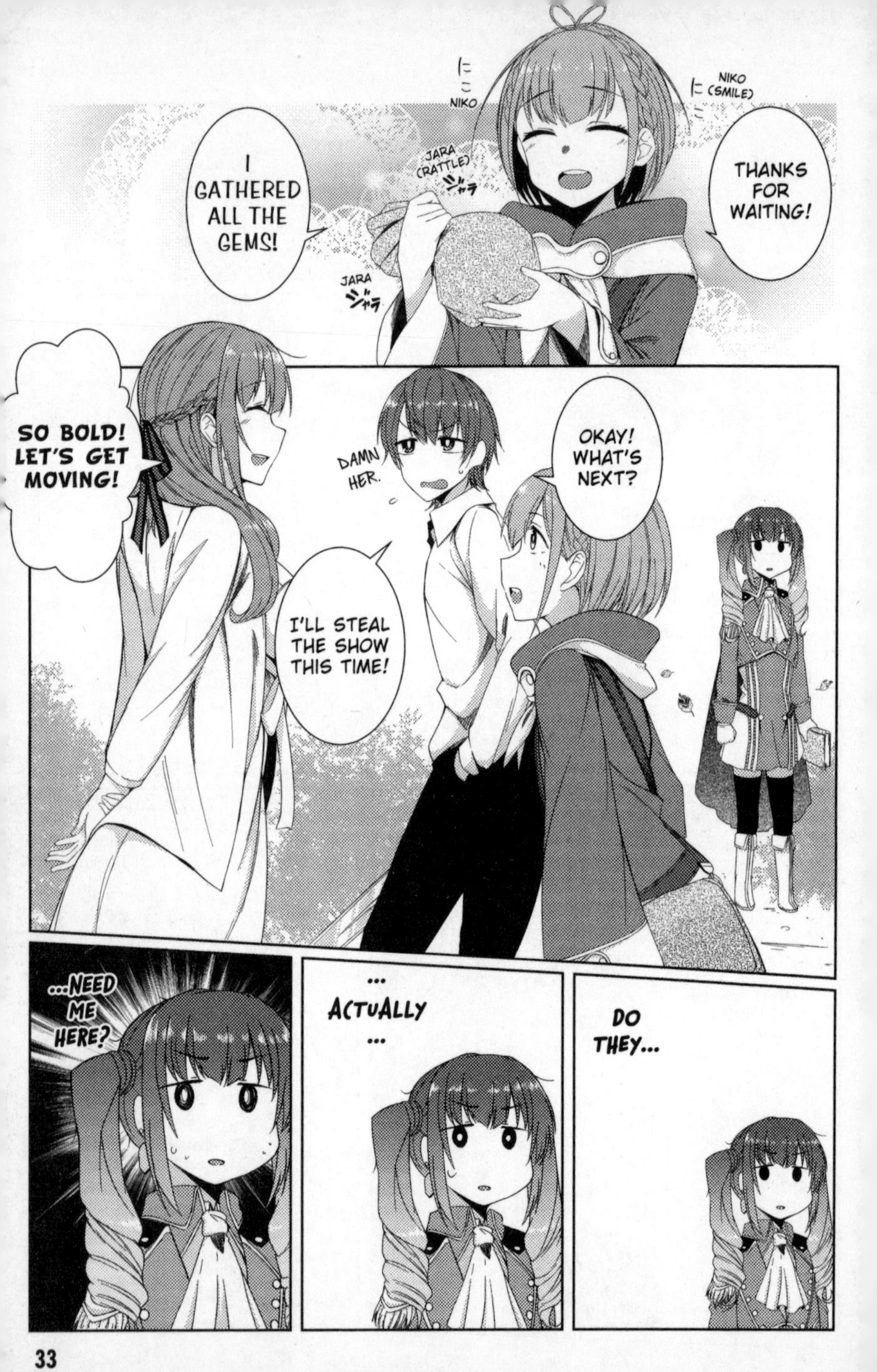

にこ NIKO (SMILE)
THANKS FOR WAITING!
にこ NIKO
JARA (RATTLE) ジャラ
I GATHERED ALL THE GEMS!
JARA ジャラ
OKAY! WHAT'S NEXT?
DAMN HER.
I'LL STEAL THE SHOW THIS TIME!
SO BOLD! LET'S GET MOVING!
DO THEY...
... ACTUALLY ...
...NEED ME HERE?

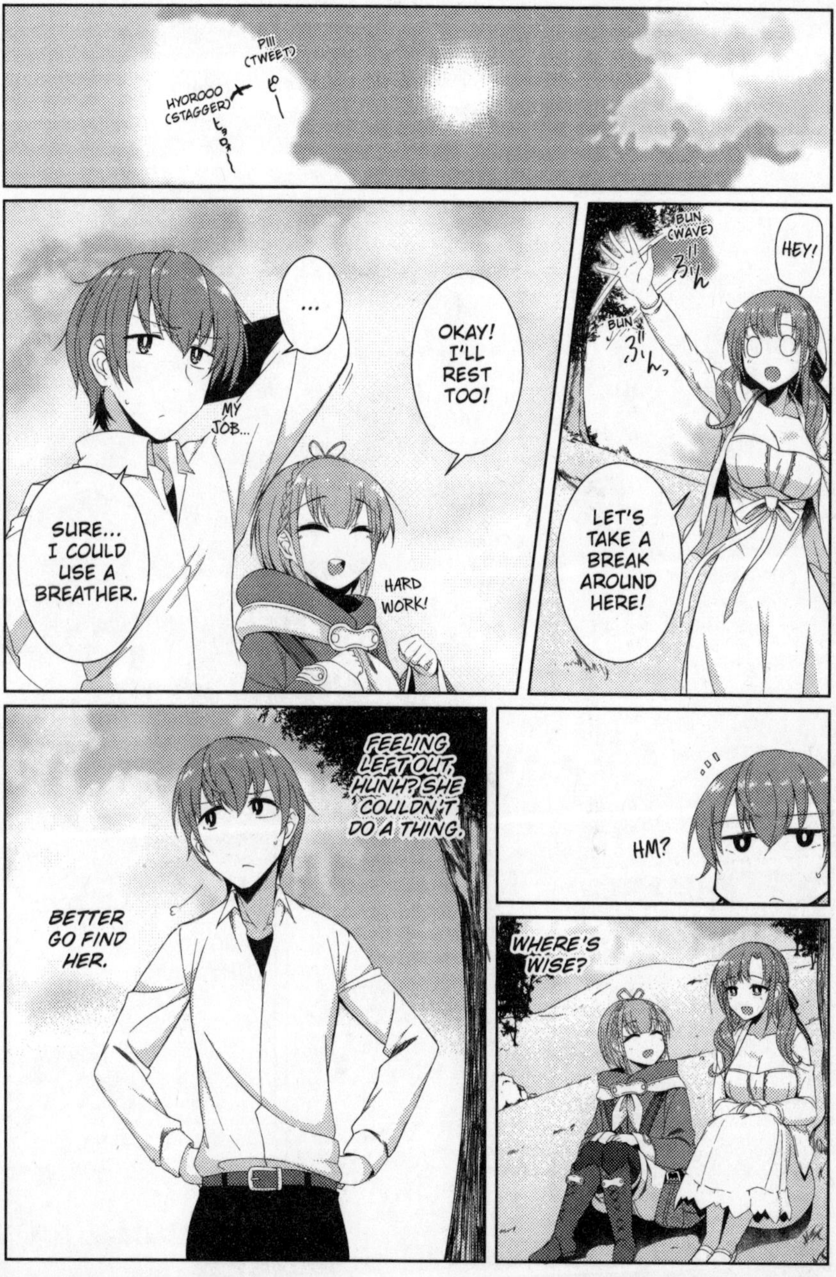
PIII (TWEET)
ぴー
HYOROOO (STAGGER)
ひょろ〜
BUN (WAVE)
ぶん!!
HEY!
BUN
ぶんっ
LET'S TAKE A BREAK AROUND HERE!
OKAY! I'LL REST TOO!
...
MY JOB...
HARD WORK!
SURE... I COULD USE A BREATHER.
HM?
WHERE'S WISE?
FEELING LEFT OUT, HUNH? SHE COULDN'T DO A THING.
BETTER GO FIND HER.

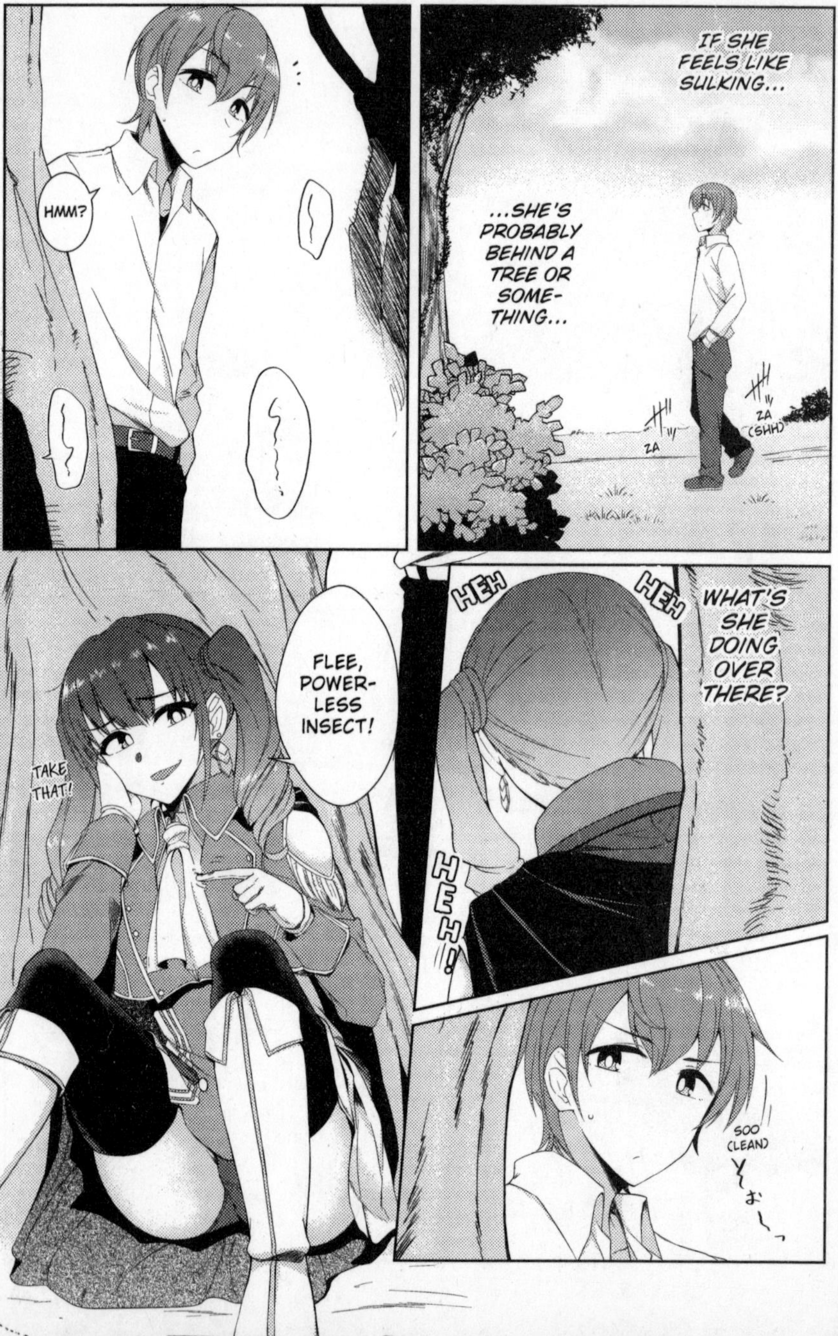
IF SHE FEELS LIKE SULKING...
...SHE'S PROBABLY BEHIND A TREE OR SOME-THING...
ZA (SHH)
ZA
HMM?
HEH
HEH
WHAT'S SHE DOING OVER THERE?
HEHEH!
SOO (CLEAN)
そ〜お〜っ
FLEE, POWER-LESS INSECT!
TAKE THAT!

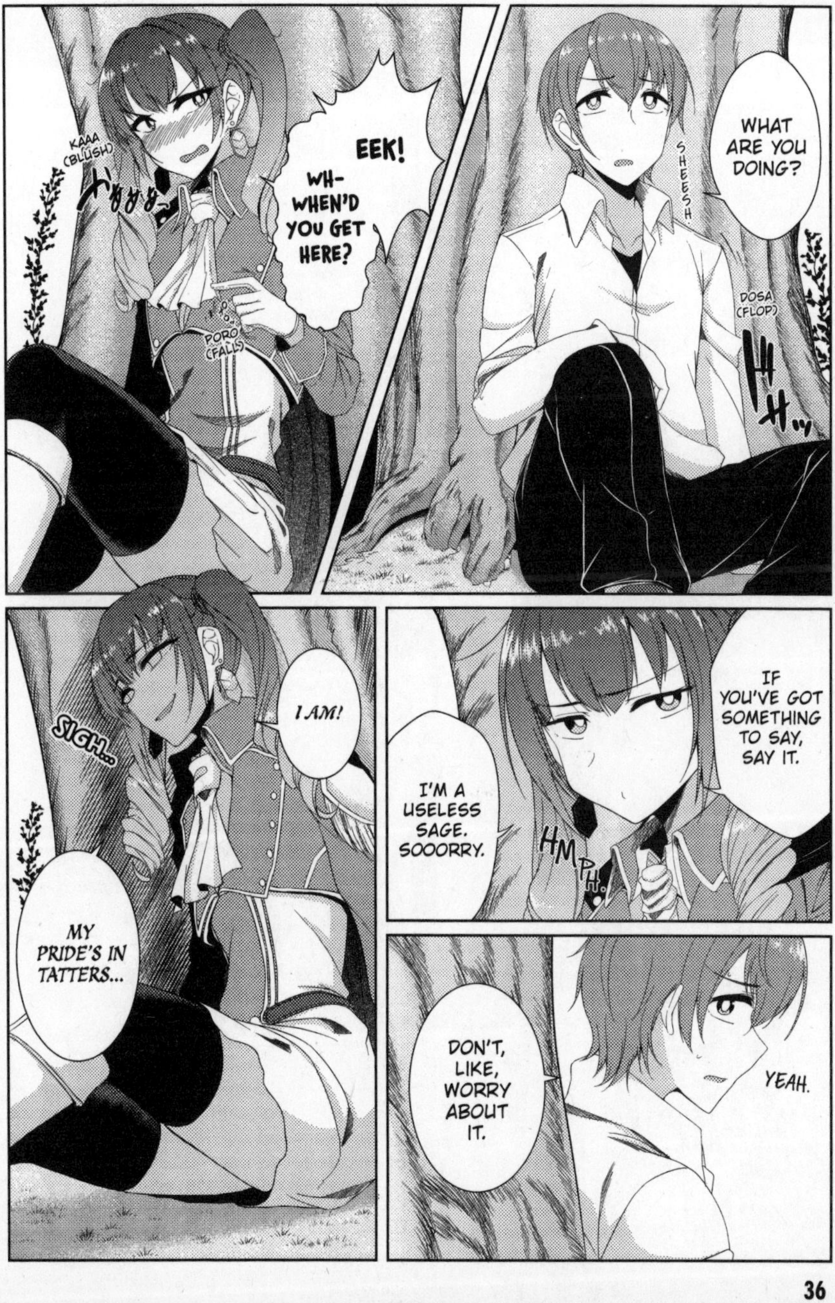
WHAT ARE YOU DOING?
SHEESH
DOSA (FLOP)
EEK!
WH- WHEN'D YOU GET HERE?
KAAA (BLUSH)
PORO (FALL)
IF YOU'VE GOT SOMETHING TO SAY, SAY IT.
I'M A USELESS SAGE. SOOORRY.
HMPH.
YEAH.
DON'T, LIKE, WORRY ABOUT IT.
I AM!
SIGH...
MY PRIDE'S IN TATTERS...

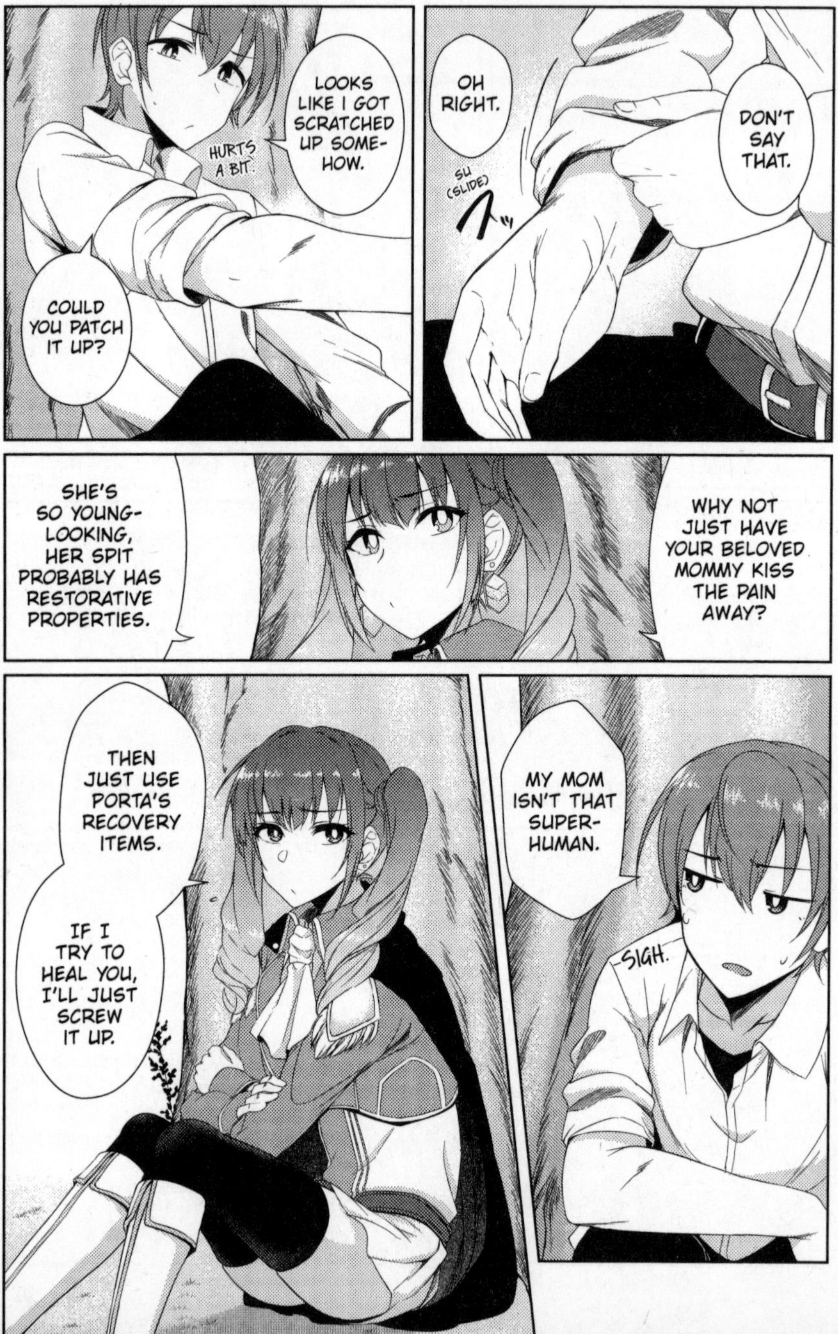
OH RIGHT.
SU (SLIDE)
DON'T SAY THAT.
LOOKS LIKE I GOT SCRATCHED UP SOME-HOW.
HURTS A BIT.
COULD YOU PATCH IT UP?
WHY NOT JUST HAVE YOUR BELOVED MOMMY KISS THE PAIN AWAY?
SHE'S SO YOUNG-LOOKING, HER SPIT PROBABLY HAS RESTORATIVE PROPERTIES.
MY MOM ISN'T THAT SUPER-HUMAN.
-SIGH.
THEN JUST USE PORTA'S RECOVERY ITEMS.
IF I TRY TO HEAL YOU, I'LL JUST SCREW IT UP.

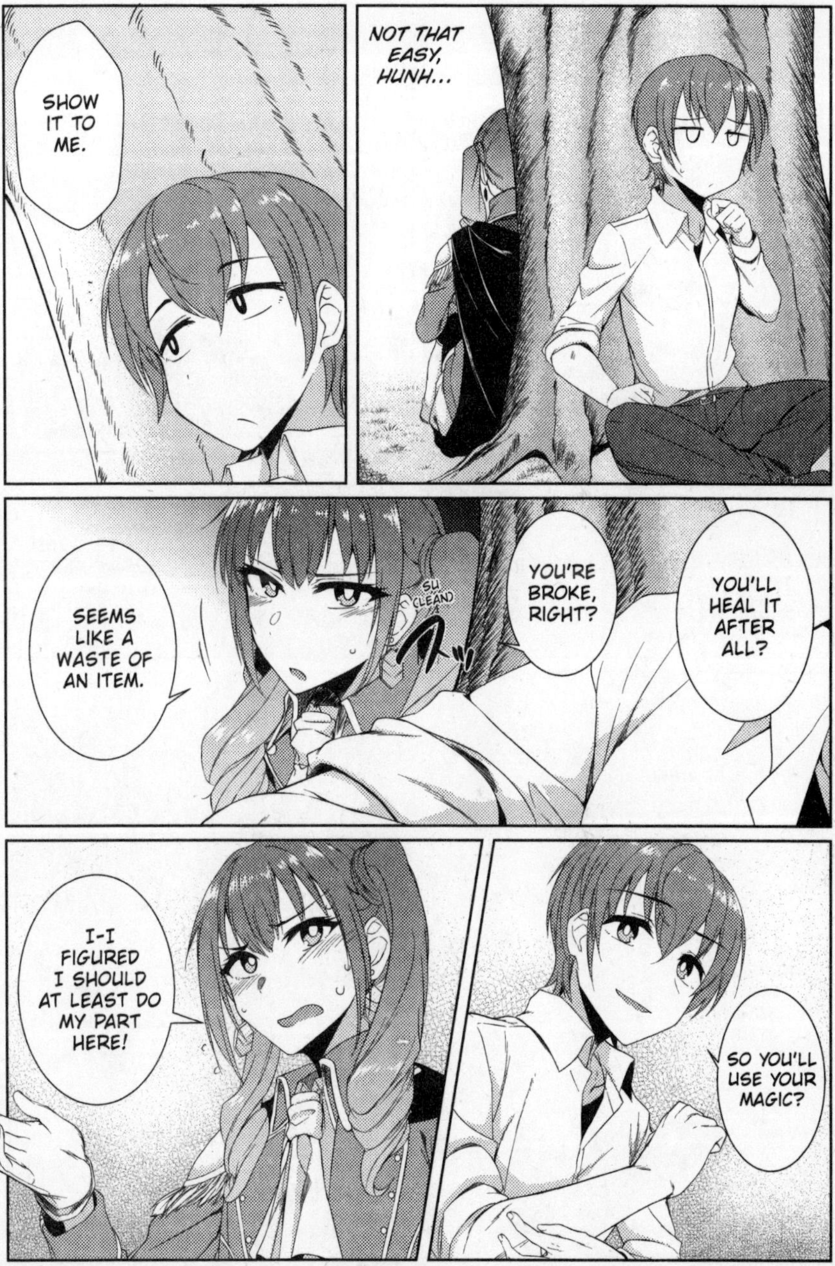
NOT THAT EASY, HUNH...
SHOW IT TO ME.
YOU'LL HEAL IT AFTER ALL?
YOU'RE BROKE, RIGHT?
SU CLEAN
SEEMS LIKE A WASTE OF AN ITEM.
SO YOU'LL USE YOUR MAGIC?
I-I FIGURED I SHOULD AT LEAST DO MY PART HERE!

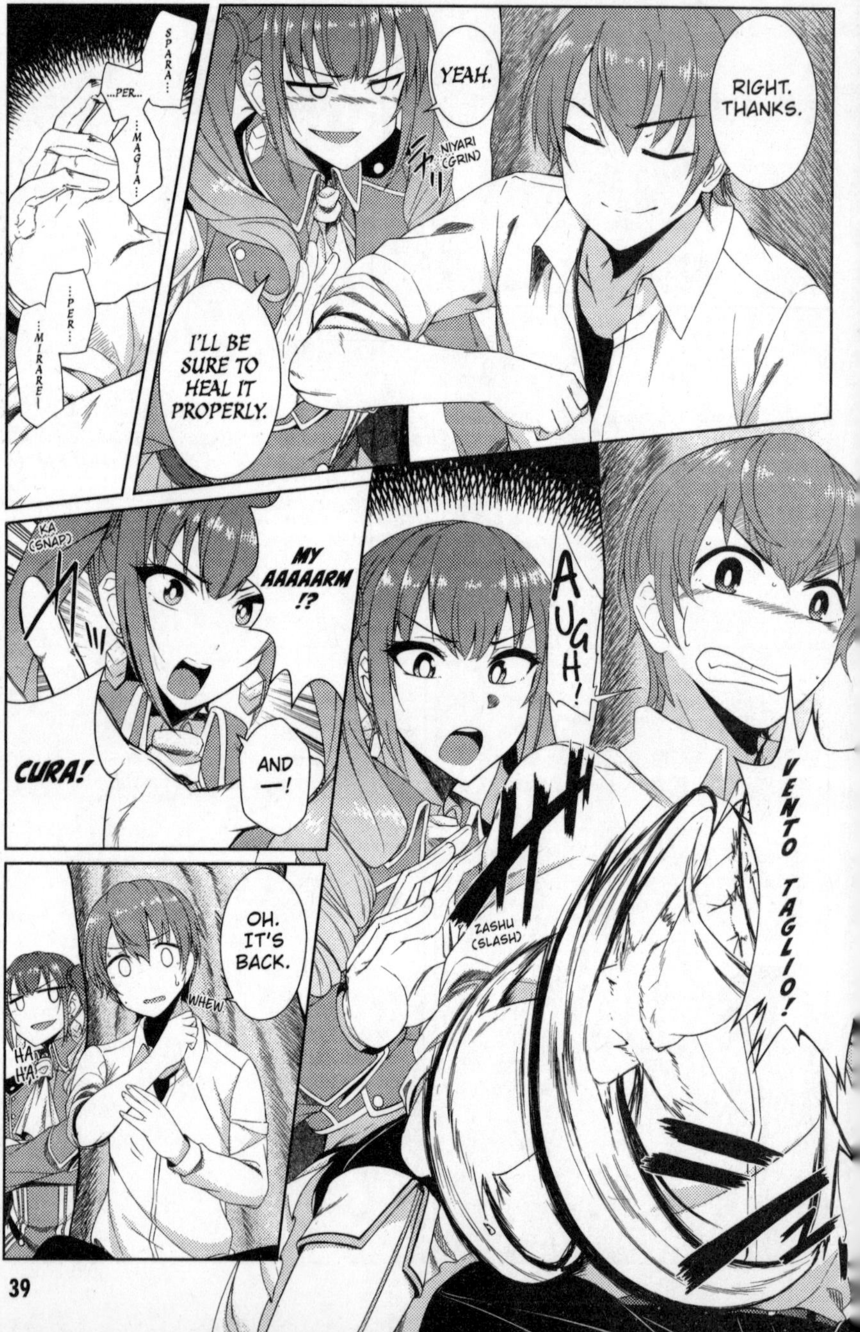
RIGHT. THANKS.
YEAH.
NIYARI (GRIN)
I'LL BE SURE TO HEAL IT PROPERLY.
SPARA...
...PER...
...MAGIA...
...PER...
...MIRARE!
AUGH!
VENTO TAGLIO!
ZASHU (SLASH)
MY AAAAARM!?
KA (SNAP)
AND—!
CURA!
OH. IT'S BACK.
WHEW.
HA HA!

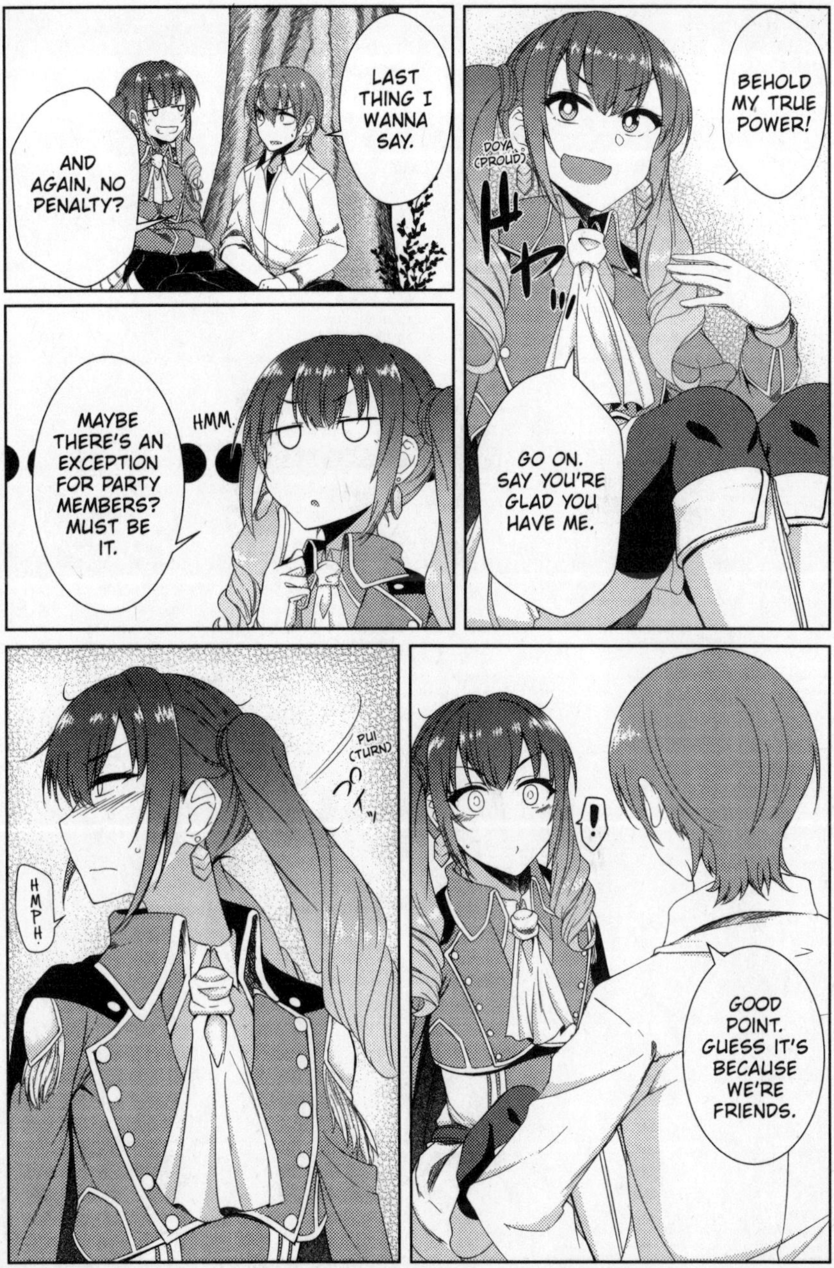

BEHOLD MY TRUE POWER!
DOYA (PROUD)
GO ON. SAY YOU'RE GLAD YOU HAVE ME.
LAST THING I WANNA SAY.
AND AGAIN, NO PENALTY?
HMM.
MAYBE THERE'S AN EXCEPTION FOR PARTY MEMBERS? MUST BE IT.
!
GOOD POINT. GUESS IT'S BECAUSE WE'RE FRIENDS.
PUI (TURN)
HMPH.

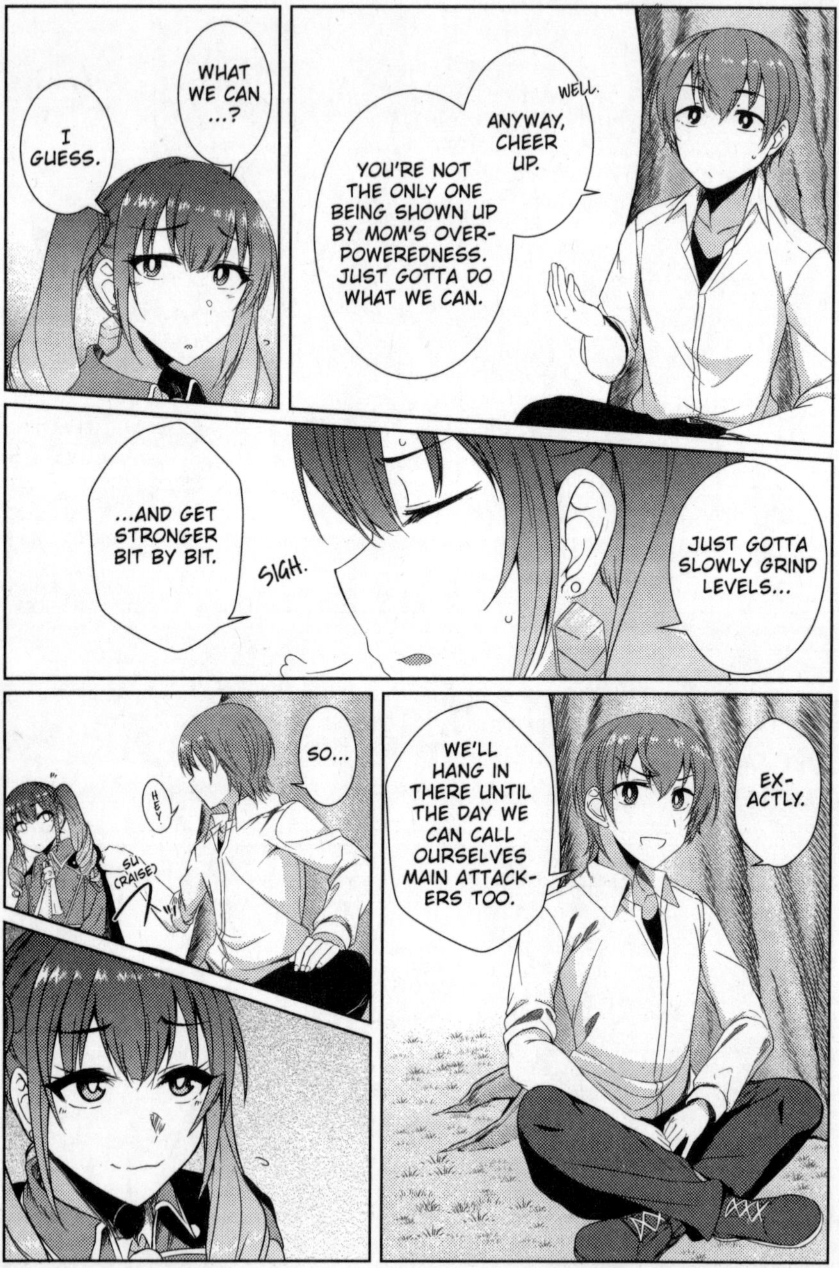
WELL.
ANYWAY, CHEER UP.
YOU'RE NOT THE ONLY ONE BEING SHOWN UP BY MOM'S OVER-POWEREDNESS. JUST GOTTA DO WHAT WE CAN.
WHAT WE CAN ...?
I GUESS.
JUST GOTTA SLOWLY GRIND LEVELS...
SIGH.
...AND GET STRONGER BIT BY BIT.
EX-ACTLY.
WE'LL HANG IN THERE UNTIL THE DAY WE CAN CALL OURSELVES MAIN ATTACK-ERS TOO.
SO...
HEY.
SU (RAISE)

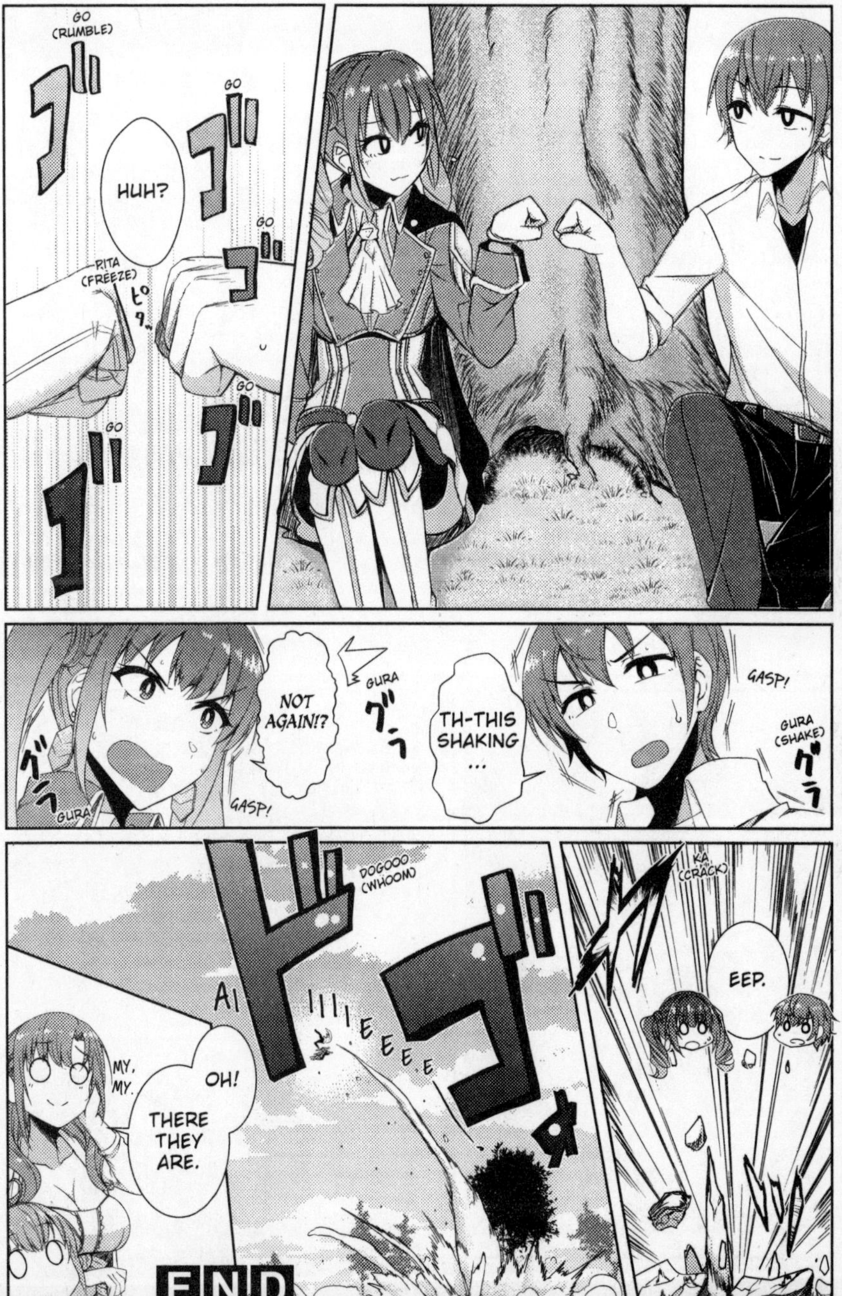

GO (RUMBLE)
GO
HUH?
GO
PITA (FREEZE)
GO
GO
GASP!
GURA (SHAKE)
TH-THIS SHAKING ...
GURA
NOT AGAIN!?
GASP!
GURA
KA (CRACK)
EEP.
DOGOOO (WHOOM)
AIIIIIEEEEE
OH! THERE THEY ARE.
MY, MY.
END

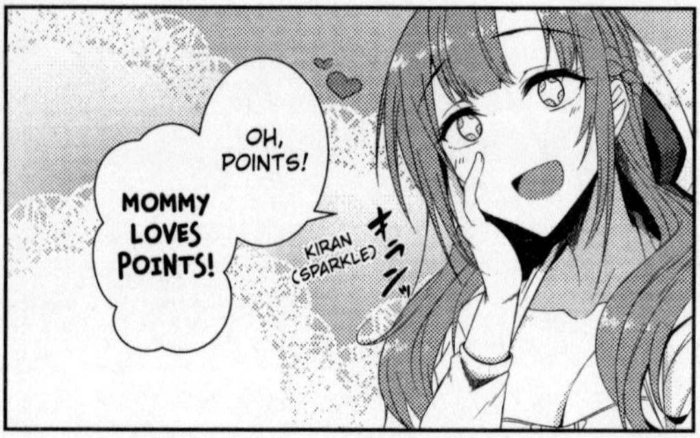
KIRAN (SPARKLE)
OH, POINTS!
MOMMY LOVES POINTS!

DO YOU LOVE YOUR MOM AND HER TWO-HIT, MULTI-TARGET ATTACKS?

COMIC: MEICHA
STORY: DACHIMA INAKA, ILLUST: IIDA POCHI.
VOLUME 2

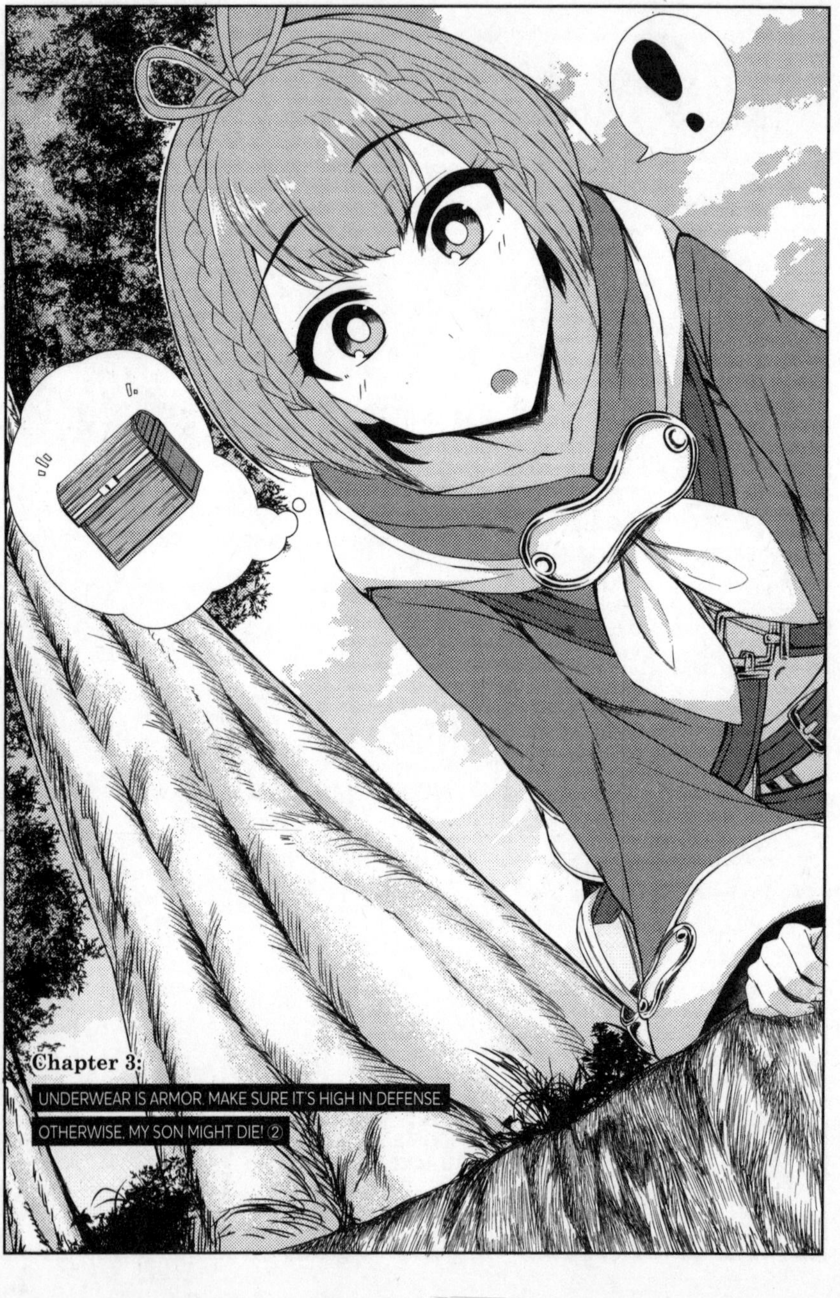
!
Chapter 3:
UNDERWEAR IS ARMOR. MAKE SURE IT'S HIGH IN DEFENSE. OTHERWISE, MY SON MIGHT DIE! ②

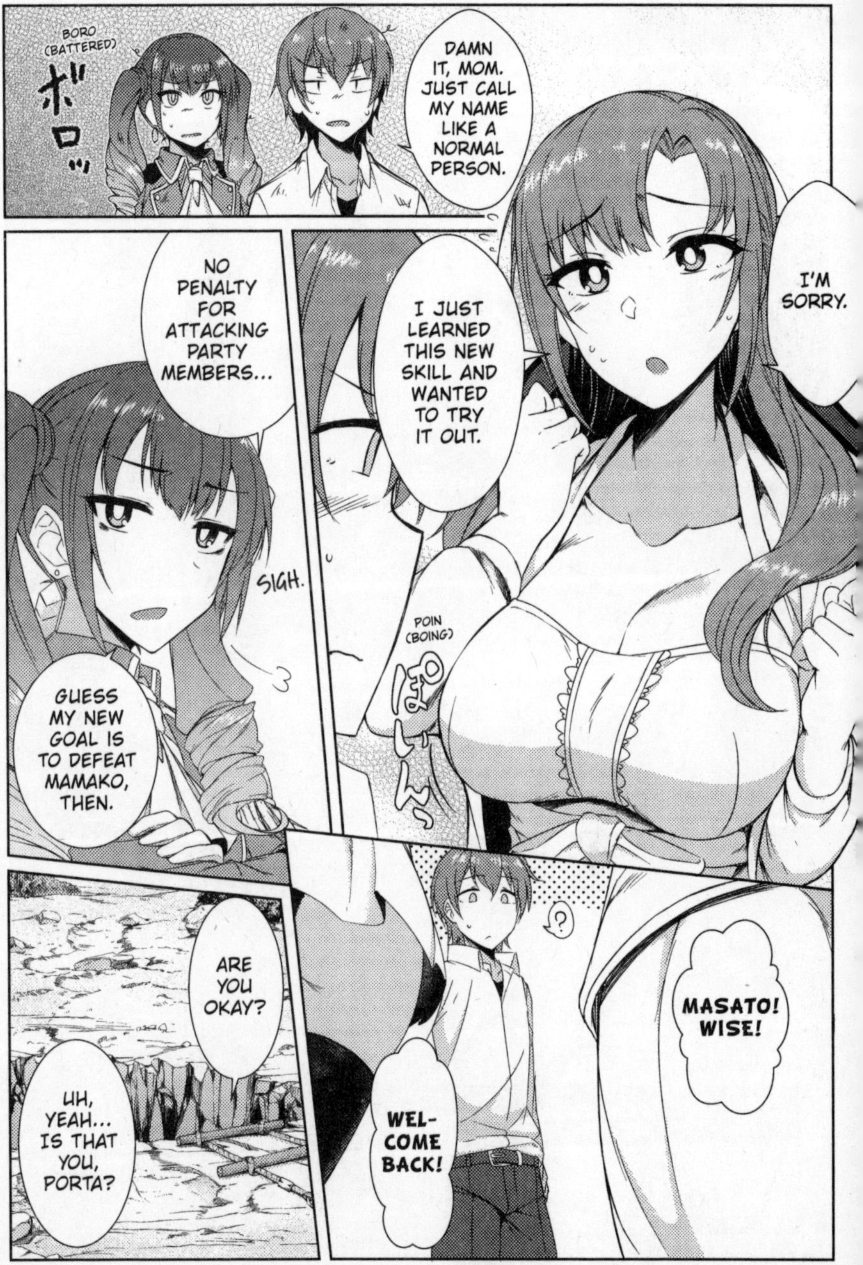
DAMN IT, MOM. JUST CALL MY NAME LIKE A NORMAL PERSON.
BORO (BATTERED)
ボロッ
I'M SORRY.
I JUST LEARNED THIS NEW SKILL AND WANTED TO TRY IT OUT.
POIN (BOING)
ぽいん
NO PENALTY FOR ATTACKING PARTY MEMBERS...
SIGH.
GUESS MY NEW GOAL IS TO DEFEAT MAMAKO, THEN.
MASATO! WISE!
WEL-COME BACK!
?
ARE YOU OKAY?
UH, YEAH... IS THAT YOU, PORTA?

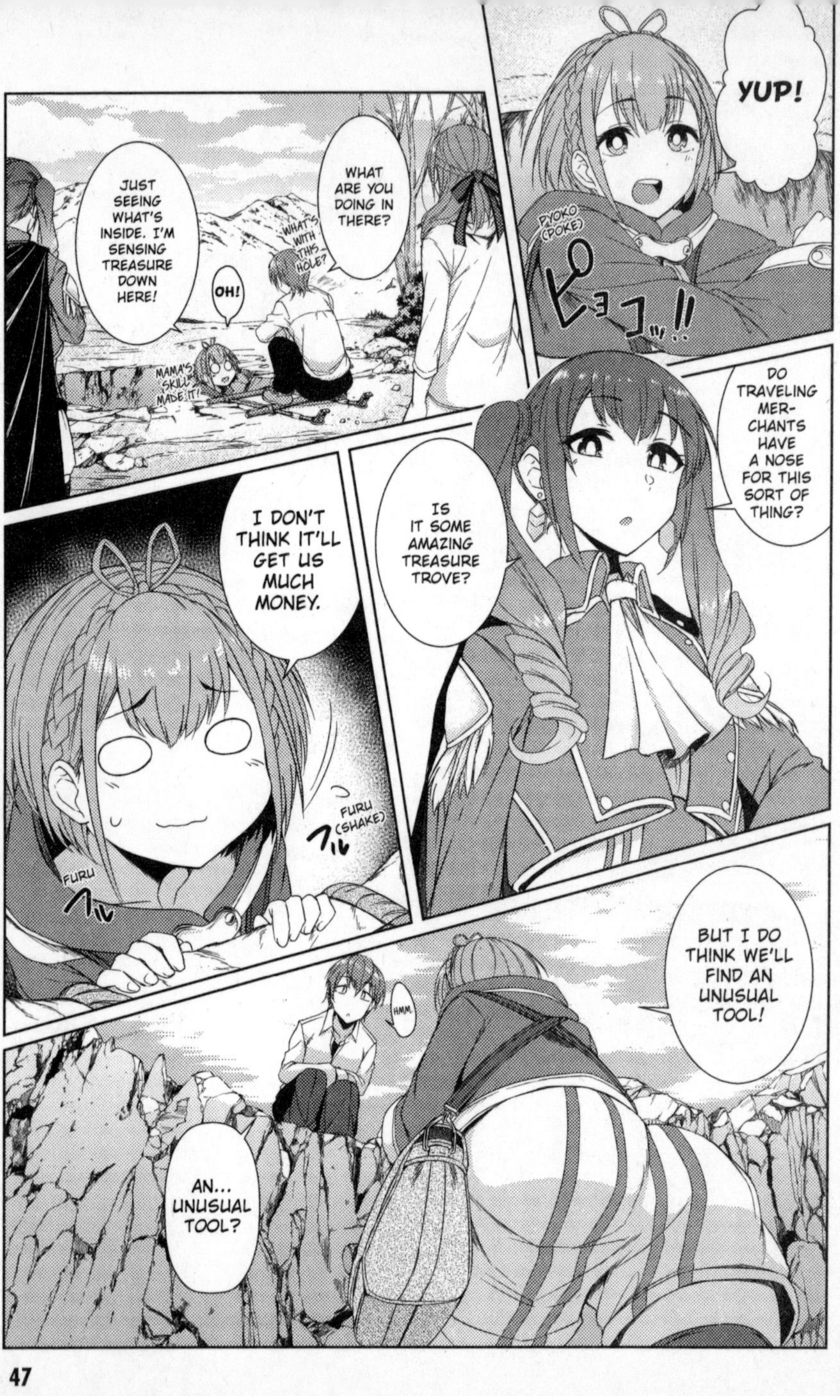
YUP!
PYOKO (POKE)
ピョコッ!!
WHAT ARE YOU DOING IN THERE?
WHAT'S WITH THIS HOLE?
JUST SEEING WHAT'S INSIDE. I'M SENSING TREASURE DOWN HERE!
OH!
MAMA'S SKILL MADE IT!
DO TRAVELING MER-CHANTS HAVE A NOSE FOR THIS SORT OF THING?
IS IT SOME AMAZING TREASURE TROVE?
I DON'T THINK IT'LL GET US MUCH MONEY.
FURU (SHAKE)
フル
FURU
フル
BUT I DO THINK WE'LL FIND AN UNUSUAL TOOL!
HMM.
AN... UNUSUAL TOOL?

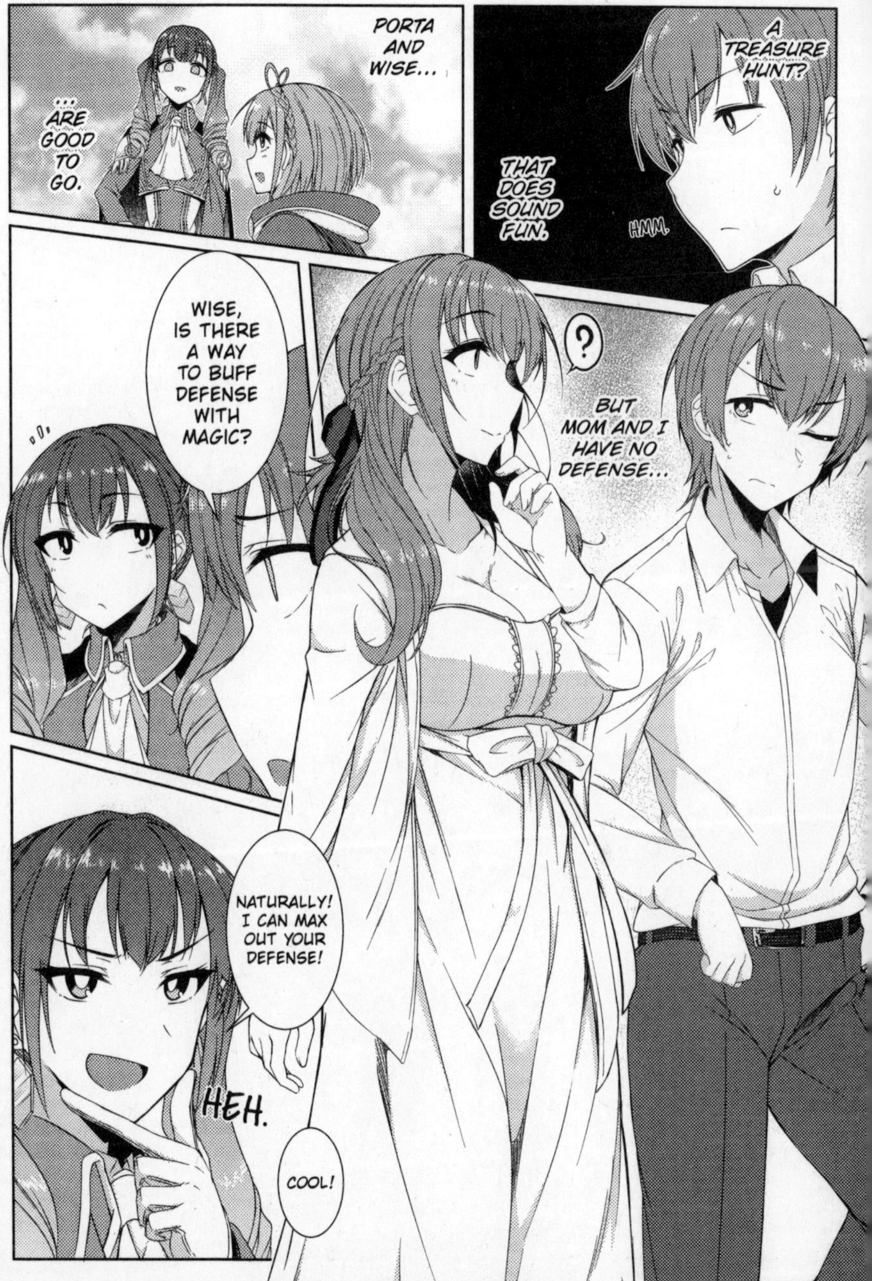
A TREASURE HUNT?
THAT DOES SOUND FUN.
HMM.
PORTA AND WISE...
...ARE GOOD TO GO.
?
BUT MOM AND I HAVE NO DEFENSE...
WISE, IS THERE A WAY TO BUFF DEFENSE WITH MAGIC?
NATURALLY! I CAN MAX OUT YOUR DEFENSE!
HEH.
COOL!

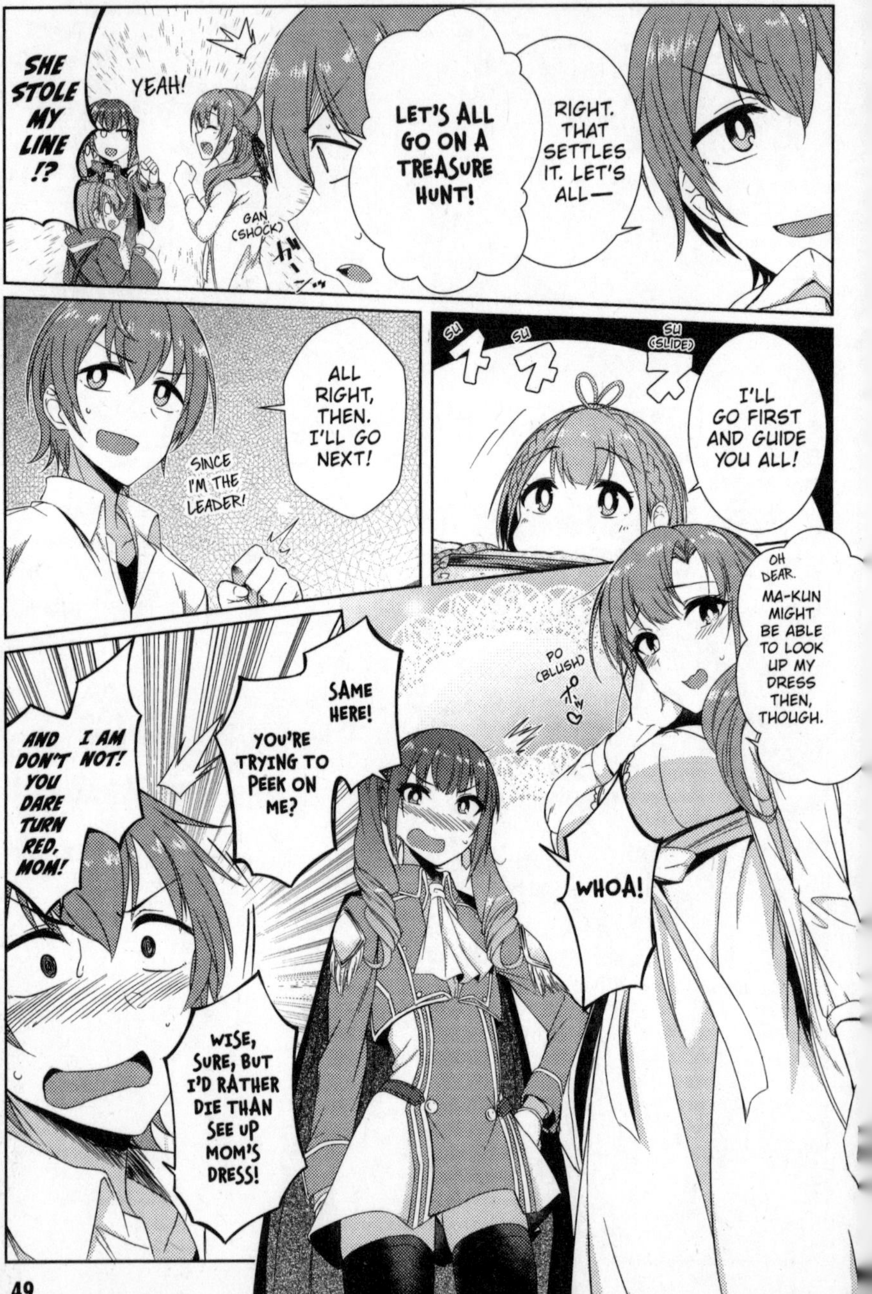
RIGHT. THAT SETTLES IT. LET'S ALL—
LET'S ALL GO ON A TREASURE HUNT!
GAN (SHOCK)
YEAH!
SHE STOLE MY LINE!?
SU (SLIDE)
SU
SU
I'LL GO FIRST AND GUIDE YOU ALL!
ALL RIGHT, THEN. I'LL GO NEXT!
SINCE I'M THE LEADER!
OH DEAR. MA-KUN MIGHT BE ABLE TO LOOK UP MY DRESS THEN, THOUGH.
PO (BLUSH)
SAME HERE!
YOU'RE TRYING TO PEEK ON ME?
WHOA!
I AM NOT!
AND DON'T YOU DARE TURN RED, MOM!
WISE, SURE, BUT I'D RATHER DIE THAN SEE UP MOM'S DRESS!

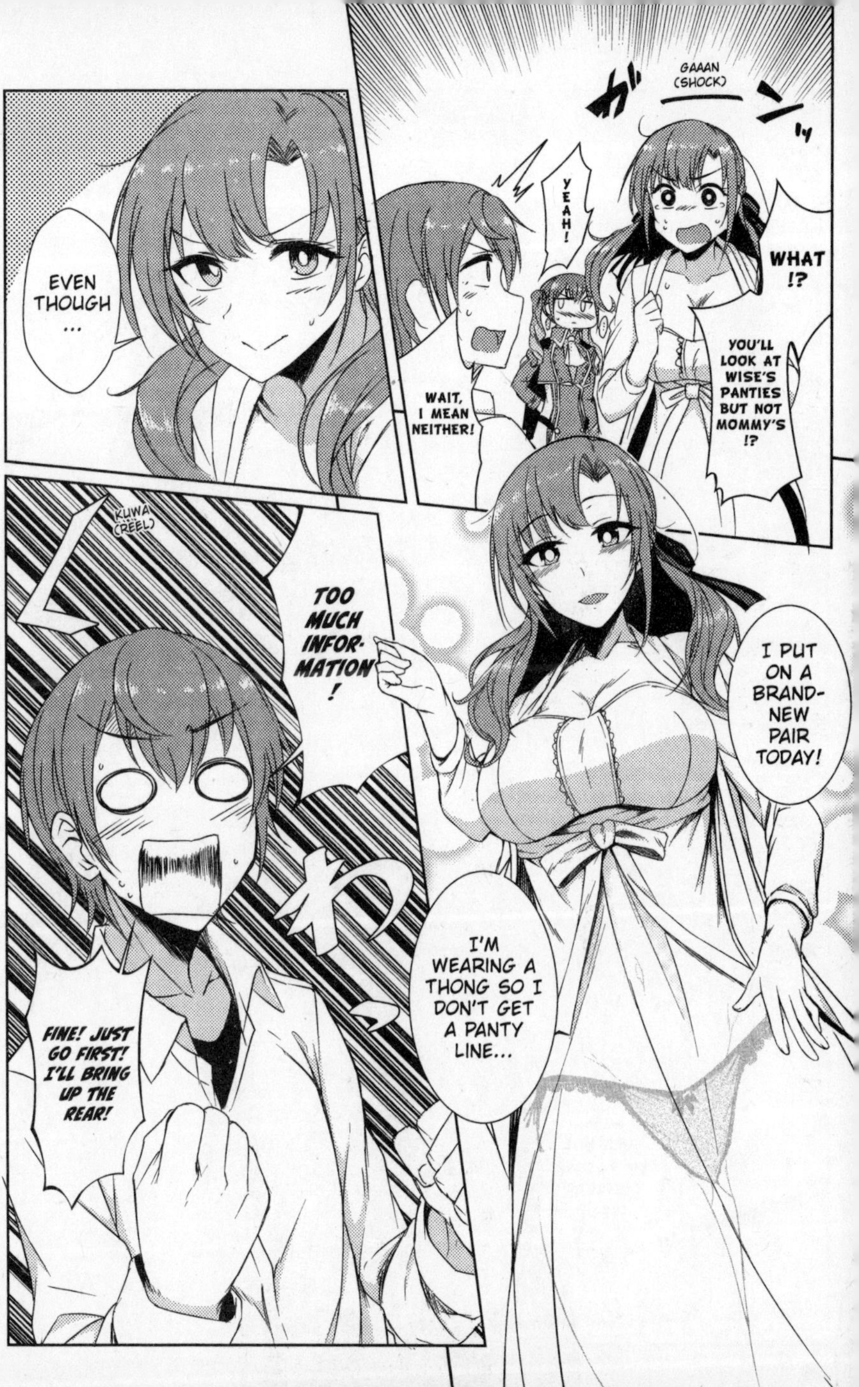
GAAAN (SHOCK)
WHAT !?
YOU'LL LOOK AT WISE'S PANTIES BUT NOT MOMMY'S !?
YEAH!
WAIT, I MEAN NEITHER!
EVEN THOUGH ...
I PUT ON A BRAND-NEW PAIR TODAY!
I'M WEARING A THONG SO I DON'T GET A PANTY LINE...
KUWA (REEL)
TOO MUCH INFORMATION !
FINE! JUST GO FIRST! I'LL BRING UP THE REAR!

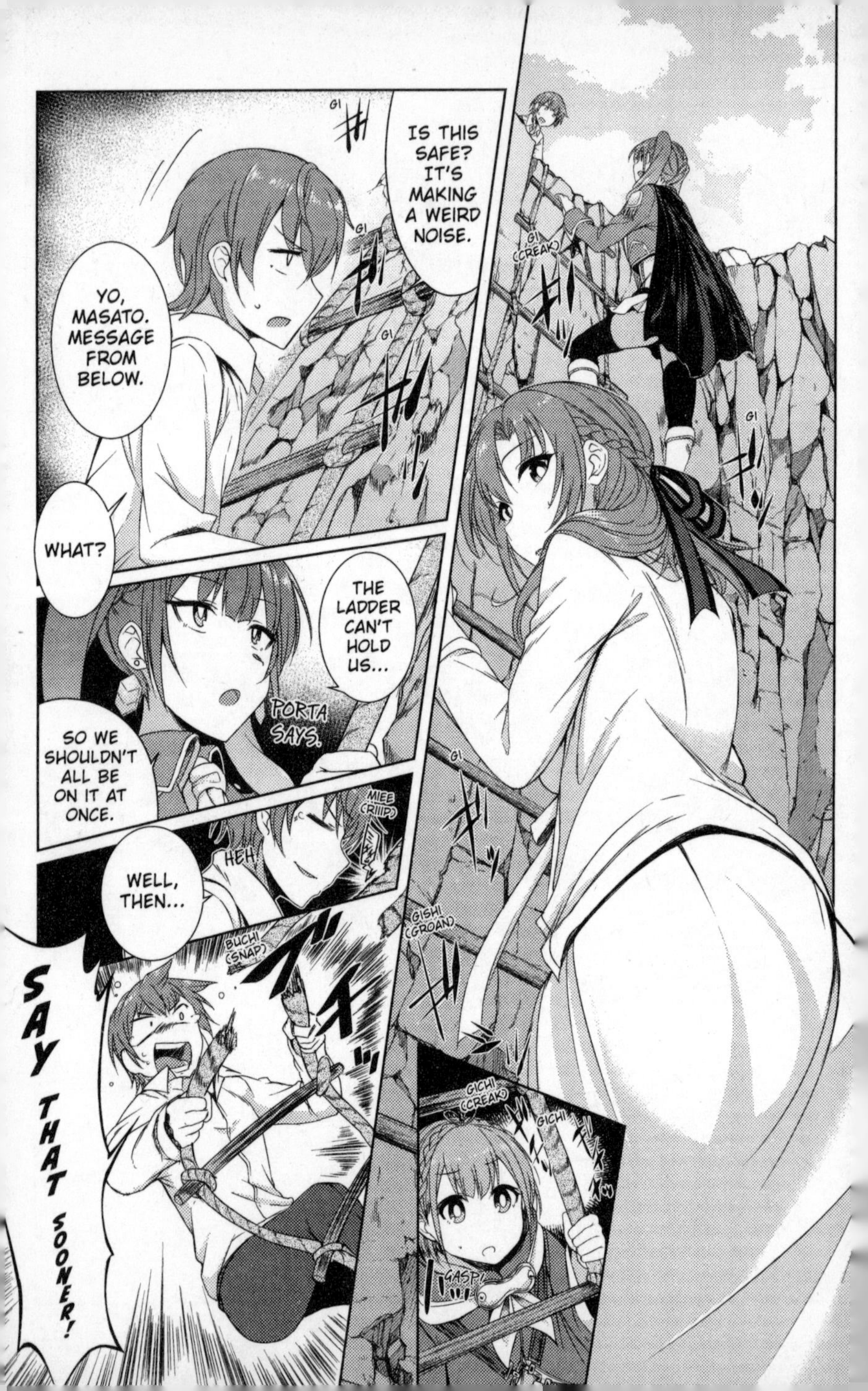
GI (CREAK)
GI
GI
GISHI (GROAN)
GI
IS THIS SAFE? IT'S MAKING A WEIRD NOISE.
GI
GI
YO, MASATO. MESSAGE FROM BELOW.
WHAT?
THE LADDER CAN'T HOLD US...
PORTA SAYS.
SO WE SHOULDN'T ALL BE ON IT AT ONCE.
MIEE (RIIIP)
HEH
WELL, THEN...
GICHI (CREAK)
GICHI
GASP!
BUCHI (SNAP)
SAY THAT SOONER!

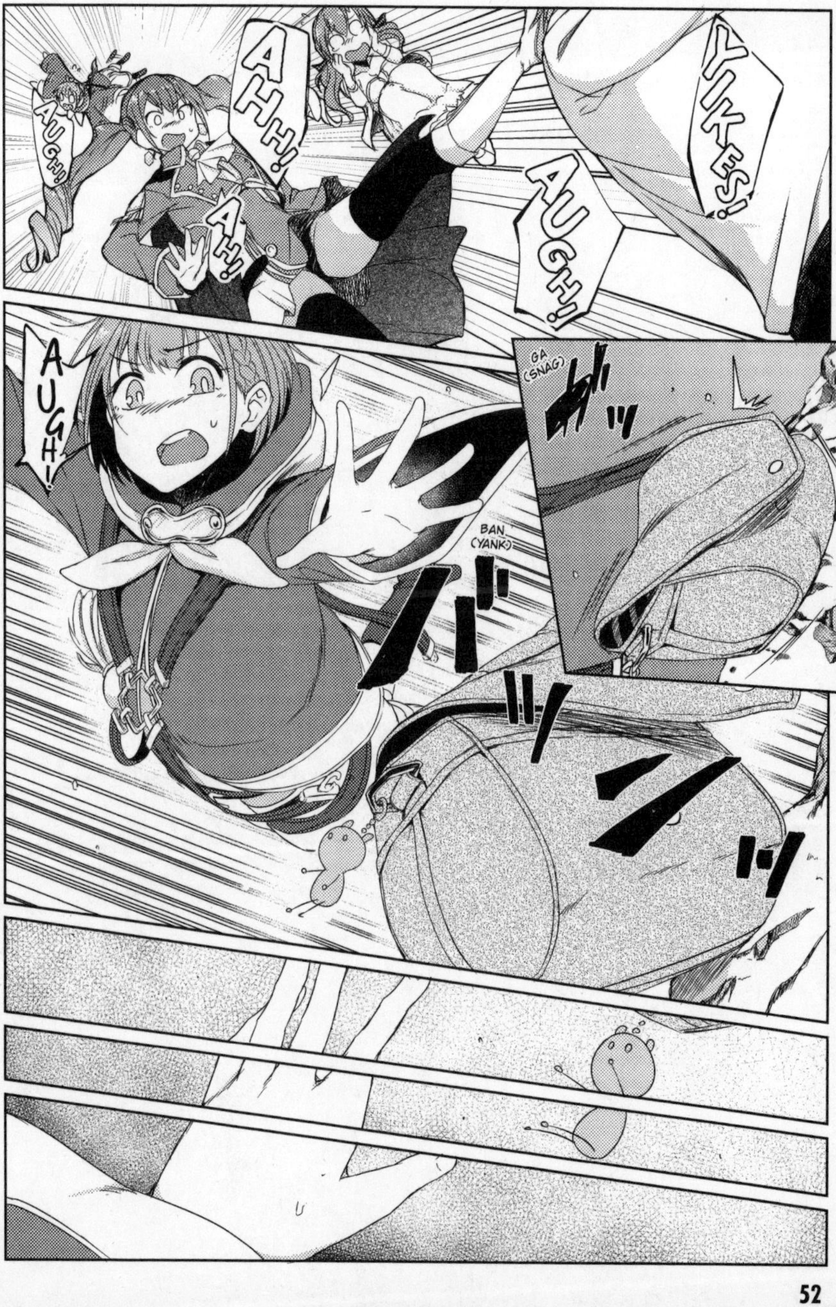
YIKES!
AUGH!
AHH!
AH!
AUGH!
GA (SNAG)
AUGH!
BAN (YANK)

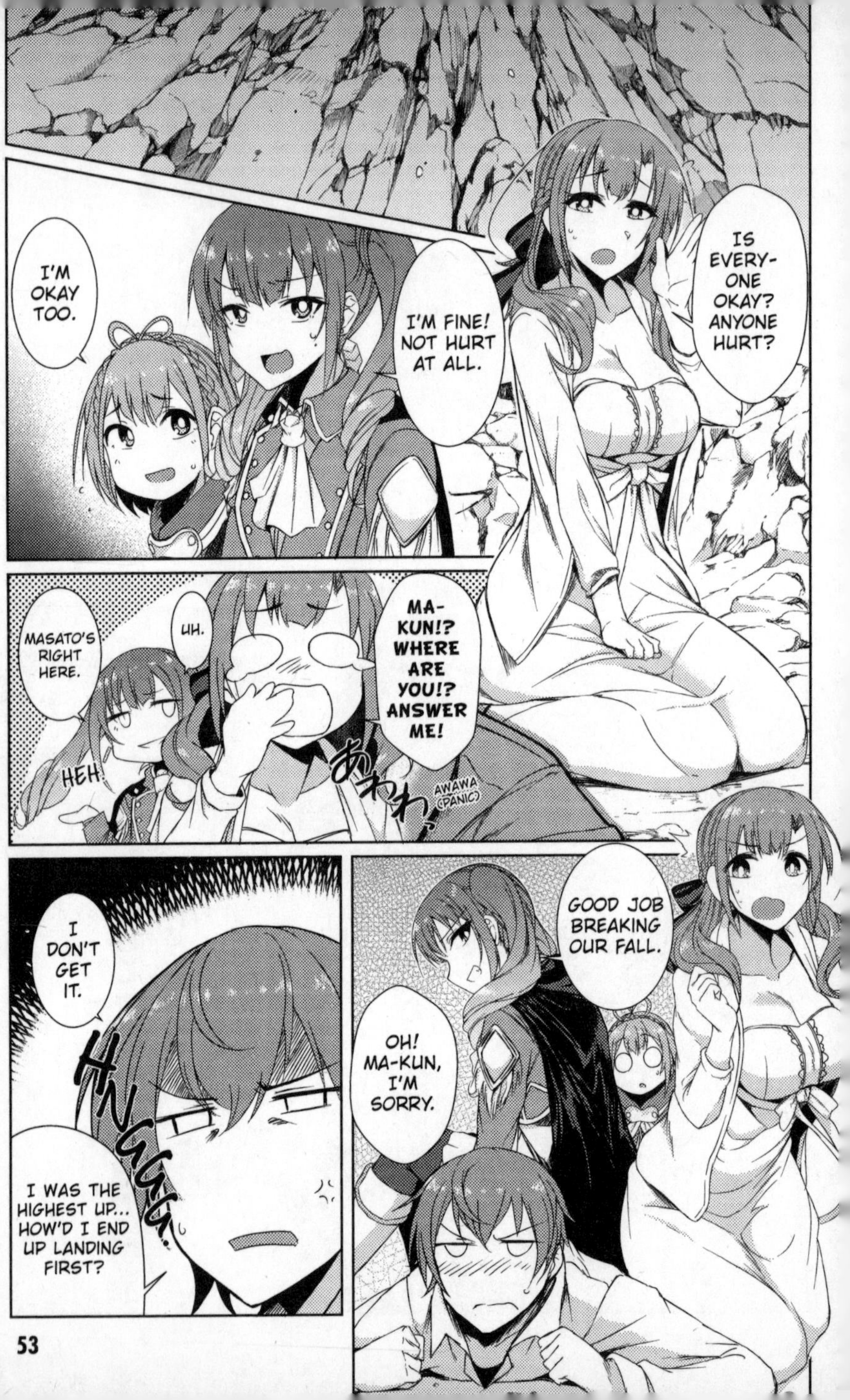
IS EVERYONE OKAY? ANYONE HURT?
I'M FINE! NOT HURT AT ALL.
I'M OKAY TOO.
MA-KUN!? WHERE ARE YOU!? ANSWER ME!
UH.
MASATO'S RIGHT HERE.
HEH
あわわ
AWAWA (PANIC)
GOOD JOB BREAKING OUR FALL.
OH! MA-KUN, I'M SORRY.
I DON'T GET IT.
HNGUU
I WAS THE HIGHEST UP... HOW'D I END UP LANDING FIRST?

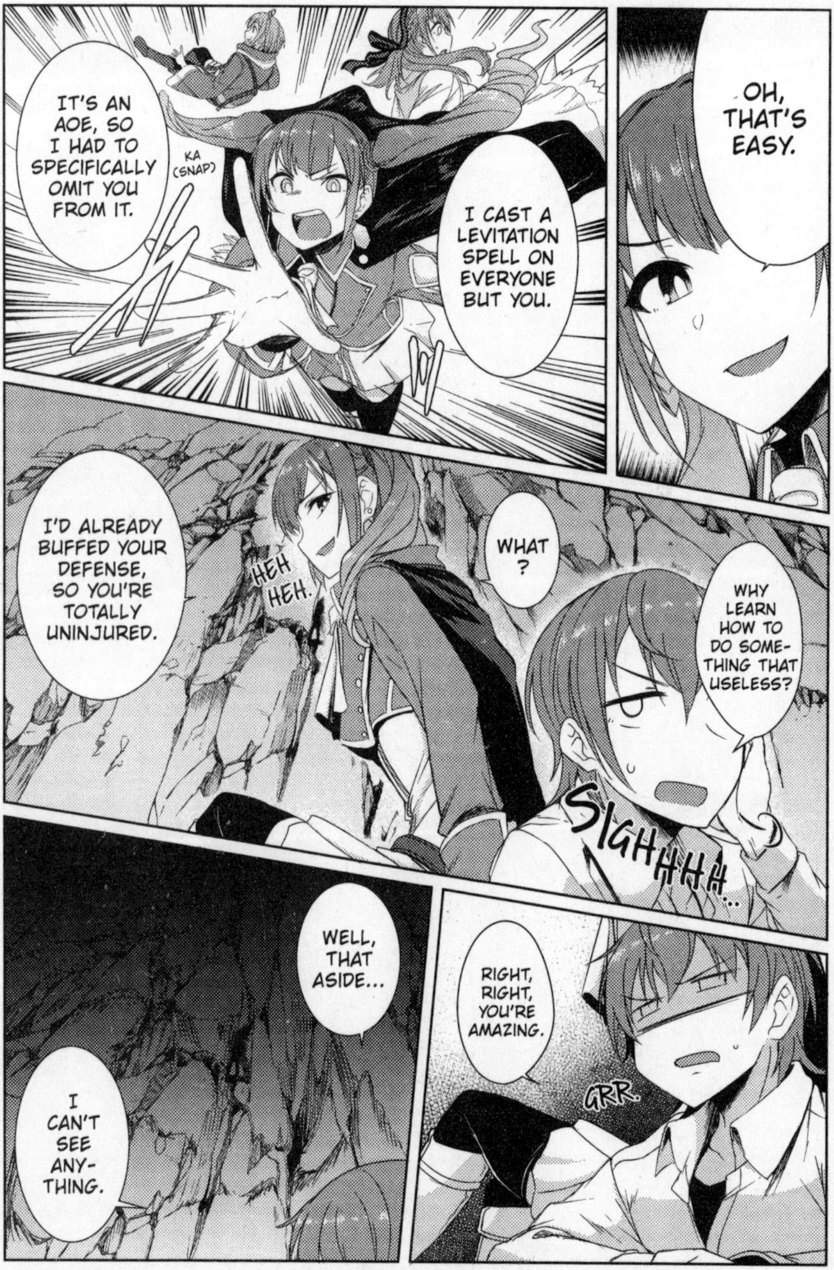
OH, THAT'S EASY.
I CAST A LEVITATION SPELL ON EVERYONE BUT YOU.
KA (SNAP)
IT'S AN AOE, SO I HAD TO SPECIFICALLY OMIT YOU FROM IT.
I'D ALREADY BUFFED YOUR DEFENSE, SO YOU'RE TOTALLY UNINJURED.
HEH HEH.
WHAT?
WHY LEARN HOW TO DO SOMETHING THAT USELESS?
SIGHHHH...
RIGHT, RIGHT, YOU'RE AMAZING.
GRR.
WELL, THAT ASIDE...
I CAN'T SEE ANYTHING.

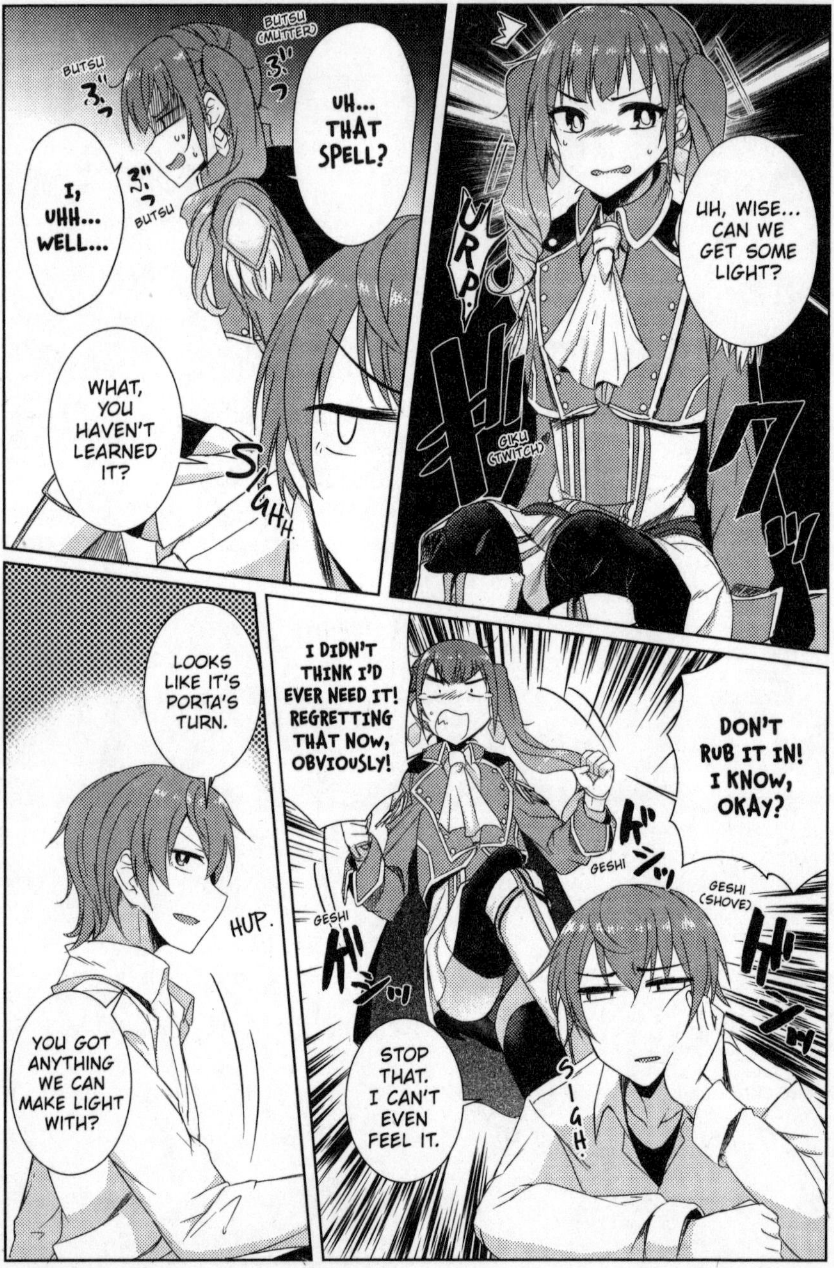
UH, WISE... CAN WE GET SOME LIGHT?
URP.
GIKU (TWITCH)
UH... THAT SPELL?
BUTSU (MUTTER)
BUTSU
I, UHH... WELL...
BUTSU
WHAT, YOU HAVEN'T LEARNED IT?
SIGHH.
DON'T RUB IT IN! I KNOW, OKAY?
I DIDN'T THINK I'D EVER NEED IT! REGRETTING THAT NOW, OBVIOUSLY!
GESHI
GESHI (SHOVE)
GESHI
STOP THAT. I CAN'T EVEN FEEL IT.
SIGH.
LOOKS LIKE IT'S PORTA'S TURN.
HUP.
YOU GOT ANYTHING WE CAN MAKE LIGHT WITH?

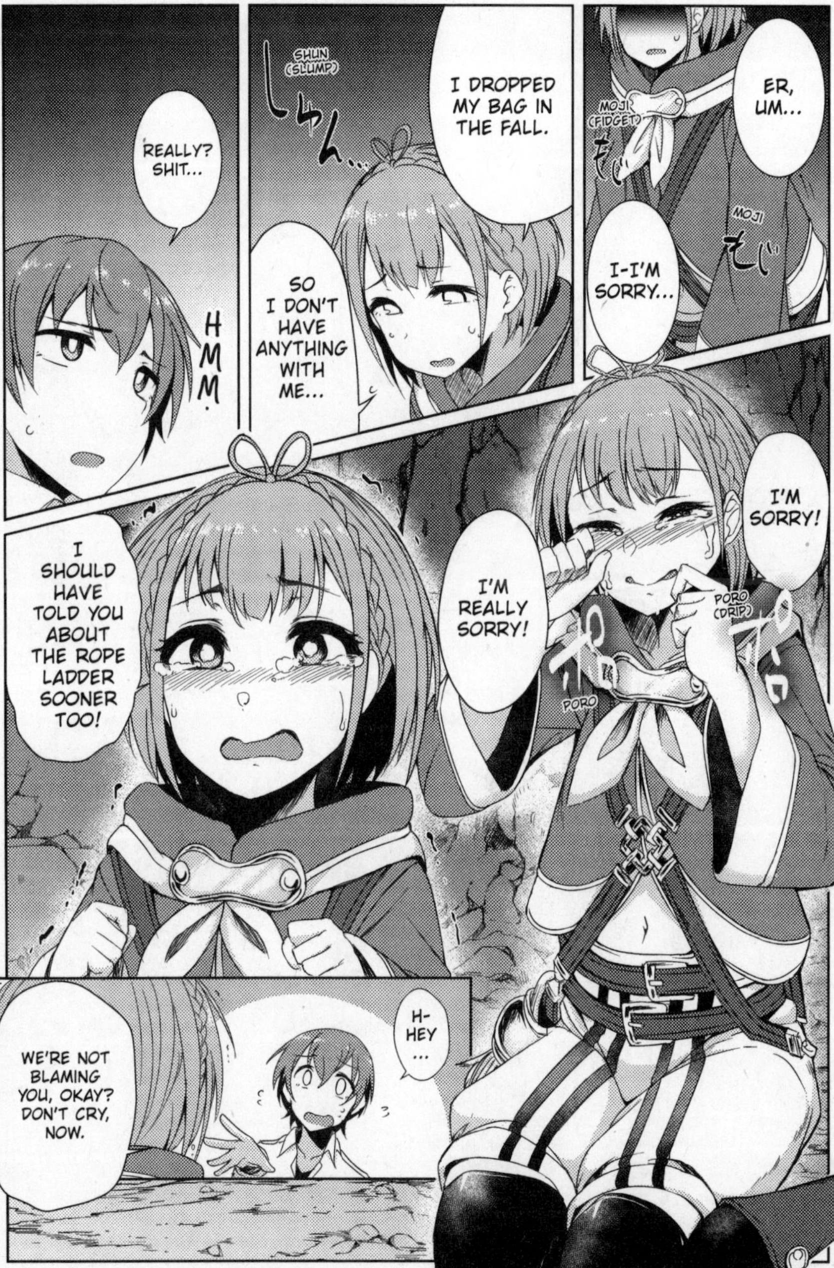

ER, UM...
MOJI (FIDGET)
もじ
MOJI
もじ
I-I'M SORRY...
SHUN (SLUMP)
しゅん...
I DROPPED MY BAG IN THE FALL.
SO I DON'T HAVE ANYTHING WITH ME...
REALLY? SHIT...
HMM.
I'M SORRY!
I'M REALLY SORRY!
PORO (DRIP)
ポロ
PORO
ポロ
I SHOULD HAVE TOLD YOU ABOUT THE ROPE LADDER SOONER TOO!
H-HEY ...
WE'RE NOT BLAMING YOU, OKAY? DON'T CRY, NOW.

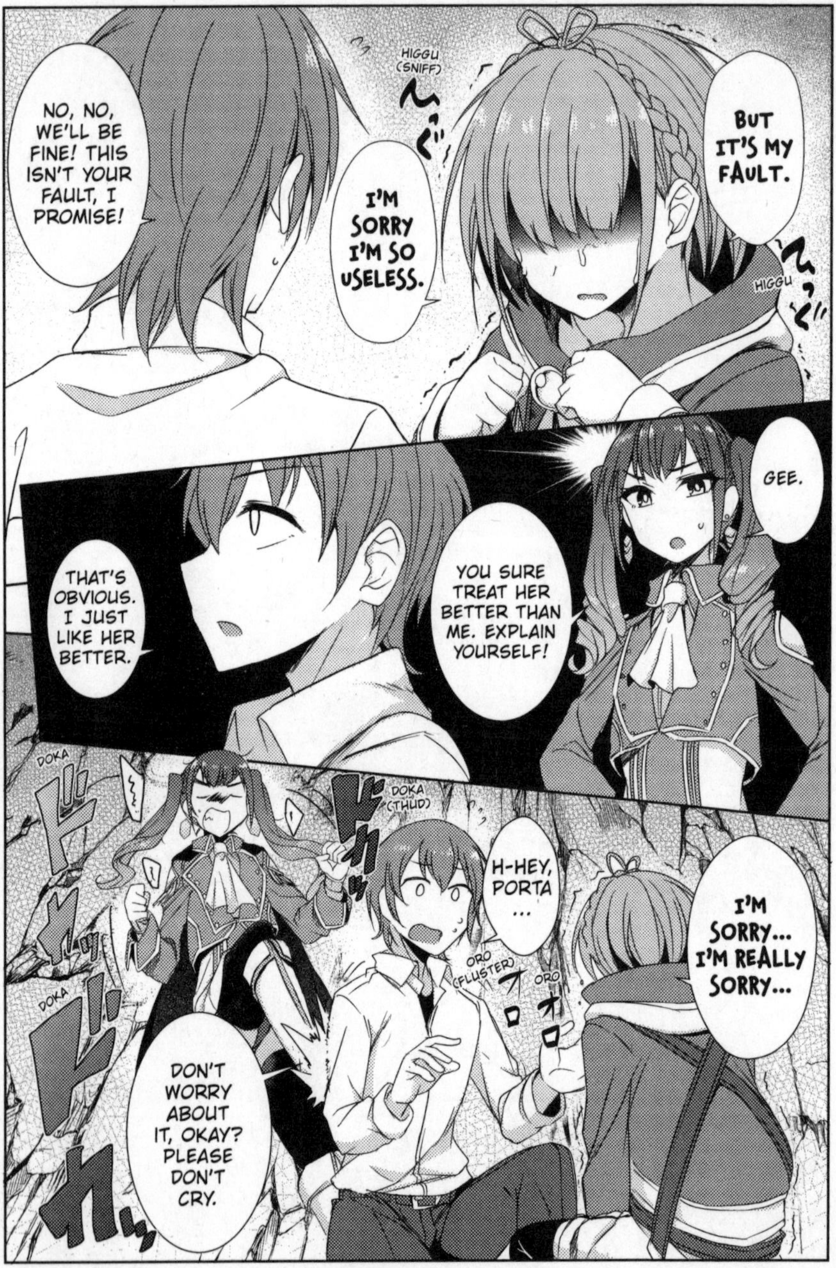
BUT IT'S MY FAULT.
HIGGU
HIGGU (SNIFF)
I'M SORRY I'M SO USELESS.
NO, NO, WE'LL BE FINE! THIS ISN'T YOUR FAULT, I PROMISE!
GEE.
YOU SURE TREAT HER BETTER THAN ME. EXPLAIN YOURSELF!
THAT'S OBVIOUS. I JUST LIKE HER BETTER.
I'M SORRY... I'M REALLY SORRY...
ORO
ORO (FLUSTER)
H-HEY, PORTA ...
DOKA (THUD)
DON'T WORRY ABOUT IT, OKAY? PLEASE DON'T CRY.
DOKA
DOKA

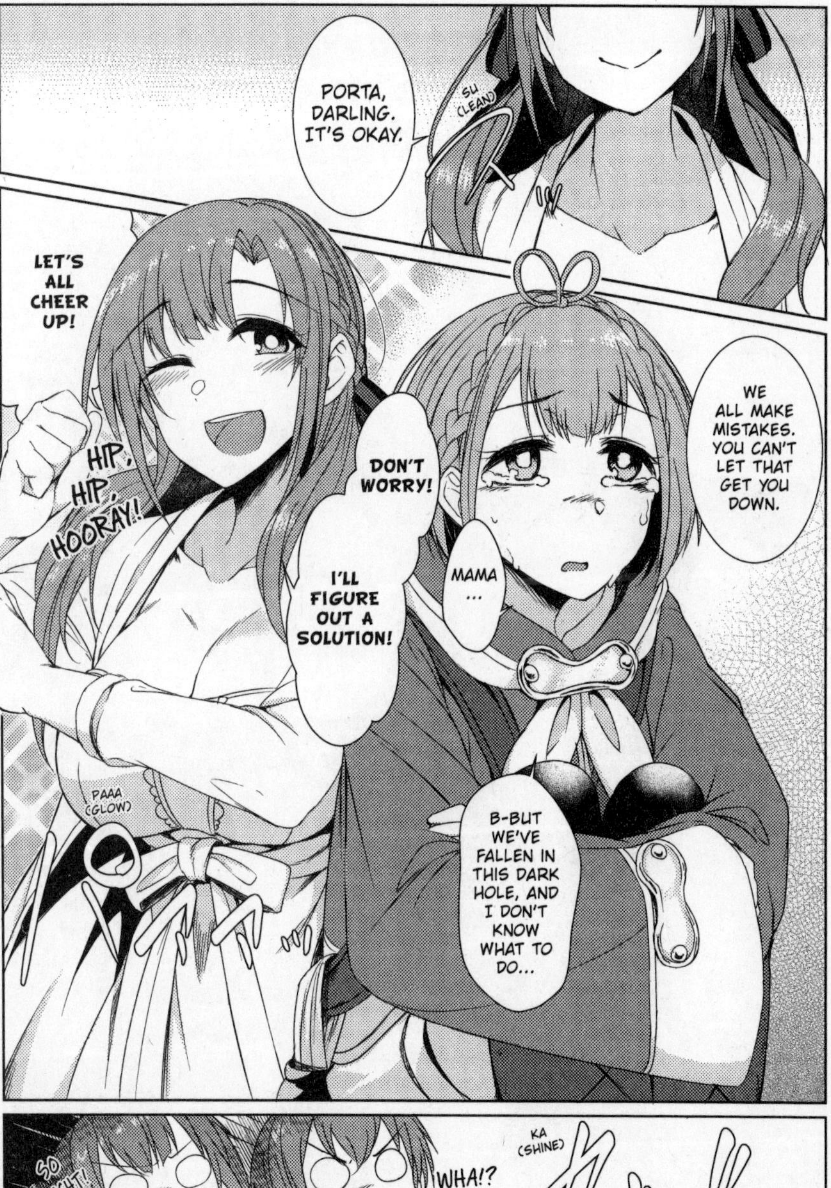
PORTA, DARLING. IT'S OKAY.
SU (LEAN)
WE ALL MAKE MISTAKES. YOU CAN'T LET THAT GET YOU DOWN.
MAMA...
B-BUT WE'VE FALLEN IN THIS DARK HOLE, AND I DON'T KNOW WHAT TO DO...
DON'T WORRY!
I'LL FIGURE OUT A SOLUTION!
LET'S ALL CHEER UP!
HIP, HIP, HOORAY!
PAAA (GLOW)
KA (SHINE)
WHA!?
SO BRIGHT!

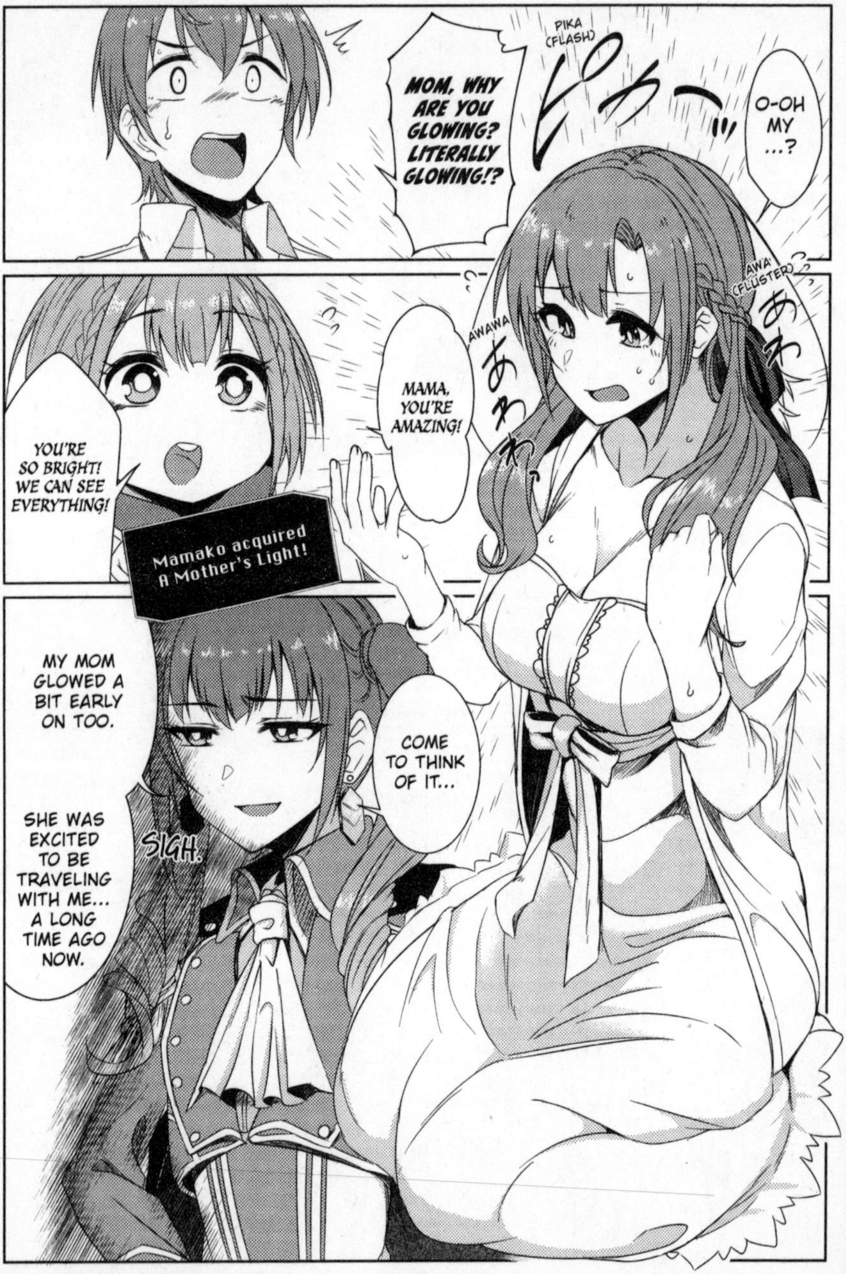

O-OH MY ...?
PIKA (FLASH)
MOM, WHY ARE YOU GLOWING? LITERALLY GLOWING!?
AWA (FLUSTER)
AWAWA
MAMA, YOU'RE AMAZING!
YOU'RE SO BRIGHT! WE CAN SEE EVERYTHING!
Mamako acquired A Mother's Light!
COME TO THINK OF IT...
MY MOM GLOWED A BIT EARLY ON TOO.
SHE WAS EXCITED TO BE TRAVELING WITH ME... A LONG TIME AGO NOW.
SIGH.

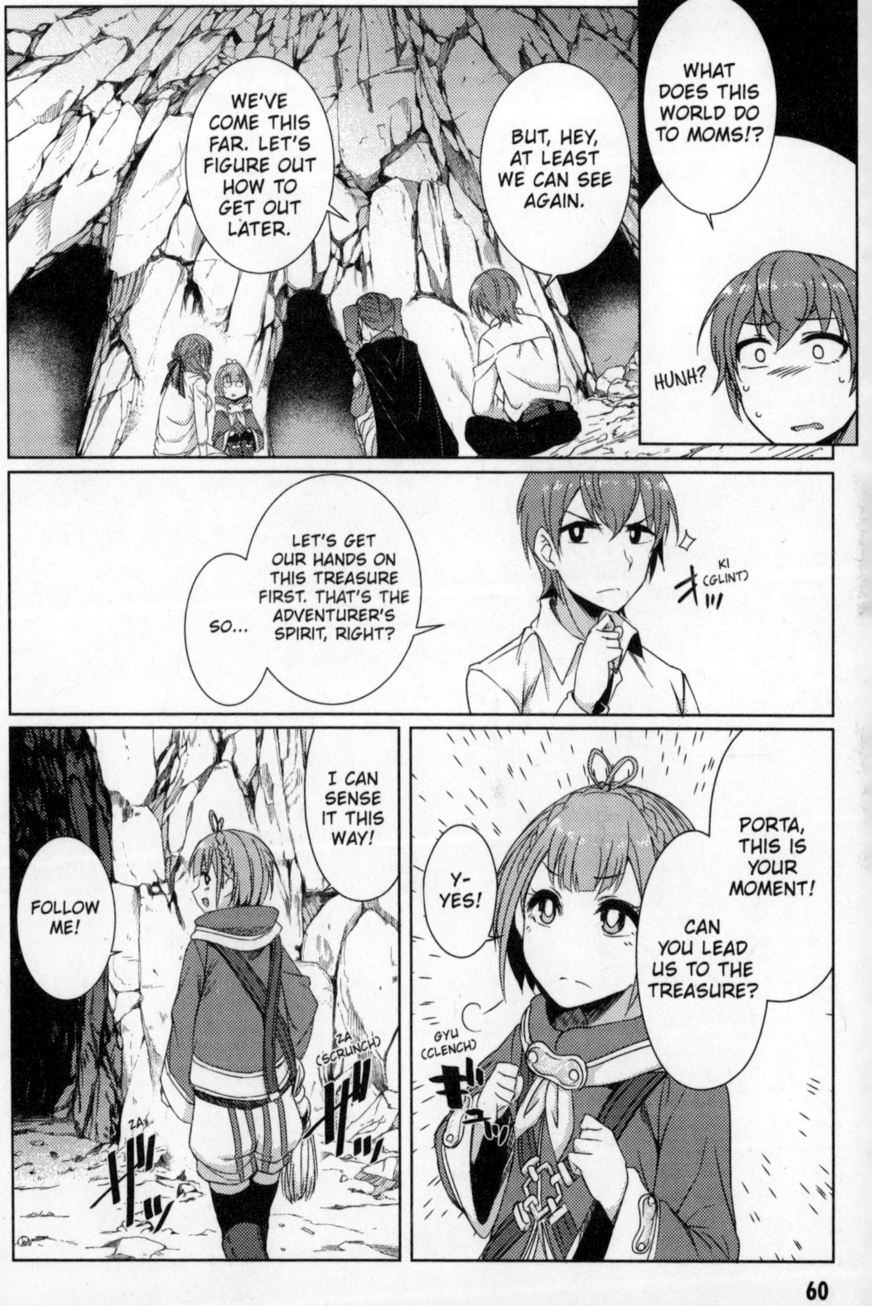
WHAT DOES THIS WORLD DO TO MOMS!?
HUNH?
BUT, HEY, AT LEAST WE CAN SEE AGAIN.
WE'VE COME THIS FAR. LET'S FIGURE OUT HOW TO GET OUT LATER.
KI (GLINT)
SO... LET'S GET OUR HANDS ON THIS TREASURE FIRST. THAT'S THE ADVENTURER'S SPIRIT, RIGHT?
PORTA, THIS IS YOUR MOMENT!
CAN YOU LEAD US TO THE TREASURE?
Y- YES!
GYU (CLENCH)
I CAN SENSE IT THIS WAY!
FOLLOW ME!
ZA (SCRUNCH)
ZA

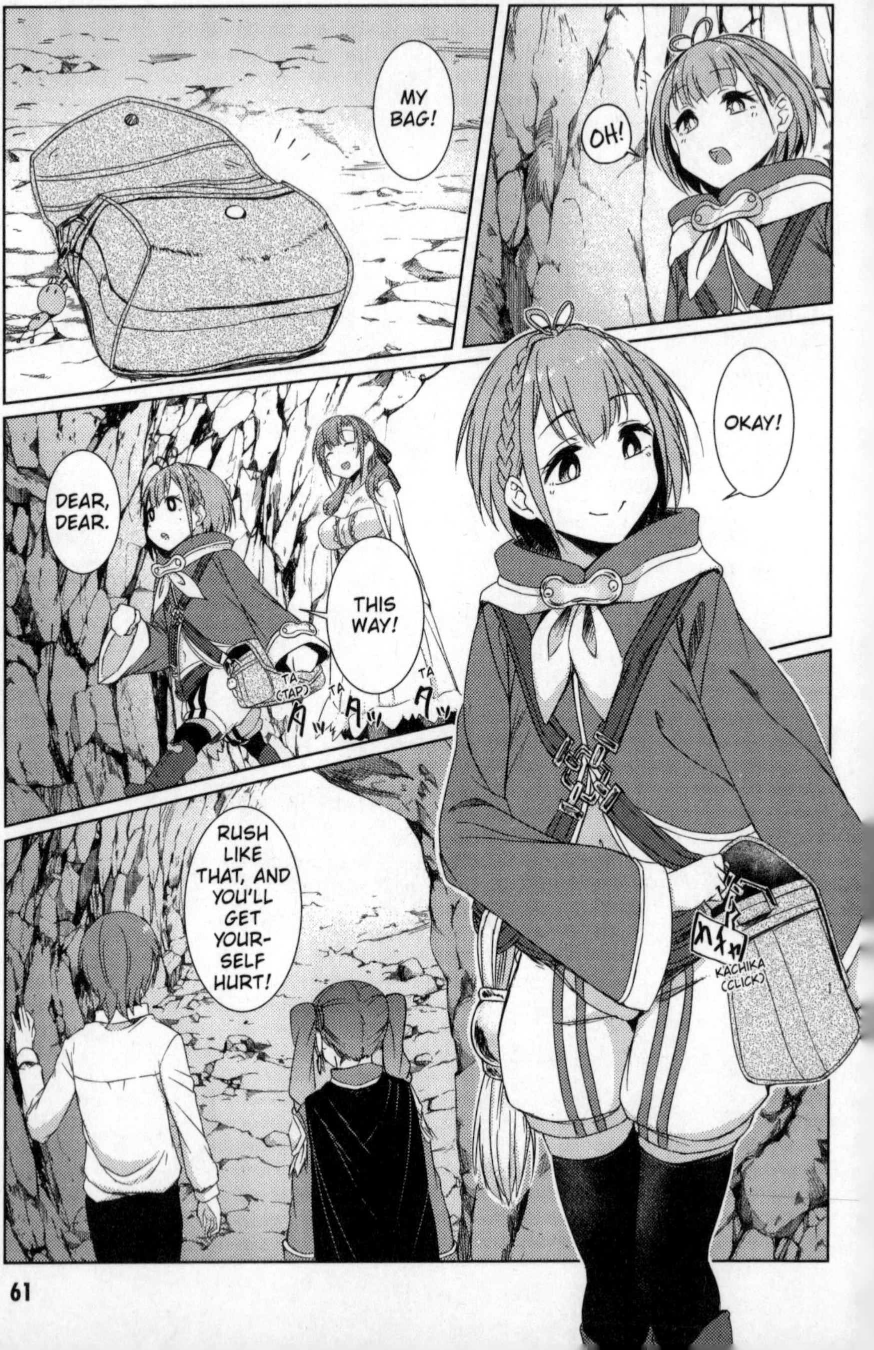
OH!
MY BAG!
OKAY!
ｶﾁｬ
KACHIKA (CLICK)
THIS WAY!
TA (TAP)
TA
TA
DEAR, DEAR.
RUSH LIKE THAT, AND YOU'LL GET YOUR-SELF HURT!

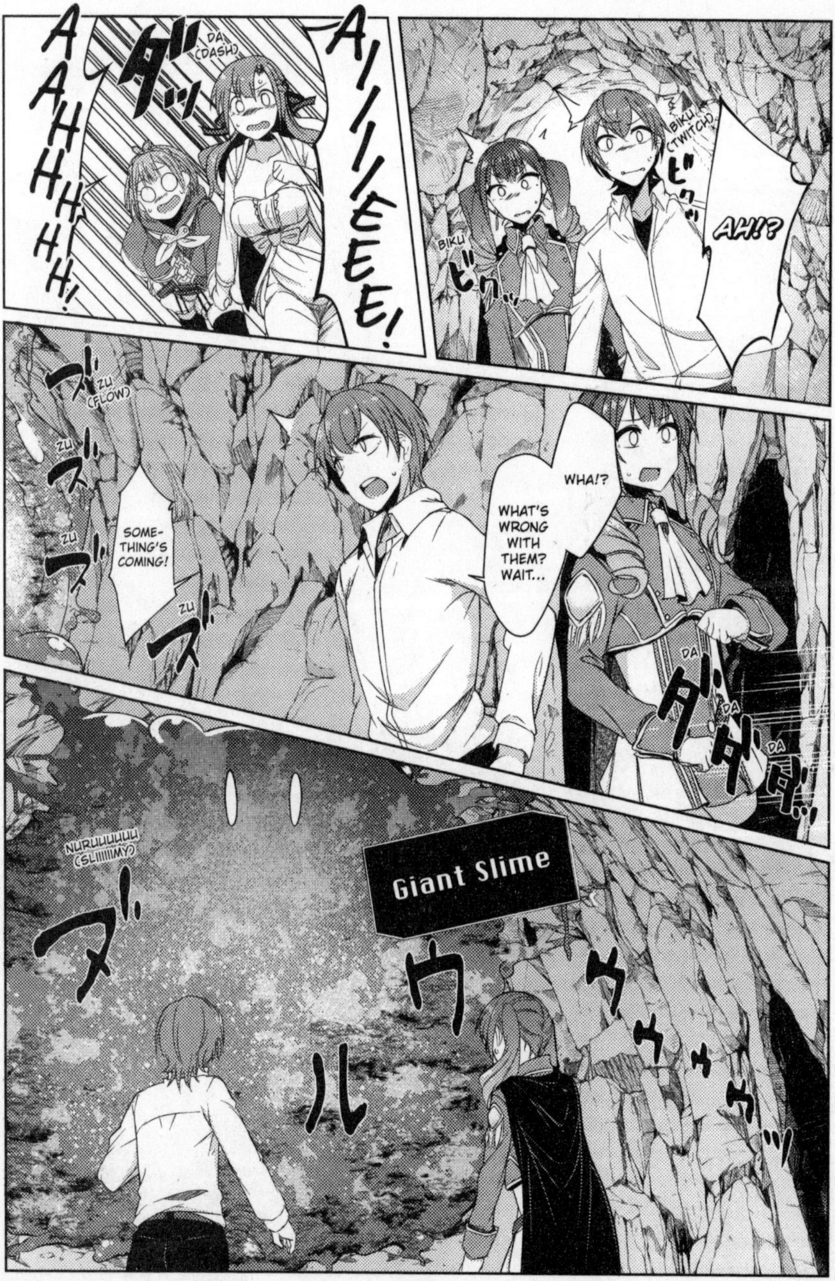
AH!?
BIKU (TWITCH)
BIKU
AIIIIIEEEE!
DA (DASH)
AAAHHHHHHH!
WHA!?
WHAT'S WRONG WITH THEM? WAIT...
DA
DA
DA
SOME-THING'S COMING!
ZU (FLOW)
ZU
ZU
ZU
Giant Slime
NURUUUUUUU (SLIIIIIMY)

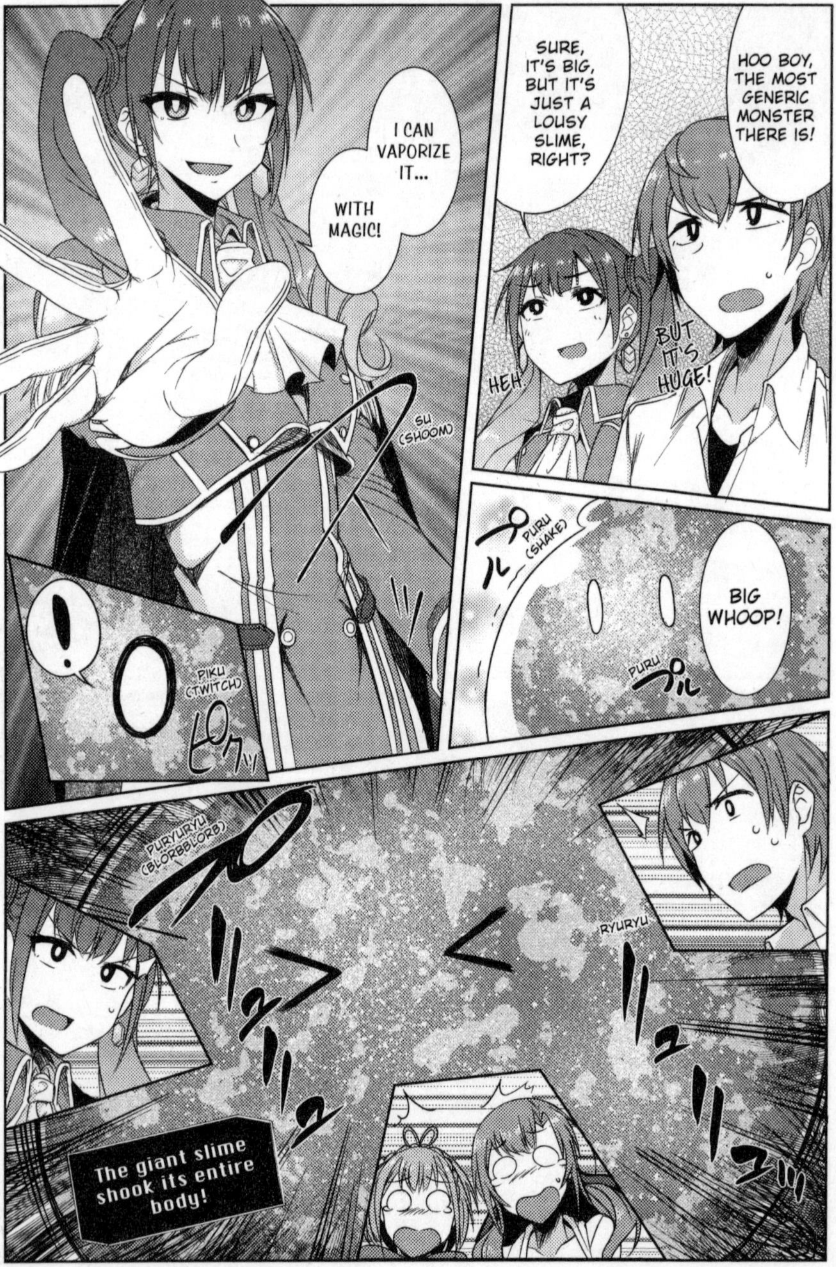
HOO BOY, THE MOST GENERIC MONSTER THERE IS!
SURE, IT'S BIG, BUT IT'S JUST A LOUSY SLIME, RIGHT?
BUT IT'S HUGE!
HEH
BIG WHOOP!
PURU (SHAKE)
PURU
I CAN VAPORIZE IT...
WITH MAGIC!
SU (SHOOM)
!
PIKU (TWITCH)
RYURYU
PURYURYU (BLORBBLORB)
The giant slime shook its entire body!

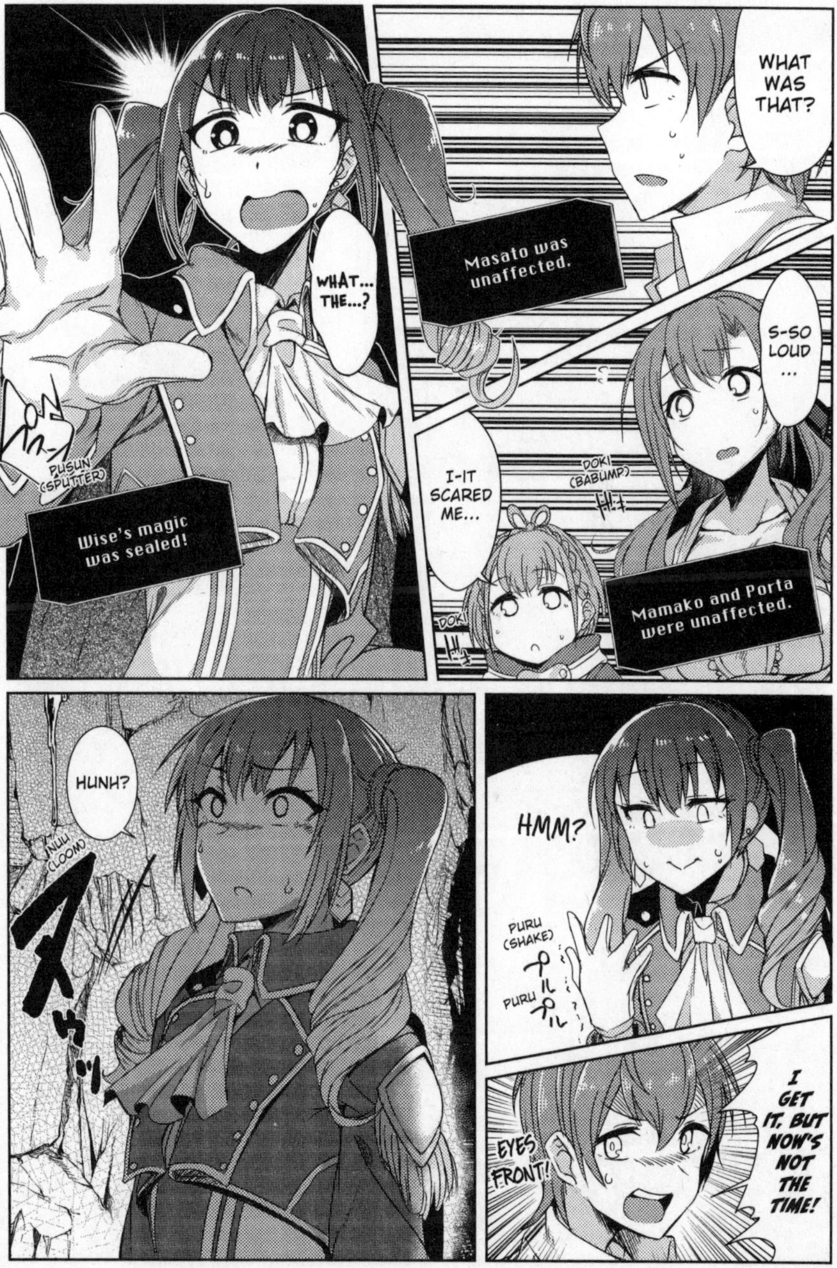
WHAT WAS THAT?
Masato was unaffected.
WHAT... THE...?
PUSUN (SPUTTER)
Wise's magic was sealed!
S-SO LOUD ...
DOKI (BABUMP)
I-IT SCARED ME...
DOKI
Mamako and Porta were unaffected.
HMM?
PURU (SHAKE)
PURU
I GET IT, BUT NOW'S NOT THE TIME!
EYES FRONT!
HUNH?
NUU (LOOM)

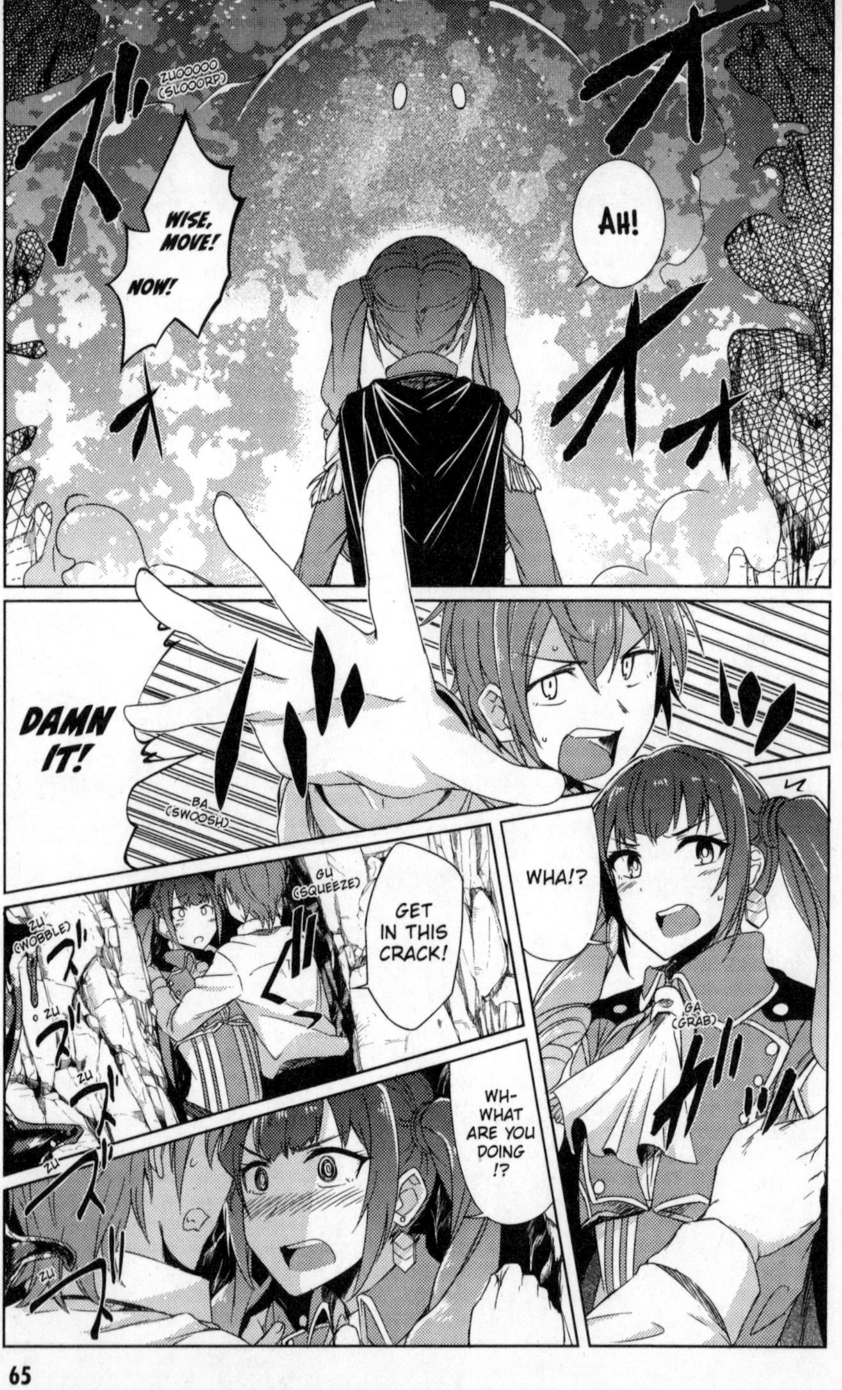
ZUOOOOO (SLOOORP)
WISE, MOVE! NOW!
AH!
DAMN IT!
BA (SWOOSH)
WHA!?
GA (GRAB)
GET IN THIS CRACK!
GU (SQUEEZE)
ZU (WOBBLE)
ZU
ZU
ZU
ZU
WH- WHAT ARE YOU DOING !?

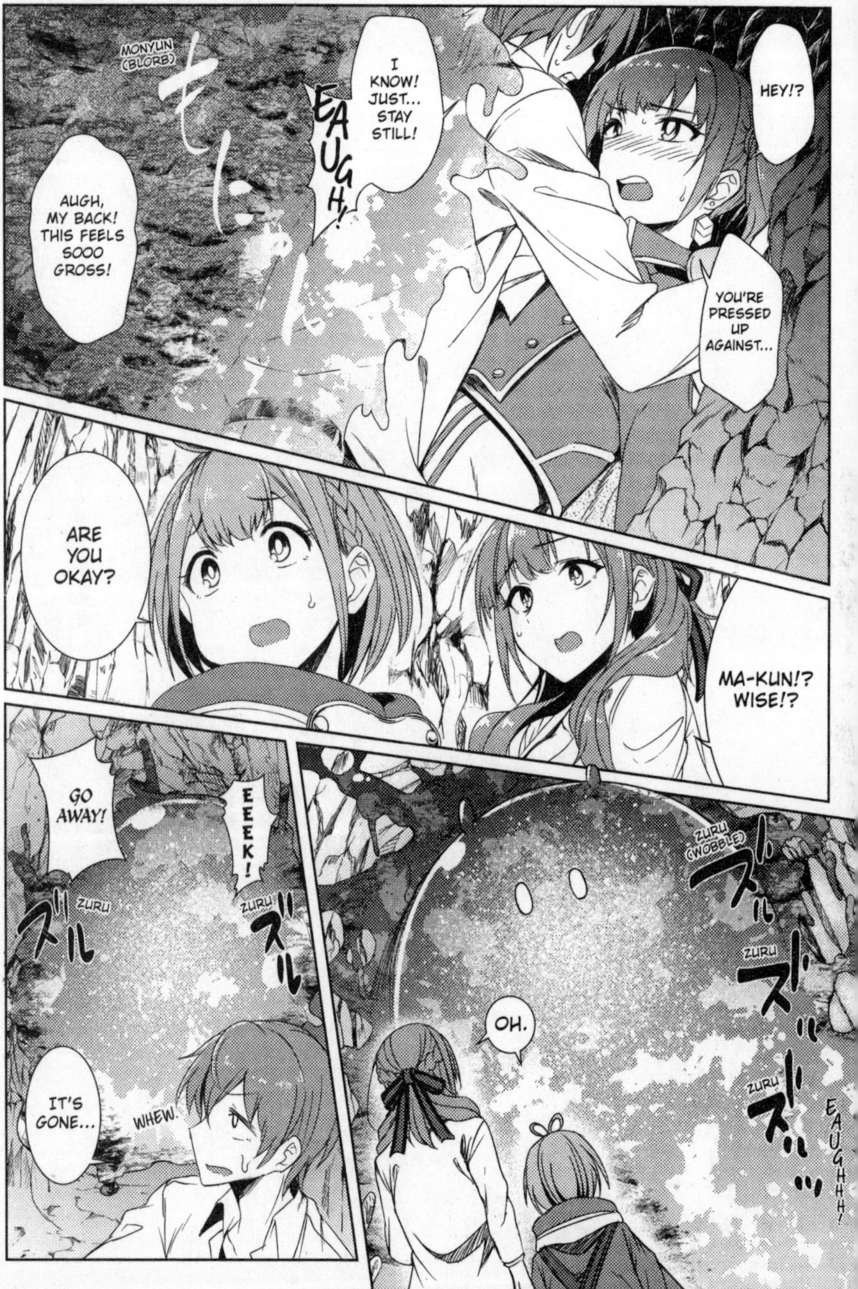
HEY!?
YOU'RE PRESSED UP AGAINST...
I KNOW! JUST... STAY STILL!
EAUGH!
MONYUN (BLORB)
AUGH, MY BACK! THIS FEELS SOOO GROSS!
MA-KUN!? WISE!?
ARE YOU OKAY?
ZURU (WOBBLE)
ZURU
ZURU
EAUGHHH!
OH.
GO AWAY!
EEEK!
ZURU
ZURU
IT'S GONE...
WHEW.

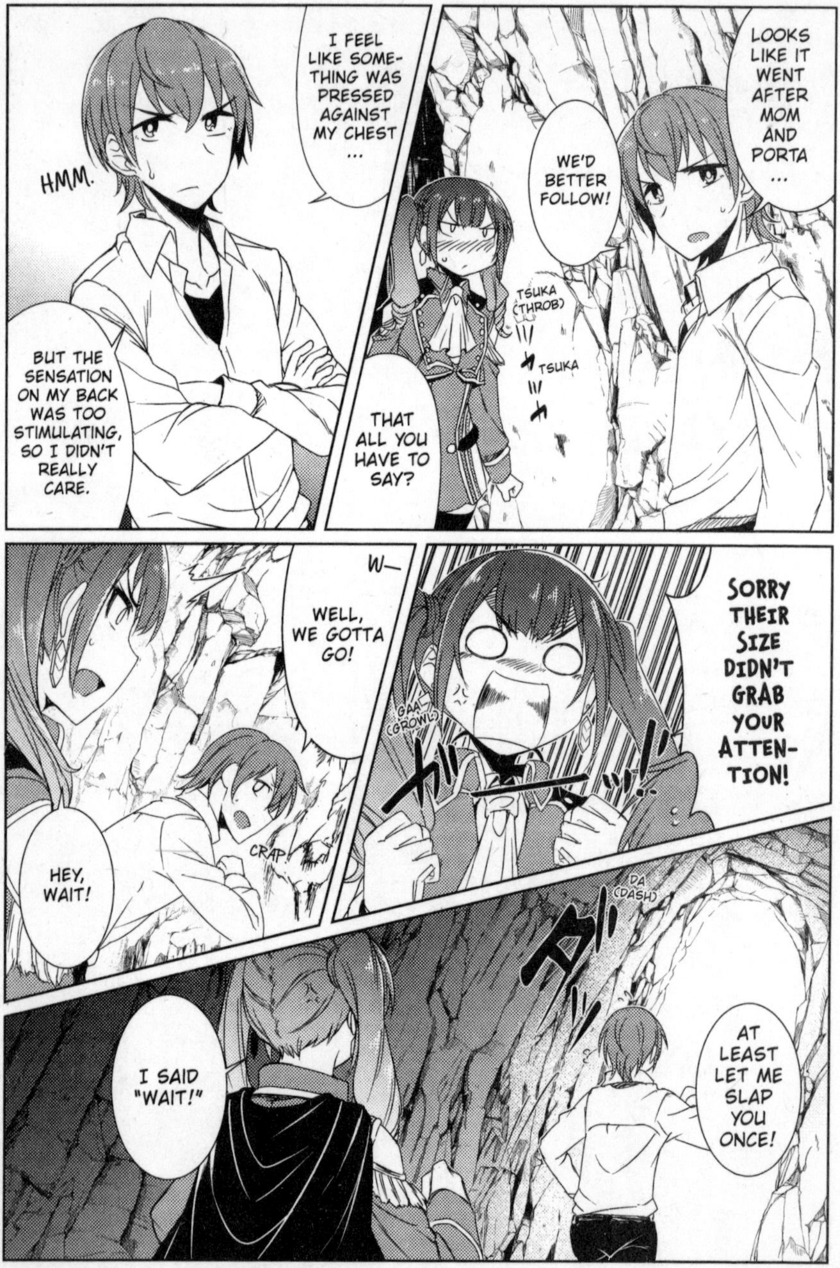
LOOKS LIKE IT WENT AFTER MOM AND PORTA ...
WE'D BETTER FOLLOW!
TSUKA (THROB)
TSUKA
THAT ALL YOU HAVE TO SAY?
I FEEL LIKE SOME-THING WAS PRESSED AGAINST MY CHEST ...
HMM.
BUT THE SENSATION ON MY BACK WAS TOO STIMULATING, SO I DIDN'T REALLY CARE.
SORRY THEIR SIZE DIDN'T GRAB YOUR ATTEN-TION!
GAA (GROWL)
W—
WELL, WE GOTTA GO!
CRAP!
HEY, WAIT!
DA (DASH)
AT LEAST LET ME SLAP YOU ONCE!
I SAID "WAIT!"

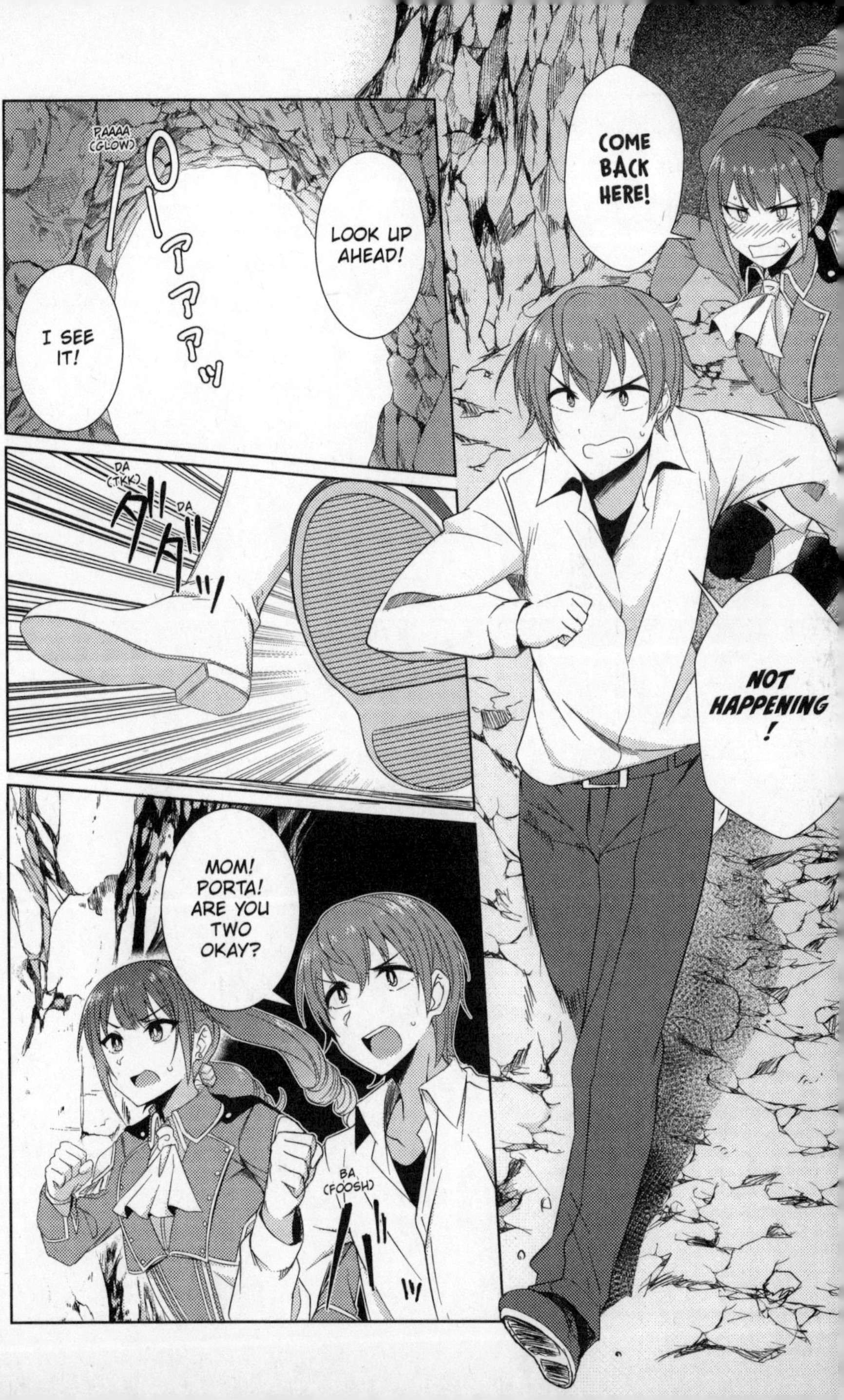
COME BACK HERE!
NOT HAPPENING!
LOOK UP AHEAD!
PAAAA (GLOW)
I SEE IT!
DA (TKK)
DA
MOM! PORTA! ARE YOU TWO OKAY?
BA (FOOSH)

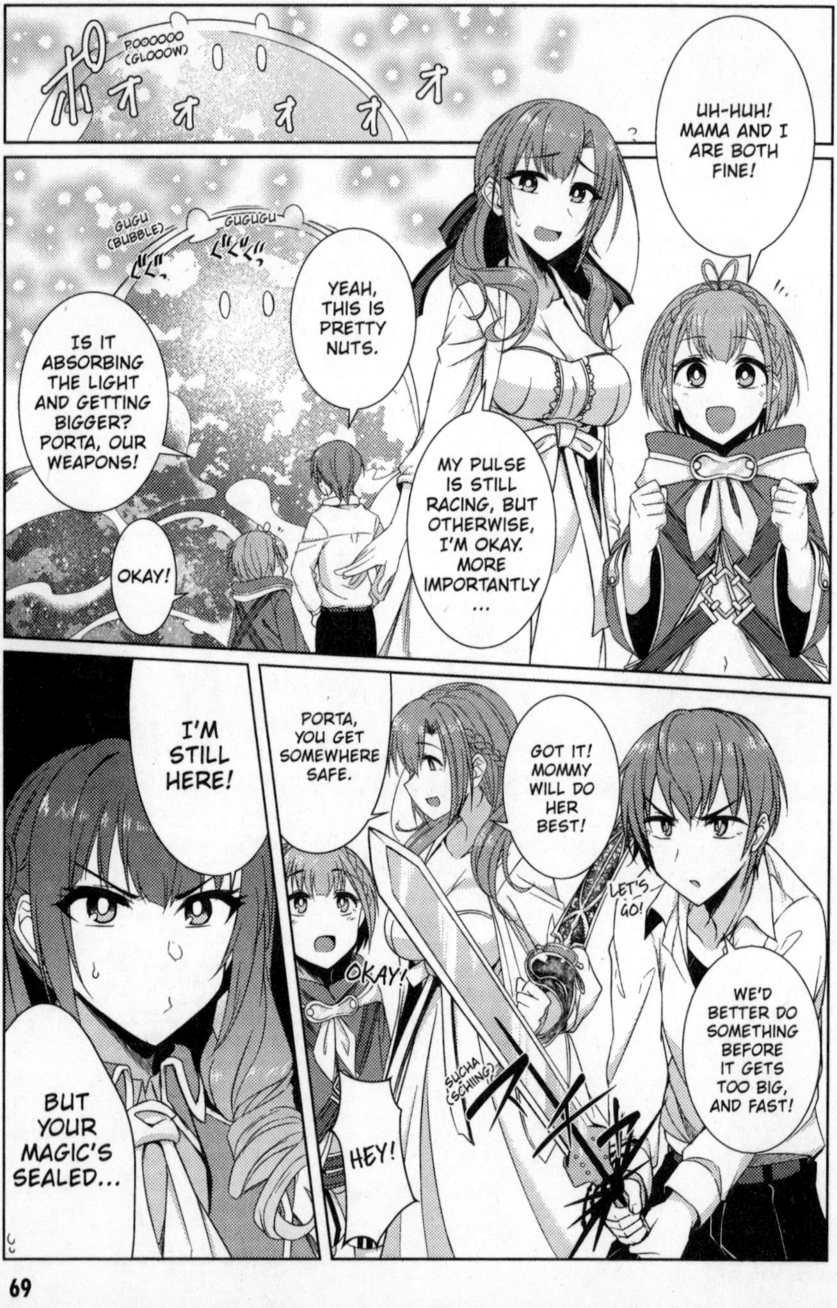
POOOOOO (GLOOOW)
ポォォォォォ
UH-HUH! MAMA AND I ARE BOTH FINE!
MY PULSE IS STILL RACING, BUT OTHERWISE, I'M OKAY. MORE IMPORTANTLY ...
YEAH, THIS IS PRETTY NUTS.
GUGUGU
ぐぐぐ
GUGU (BUBBLE)
ぐぐ
IS IT ABSORBING THE LIGHT AND GETTING BIGGER? PORTA, OUR WEAPONS!
OKAY!
GOT IT! MOMMY WILL DO HER BEST!
PORTA, YOU GET SOMEWHERE SAFE.
LET'S GO!
WE'D BETTER DO SOMETHING BEFORE IT GETS TOO BIG, AND FAST!
OKAY!
SUCHA (SCHIING)
HEY!
I'M STILL HERE!
BUT YOUR MAGIC'S SEALED...

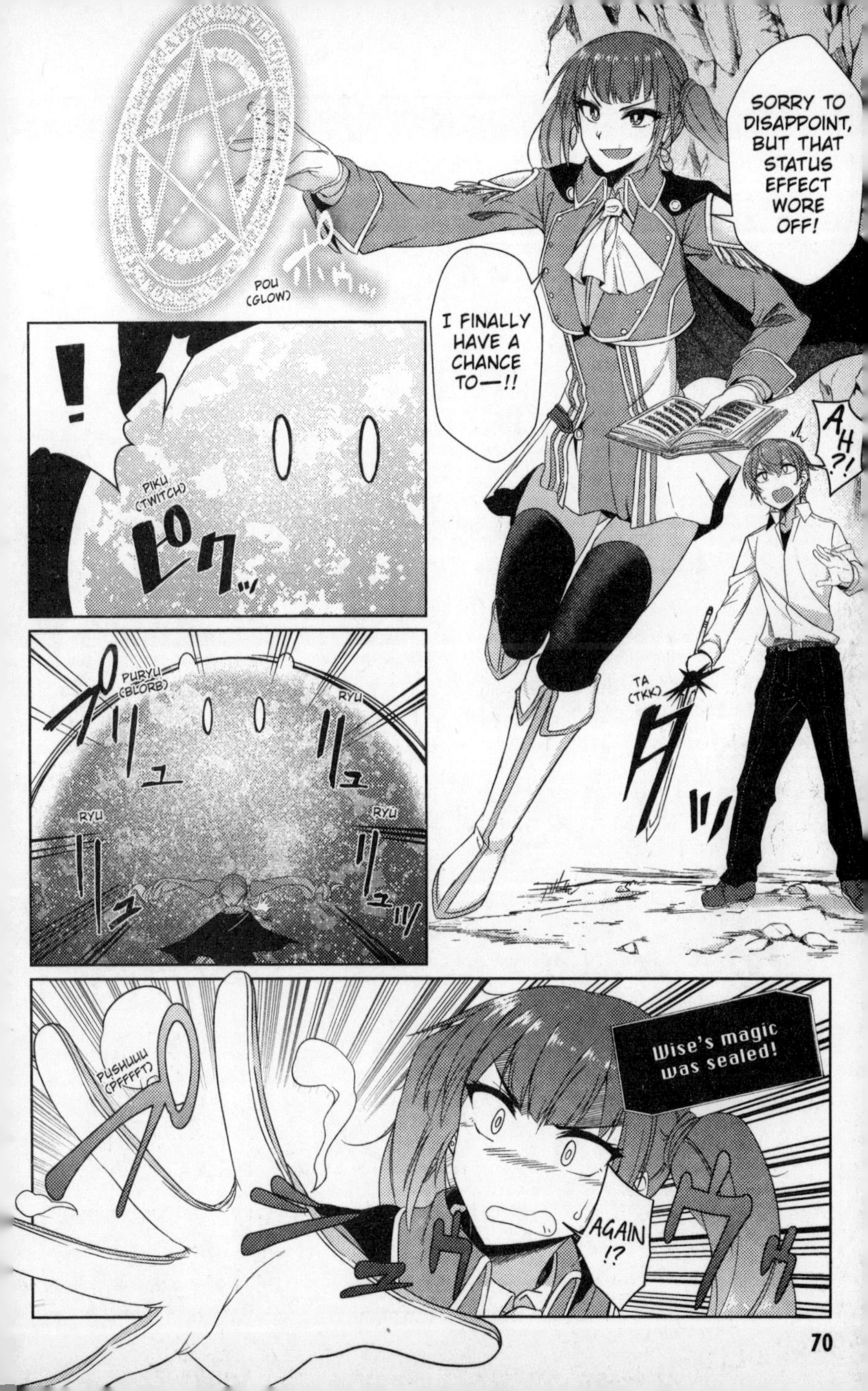
SORRY TO DISAPPOINT, BUT THAT STATUS EFFECT WORE OFF!
I FINALLY HAVE A CHANCE TO—!!
POU (GLOW)
AH?!
TA (TKK)
!
PIKU (TWITCH)
PURYU (BLORB)
RYU
RYU
RYU
Wise's magic was sealed!
PUSHUUU (PFFFFT)
AGAIN!?

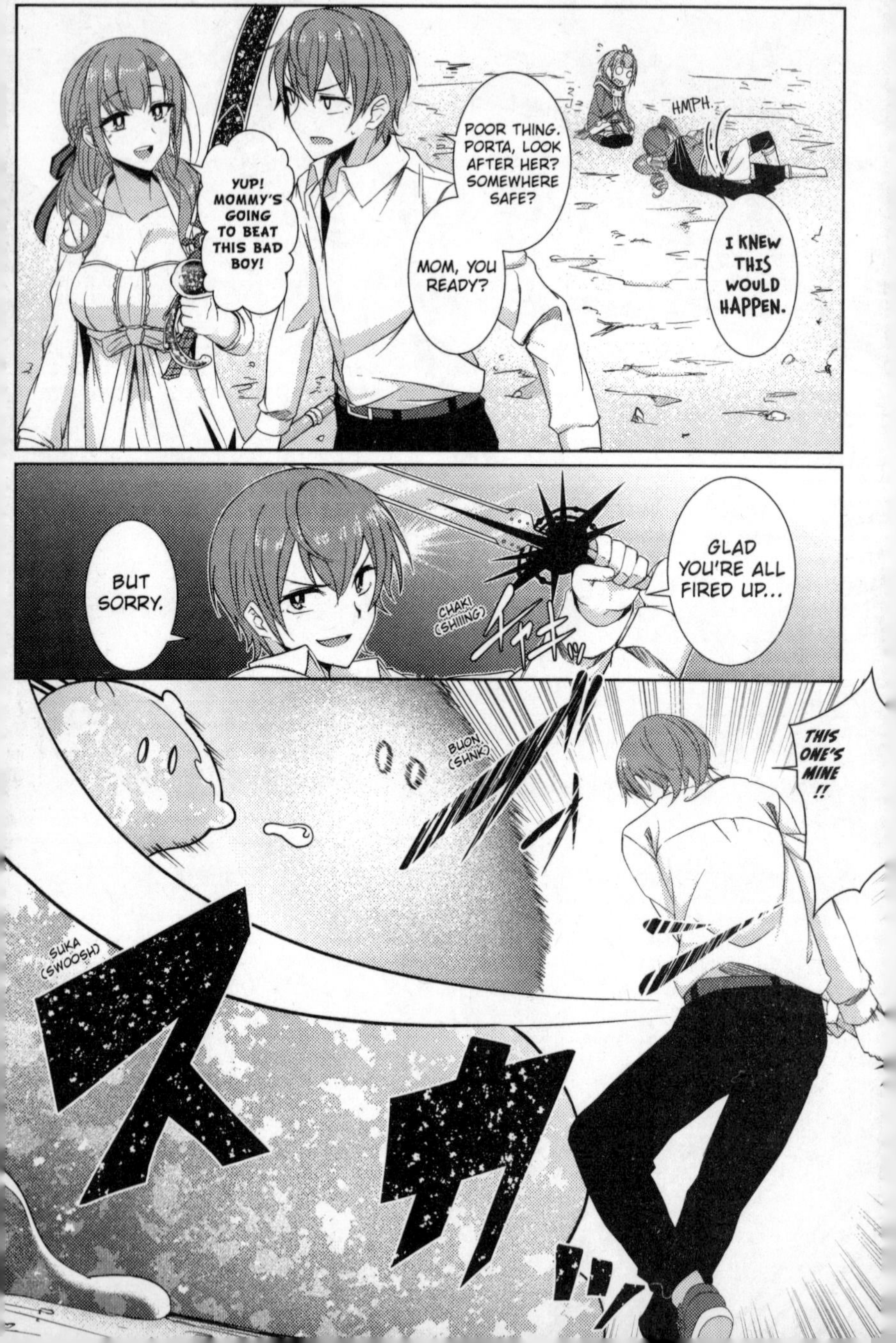
HMPH.
I KNEW THIS WOULD HAPPEN.
POOR THING. PORTA, LOOK AFTER HER? SOMEWHERE SAFE?
MOM, YOU READY?
YUP! MOMMY'S GOING TO BEAT THIS BAD BOY!
GLAD YOU'RE ALL FIRED UP...
CHAKI (SHIIING)
BUT SORRY.
THIS ONE'S MINE!!
BUON (SHNK)
SUKA (SWOOSH)

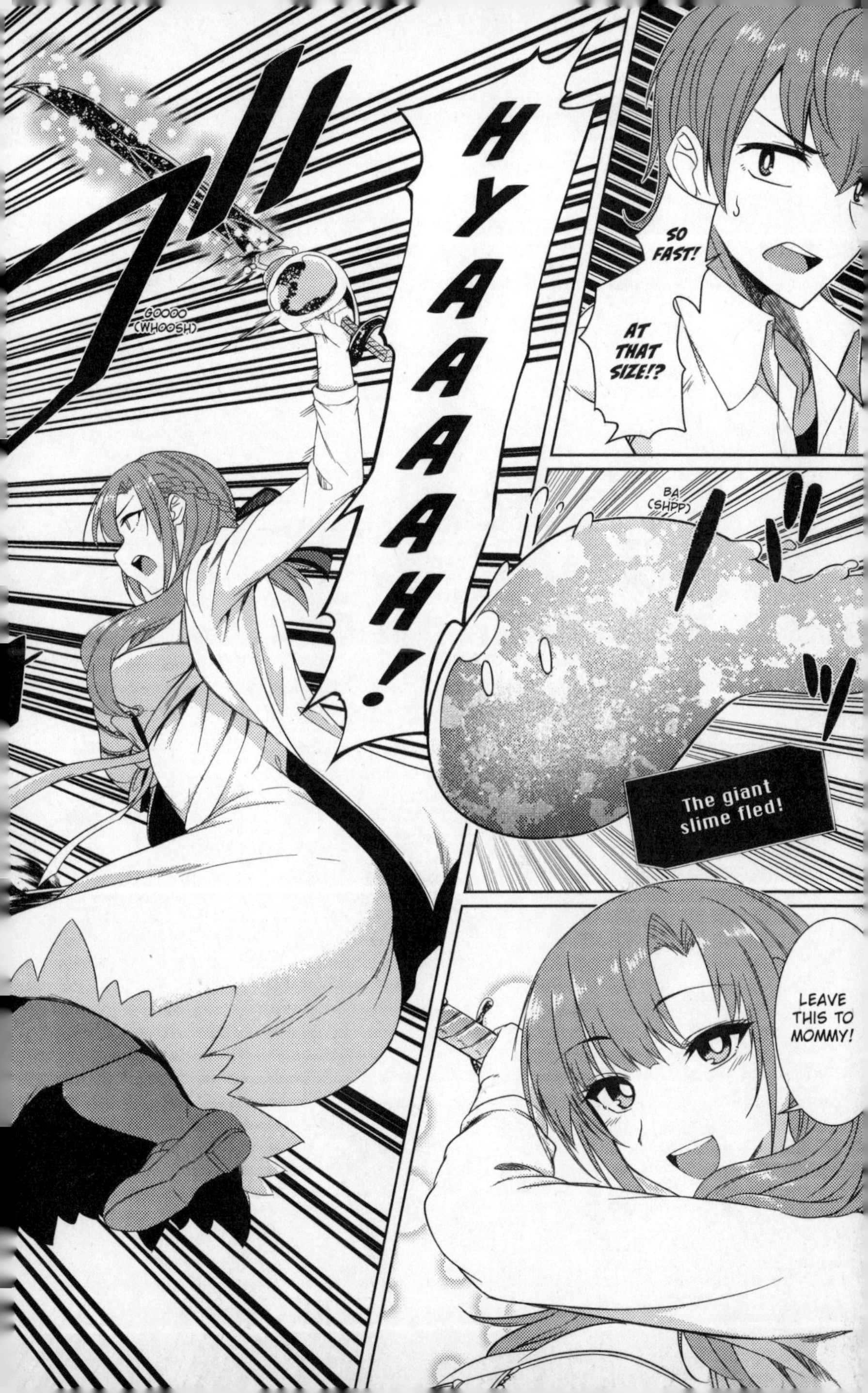
SO FAST!
AT THAT SIZE!?
BA (SHPP)
The giant slime fled!
LEAVE THIS TO MOMMY!
HYAAAAAH!
GOOOO (WHOOSH)

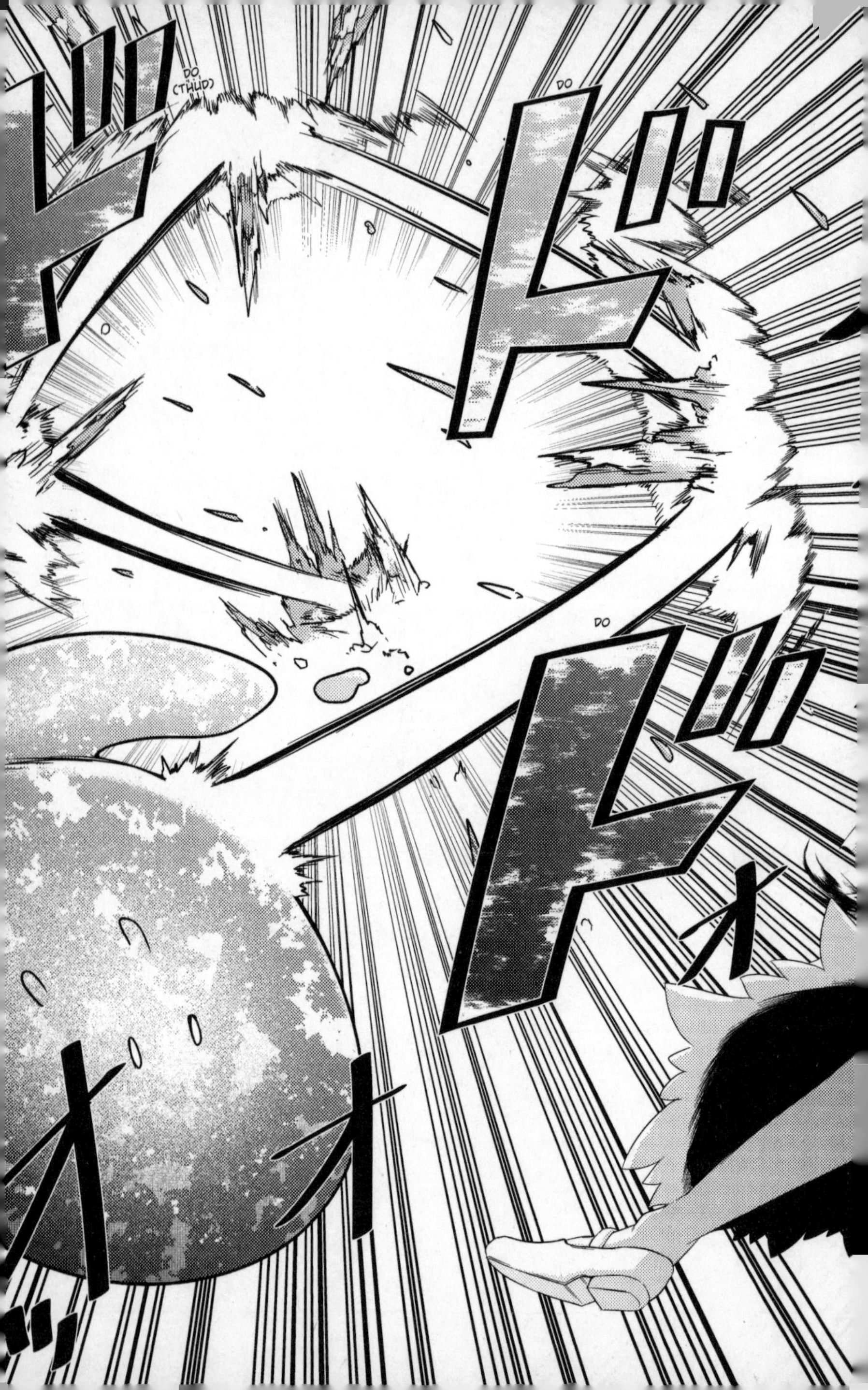
DO
DO
(THUD)
DO

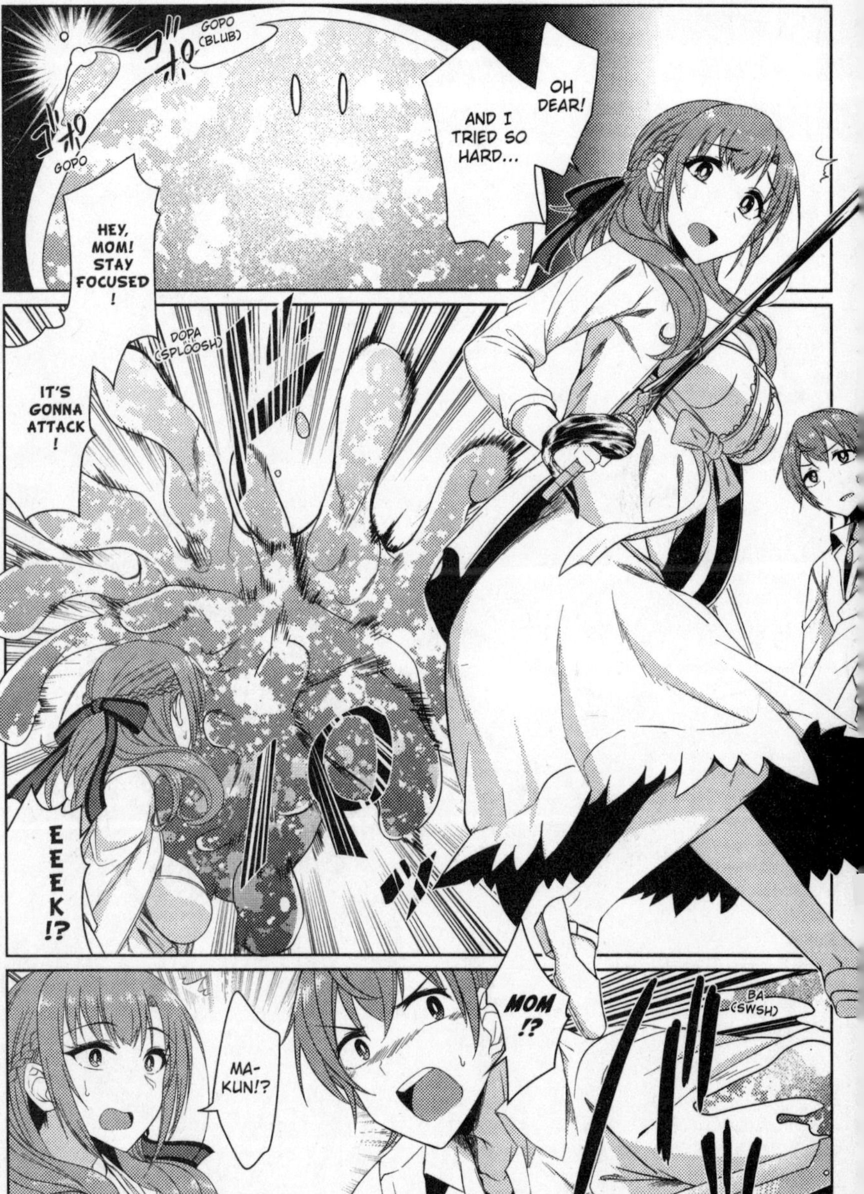
OH DEAR!
AND I TRIED SO HARD...
GOPO (BLUB)
GOPO
HEY, MOM! STAY FOCUSED!
DOPA (SPLOOSH)
IT'S GONNA ATTACK!
EEEEK!?
BA (SWSH)
MOM!?
MA-KUN!?

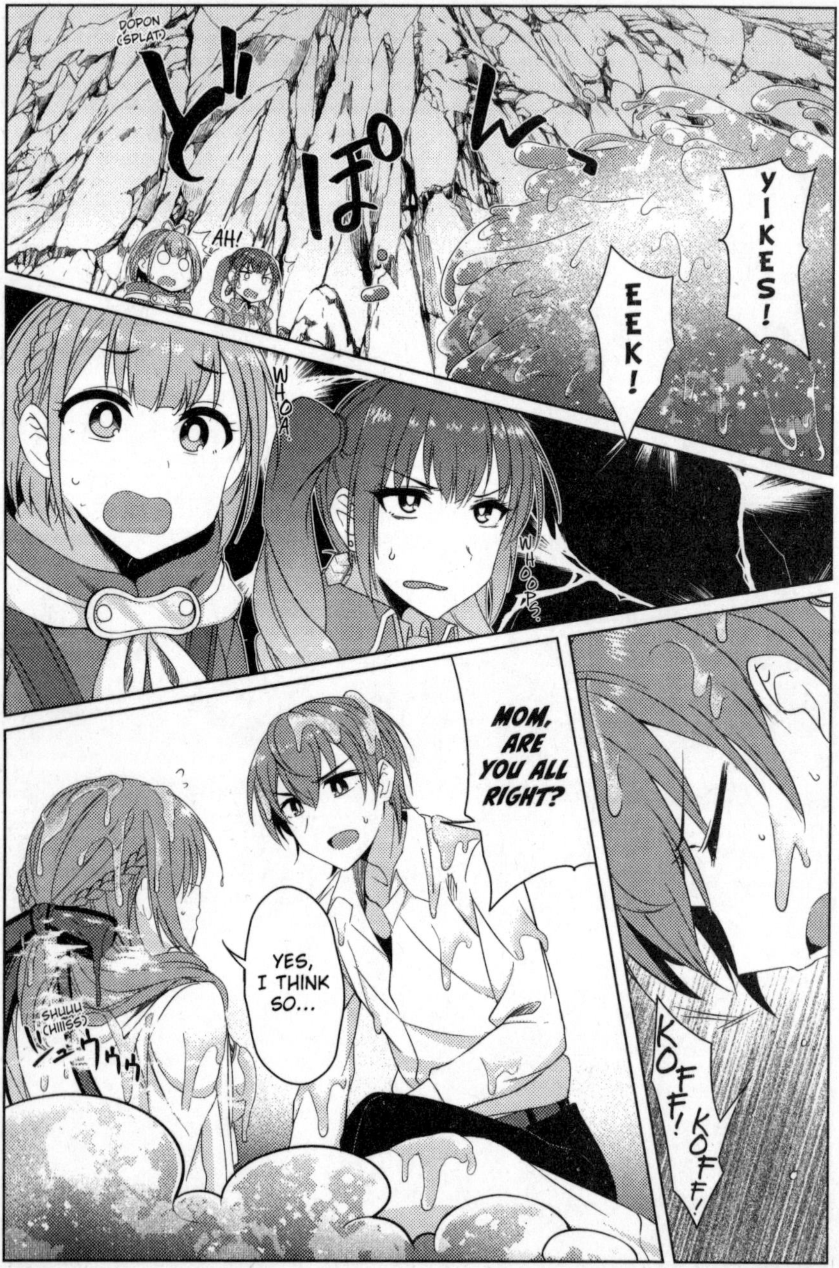
DOPON (SPLAT)
どぽん
YIKES!
EEK!
AH!
WHOOPS.
WHOA
KOFF! KOFF!
MOM, ARE YOU ALL RIGHT?
YES, I THINK SO...
SHUUU (HIIISS)
シュウウウ

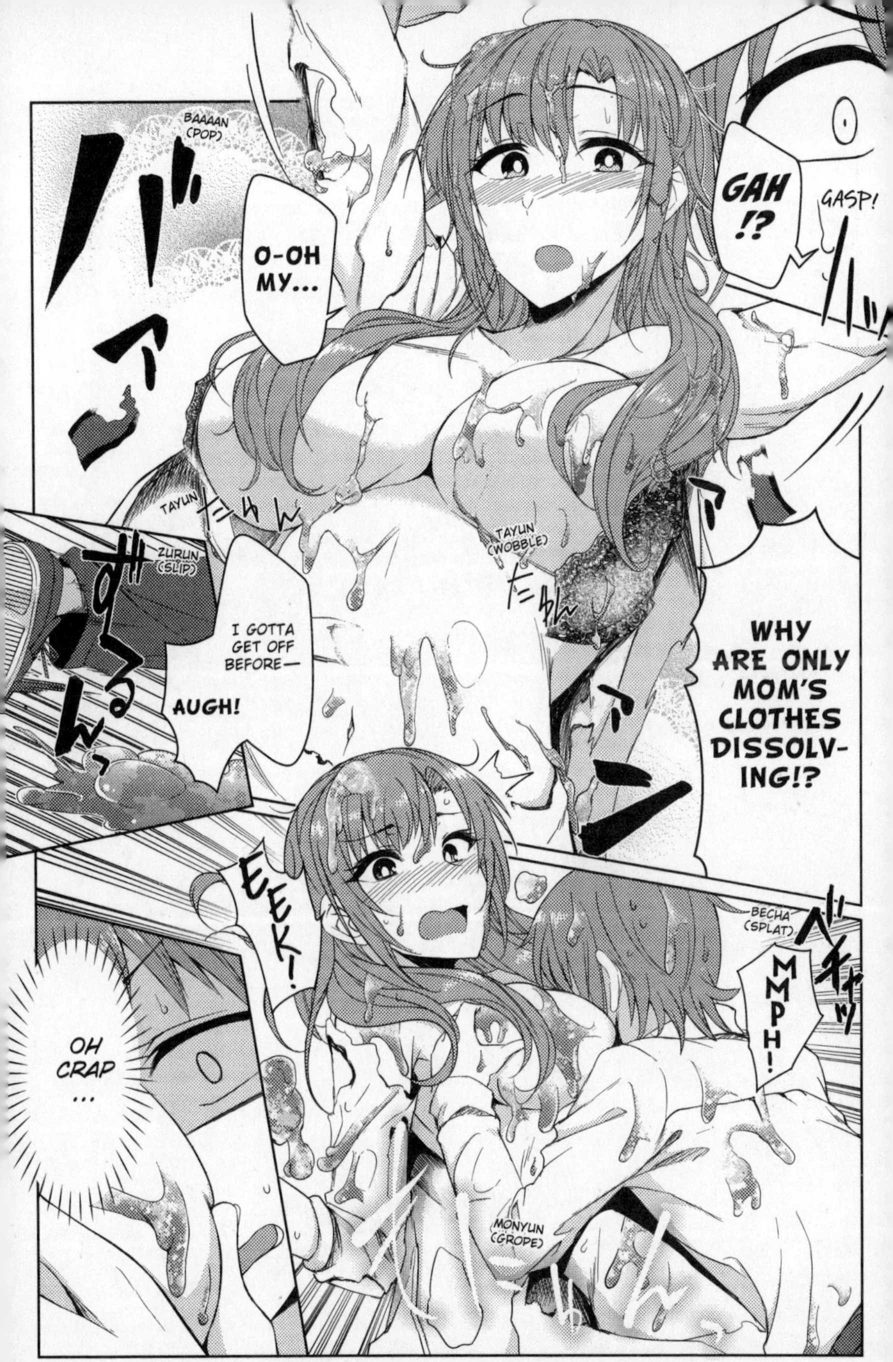
GAH!?
GASP!
O-OH MY...
BAAAAN (POP)
WHY ARE ONLY MOM'S CLOTHES DISSOLVING!?
TAYUN (WOBBLE)
TAYUN
I GOTTA GET OFF BEFORE—
AUGH!
ZURUN (SLIP)
BECHA (SPLAT)
MMPH!
EEEK!
MONYUN (GROPE)
OH CRAP...

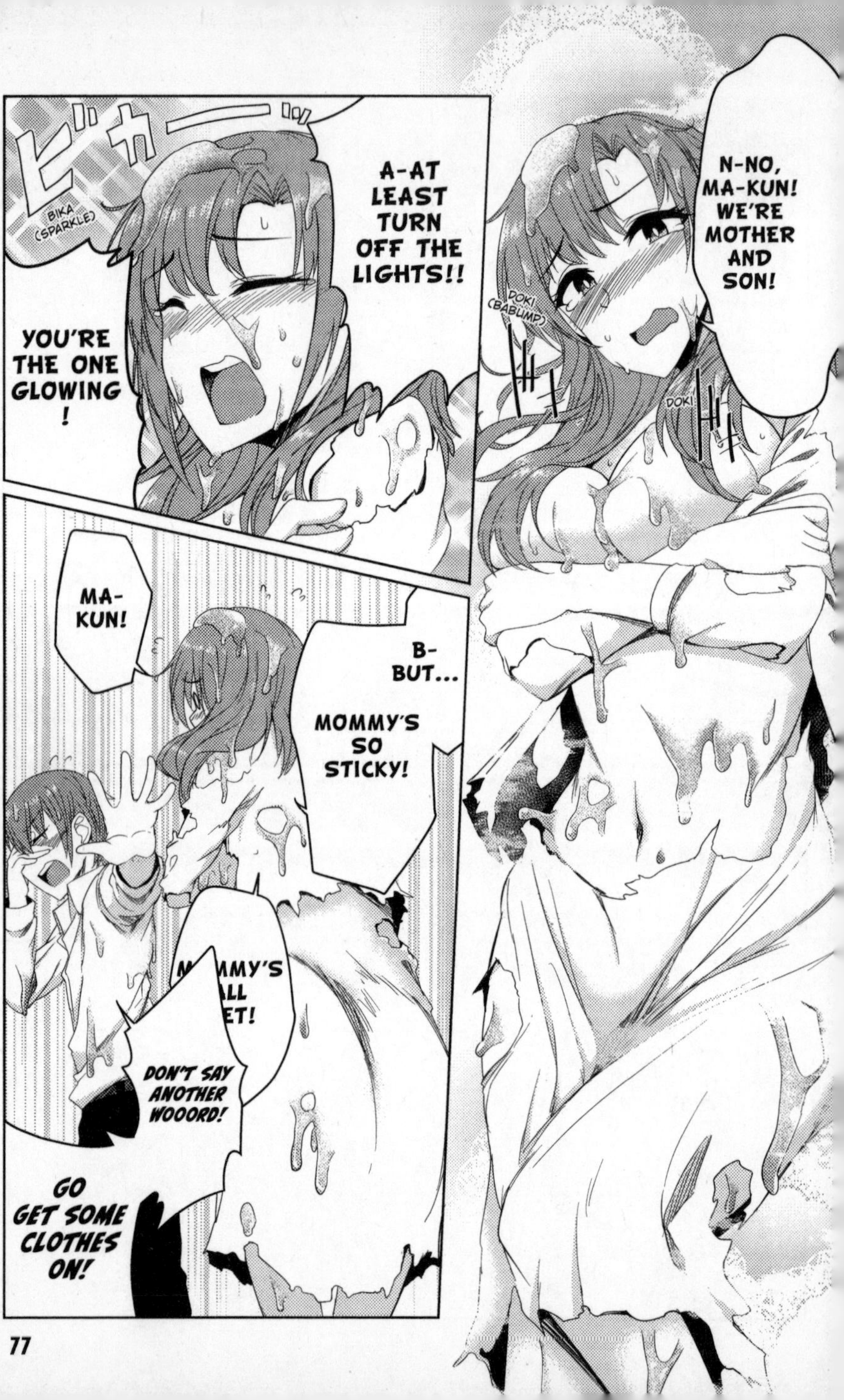
N-NO, MA-KUN! WE'RE MOTHER AND SON!
DOKI (BABUMP)
DOKI
ビカーーッ
BIKA (SPARKLE)
A-AT LEAST TURN OFF THE LIGHTS!!
YOU'RE THE ONE GLOWING!
B-BUT...
MOMMY'S SO STICKY!
MA-KUN!
DON'T SAY ANOTHER WOOORD!
GO GET SOME CLOTHES ON!

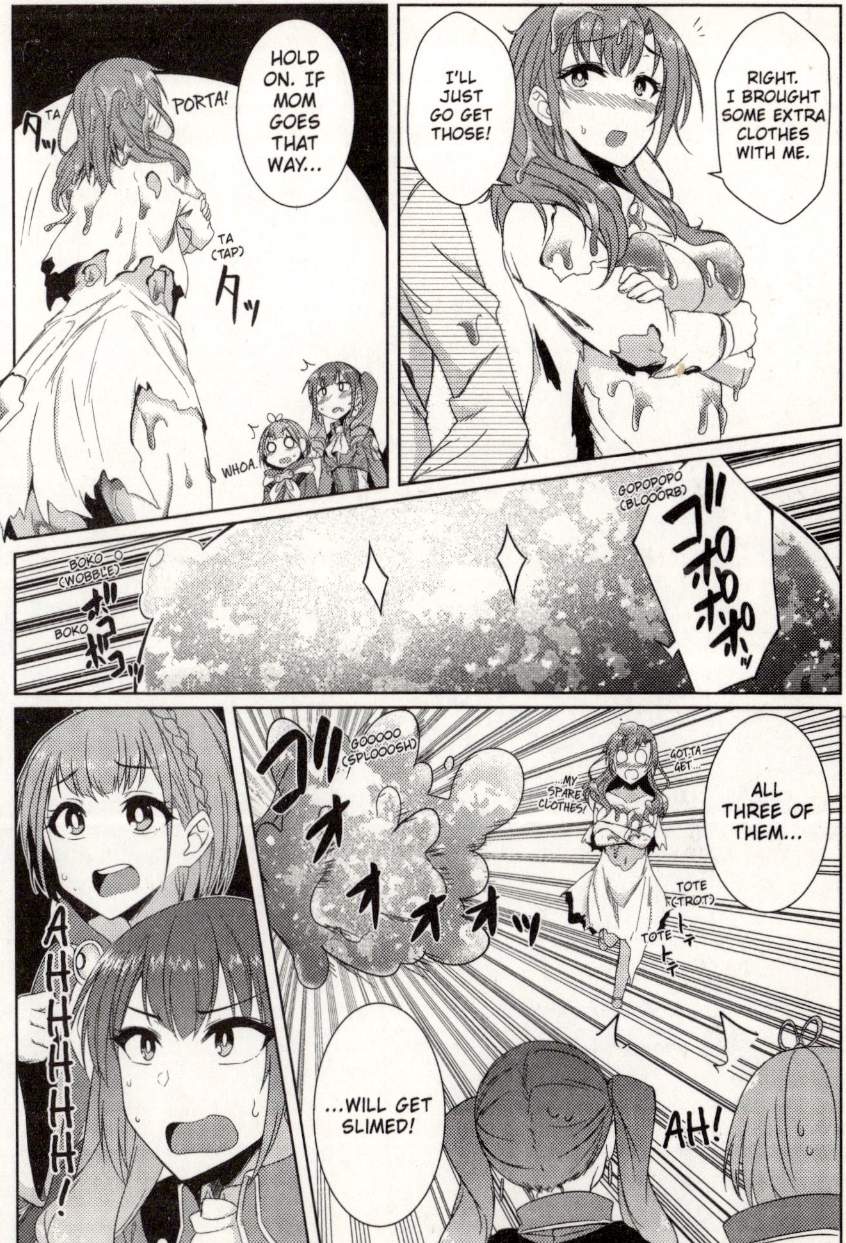
RIGHT. I BROUGHT SOME EXTRA CLOTHES WITH ME.
I'LL JUST GO GET THOSE!
HOLD ON. IF MOM GOES THAT WAY...
PORTA!
TA
TA (TAP)
WHOA.
GOPOPOPO (BLOOORB)
BOKO (WOBBLE)
BOKO
ALL THREE OF THEM...
GOTTA GET...
...MY SPARE CLOTHES!
TOTE (TROT)
TOTE
GOOOOO (SPLOOOSH)
...WILL GET SLIMED!
AH!
AHHHHHH!

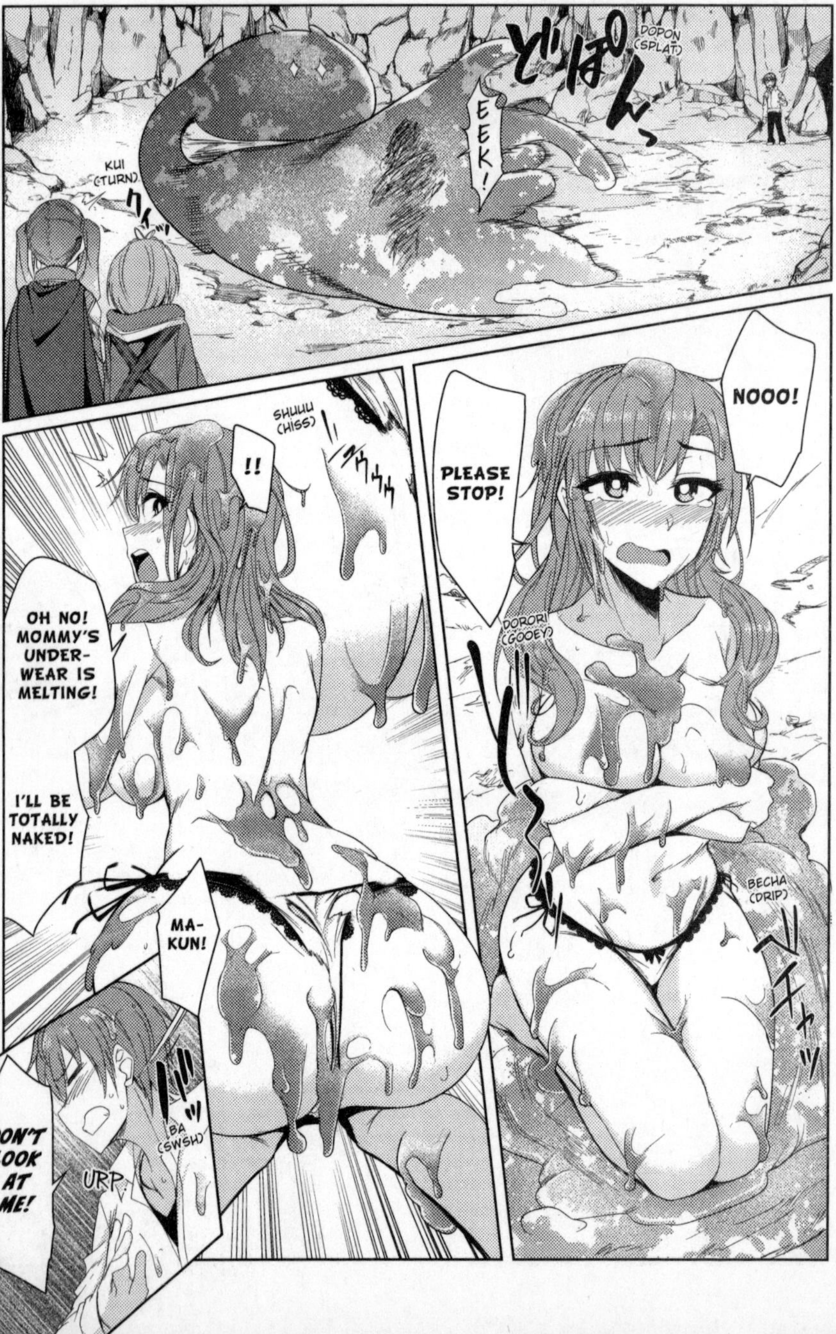
DOPON (SPLAT)
EEK!
KUI (TURN)
NOOO!
PLEASE STOP!
DORORI (GOOEY)
BECHA (DRIP)
SHUUU (HISS)
!!
OH NO! MOMMY'S UNDER-WEAR IS MELTING!
I'LL BE TOTALLY NAKED!
MA-KUN!
BA (SWSH)
URP.
DON'T LOOK AT ME!

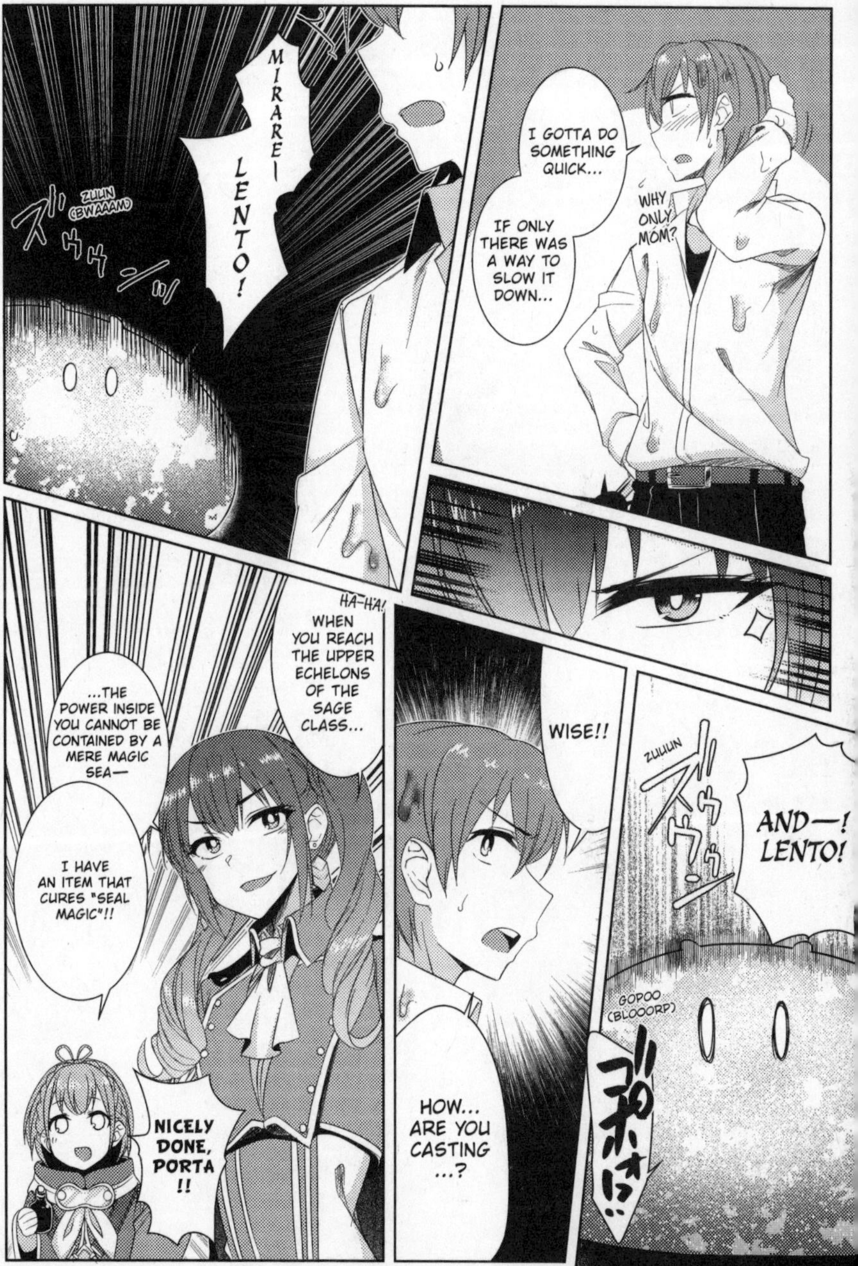
I GOTTA DO SOMETHING QUICK...
IF ONLY THERE WAS A WAY TO SLOW IT DOWN...
WHY ONLY MOM?
MIRARE LENTO!
ZUUN (BWAAAM)
ZUUUN
AND—! LENTO!
GOPOO (BLOOORP)
WISE!!
HOW... ARE YOU CASTING...?
HA-HA! WHEN YOU REACH THE UPPER ECHELONS OF THE SAGE CLASS...
...THE POWER INSIDE YOU CANNOT BE CONTAINED BY A MERE MAGIC SEA—
I HAVE AN ITEM THAT CURES "SEAL MAGIC"!!
NICELY DONE, PORTA!!

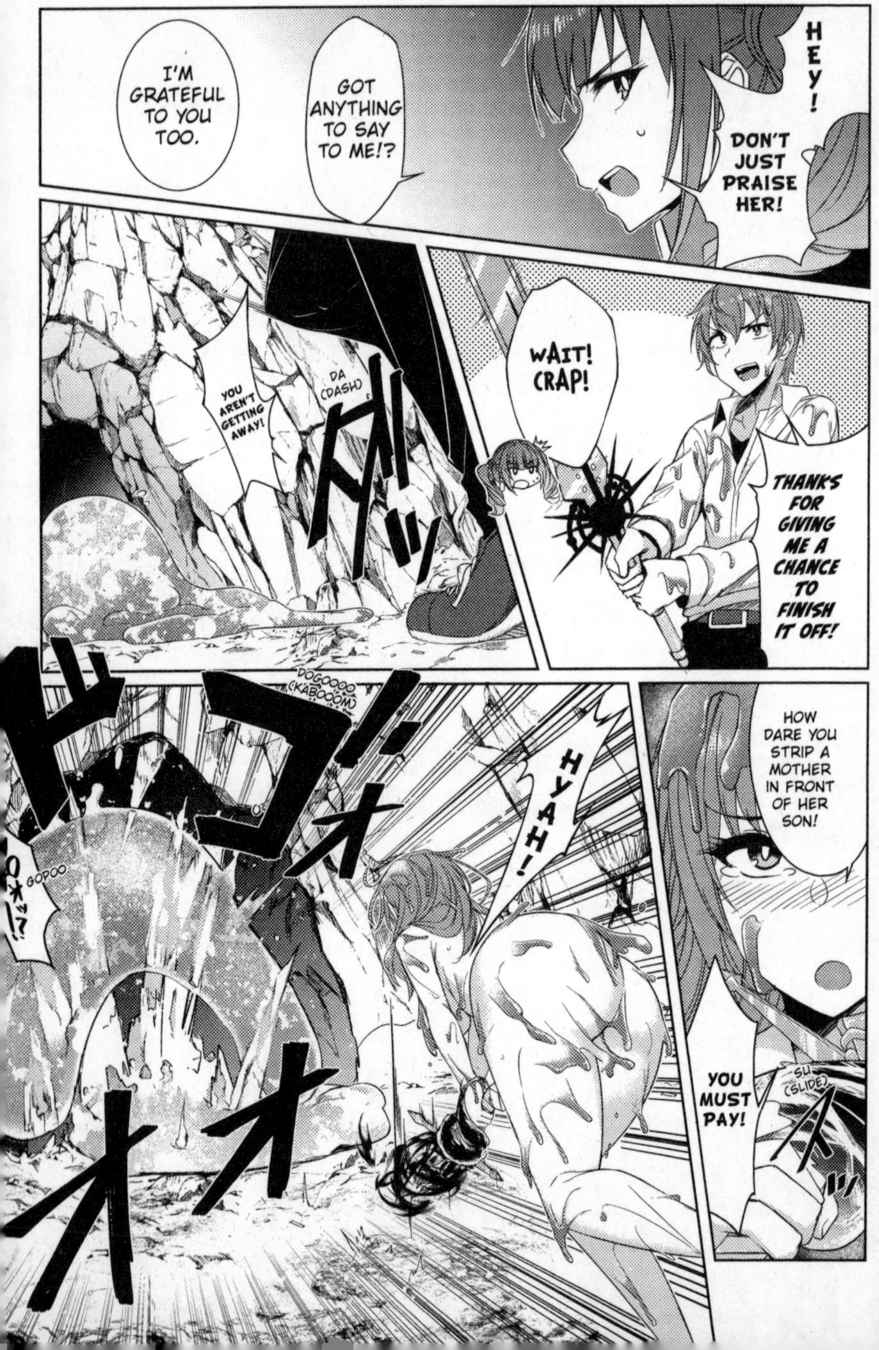
HEY!
DON'T JUST PRAISE HER!
GOT ANYTHING TO SAY TO ME!?
I'M GRATEFUL TO YOU TOO.
WAIT! CRAP!
THANKS FOR GIVING ME A CHANCE TO FINISH IT OFF!
DA (DASH)
YOU AREN'T GETTING AWAY!
HOW DARE YOU STRIP A MOTHER IN FRONT OF HER SON!
YOU MUST PAY!
SU (SLIDE)
HYAH!
DOGOOOO (KABOOOM)
GOPOO

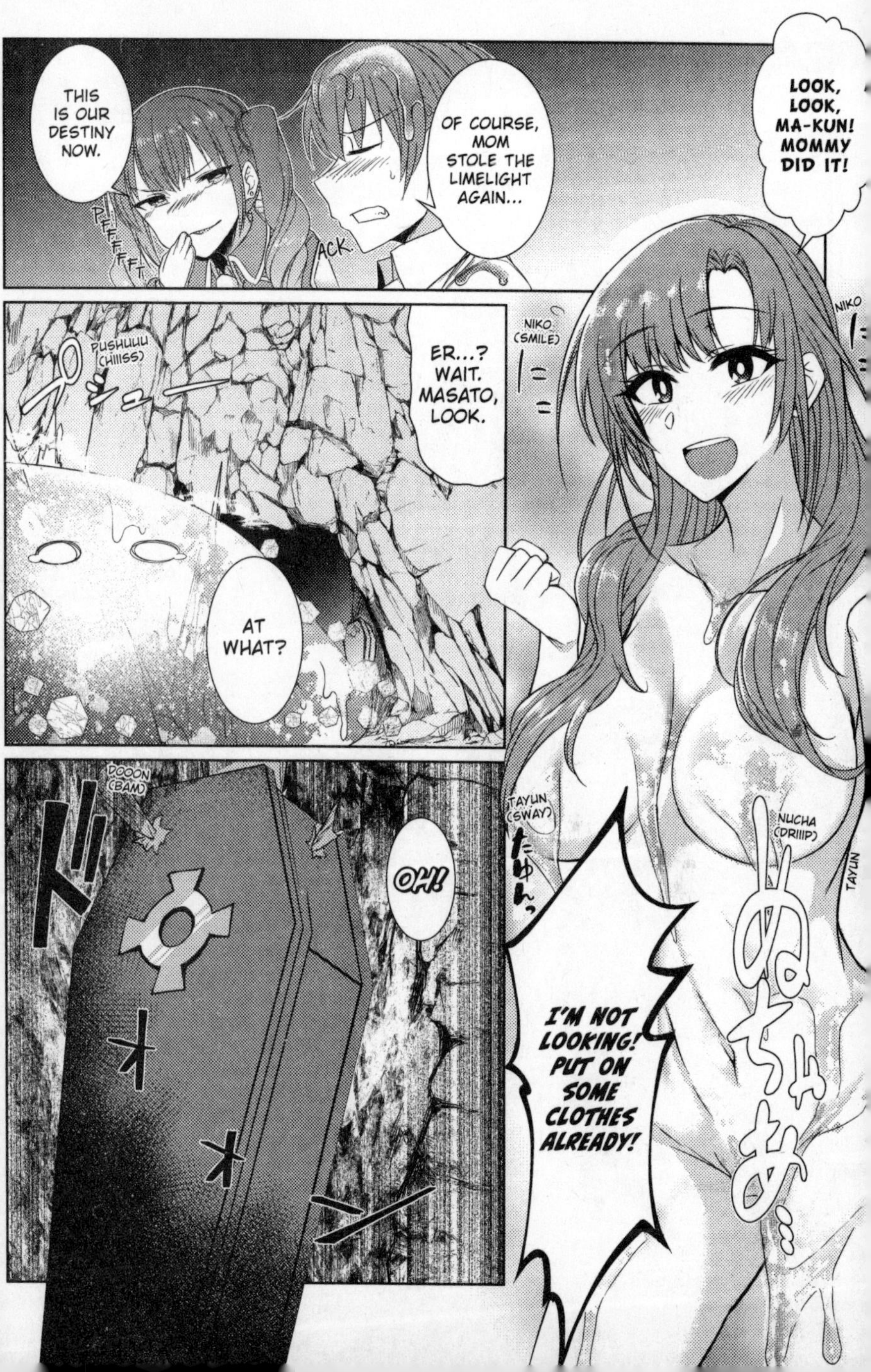
OF COURSE, MOM STOLE THE LIMELIGHT AGAIN...
ACK.
THIS IS OUR DESTINY NOW.
PFFFFFT
ER...? WAIT. MASATO, LOOK.
PUSHUUU (HIIISS)
AT WHAT?
DOOON (BAM)
OH!
LOOK, LOOK, MA-KUN! MOMMY DID IT!
NIKO
NIKO (SMILE)
TAYUN
NUCHA (DRIIIP)
TAYUN (SWAY)
I'M NOT LOOKING! PUT ON SOME CLOTHES ALREADY!

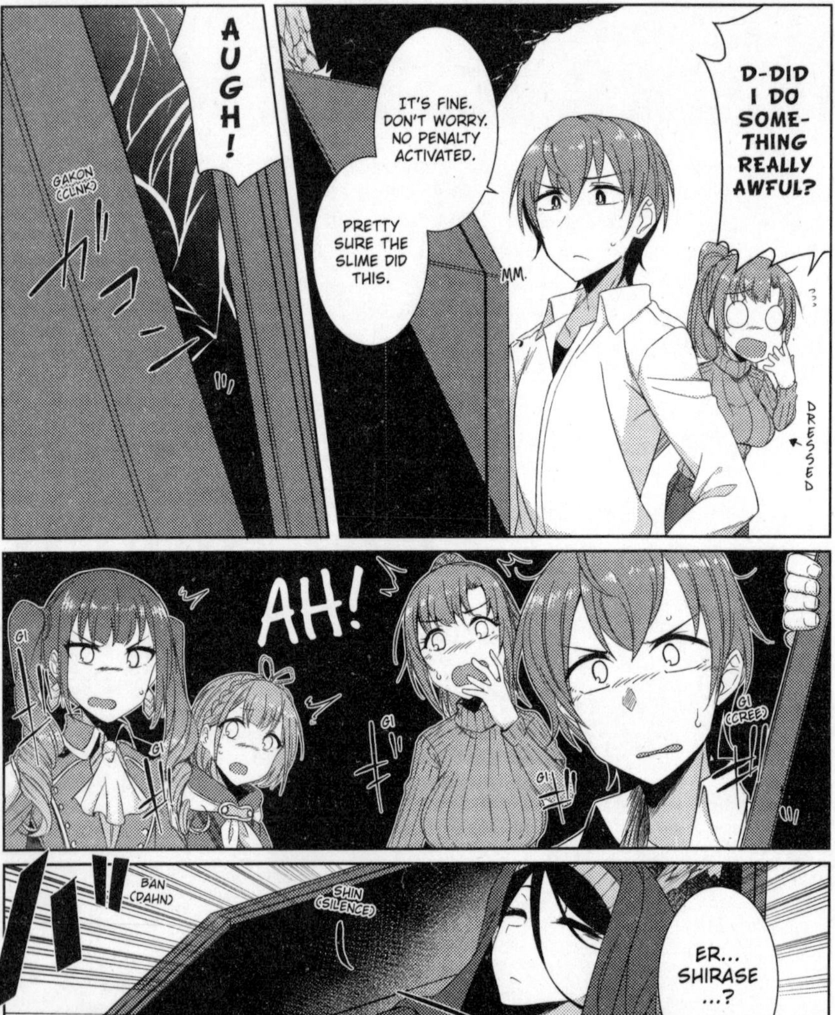
D-DID I DO SOMETHING REALLY AWFUL?
IT'S FINE. DON'T WORRY. NO PENALTY ACTIVATED.
PRETTY SURE THE SLIME DID THIS.
MM.
DRESSED
AUGH!
GAKON (CLNK)
GI (CREE)
GI
AH!
GI
GI
GI
ER... SHIRASE ...?
SHIN (SILENCE)
BAN (DAHN)
The corpse did not reply.

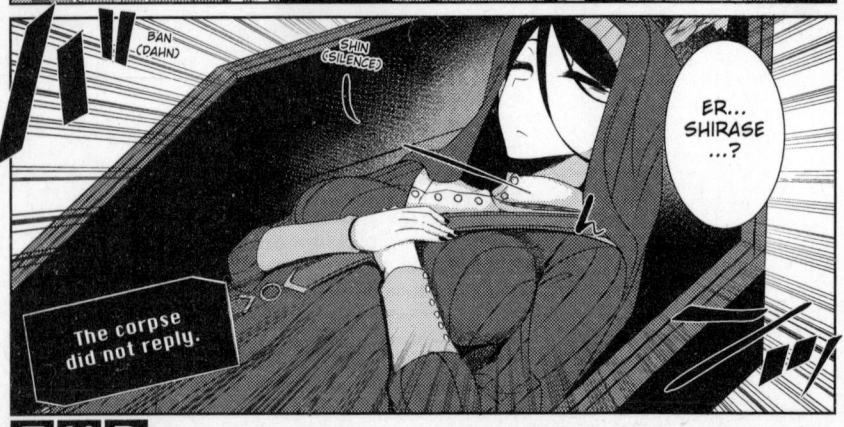

END

Do You Love Your Mom?

DO YOU LOVE YOUR MOM?

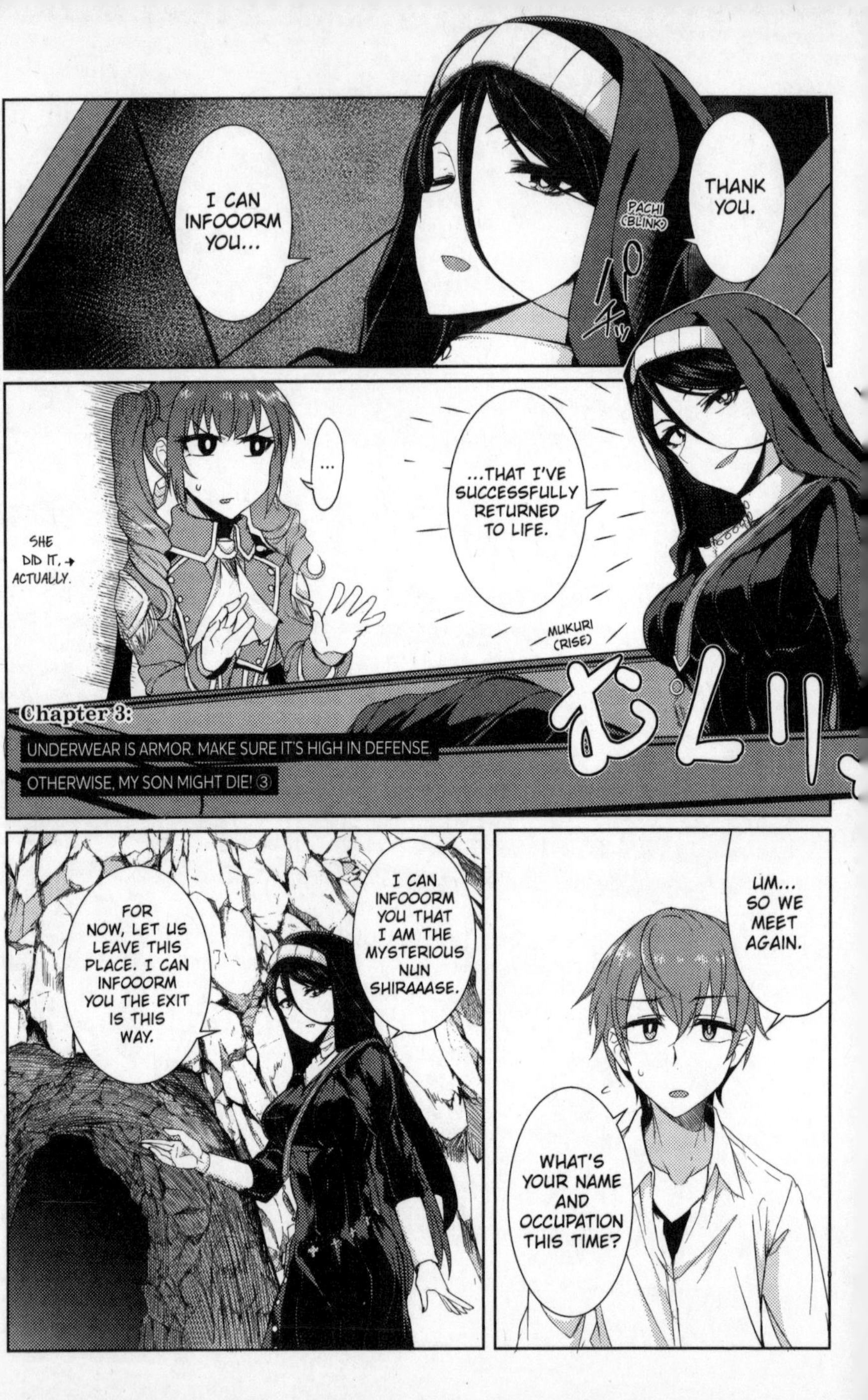
THANK YOU.
PACHI (BLINK)
I CAN INFOOORM YOU...
...THAT I'VE SUCCESSFULLY RETURNED TO LIFE.
...
SHE DID IT, ACTUALLY.
MUKURI (RISE)
Chapter 3:
UNDERWEAR IS ARMOR. MAKE SURE IT'S HIGH IN DEFENSE. OTHERWISE, MY SON MIGHT DIE! ③
UM... SO WE MEET AGAIN.
WHAT'S YOUR NAME AND OCCUPATION THIS TIME?
I CAN INFOOORM YOU THAT I AM THE MYSTERIOUS NUN SHIRAAASE.
FOR NOW, LET US LEAVE THIS PLACE. I CAN INFOOORM YOU THE EXIT IS THIS WAY.

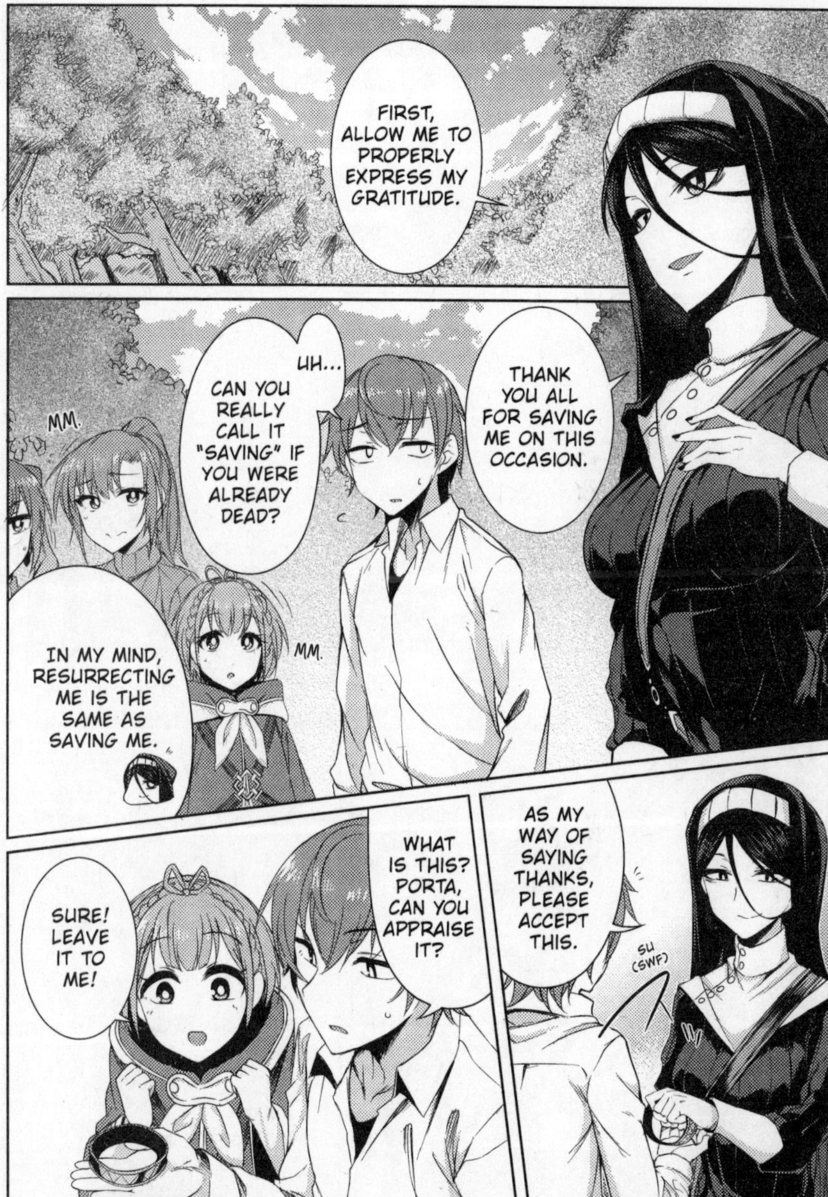
FIRST, ALLOW ME TO PROPERLY EXPRESS MY GRATITUDE.
THANK YOU ALL FOR SAVING ME ON THIS OCCASION.
UH... CAN YOU REALLY CALL IT "SAVING" IF YOU WERE ALREADY DEAD?
MM.
MM.
IN MY MIND, RESURRECTING ME IS THE SAME AS SAVING ME.
AS MY WAY OF SAYING THANKS, PLEASE ACCEPT THIS.
SU (SWF)
WHAT IS THIS? PORTA, CAN YOU APPRAISE IT?
SURE! LEAVE IT TO ME!

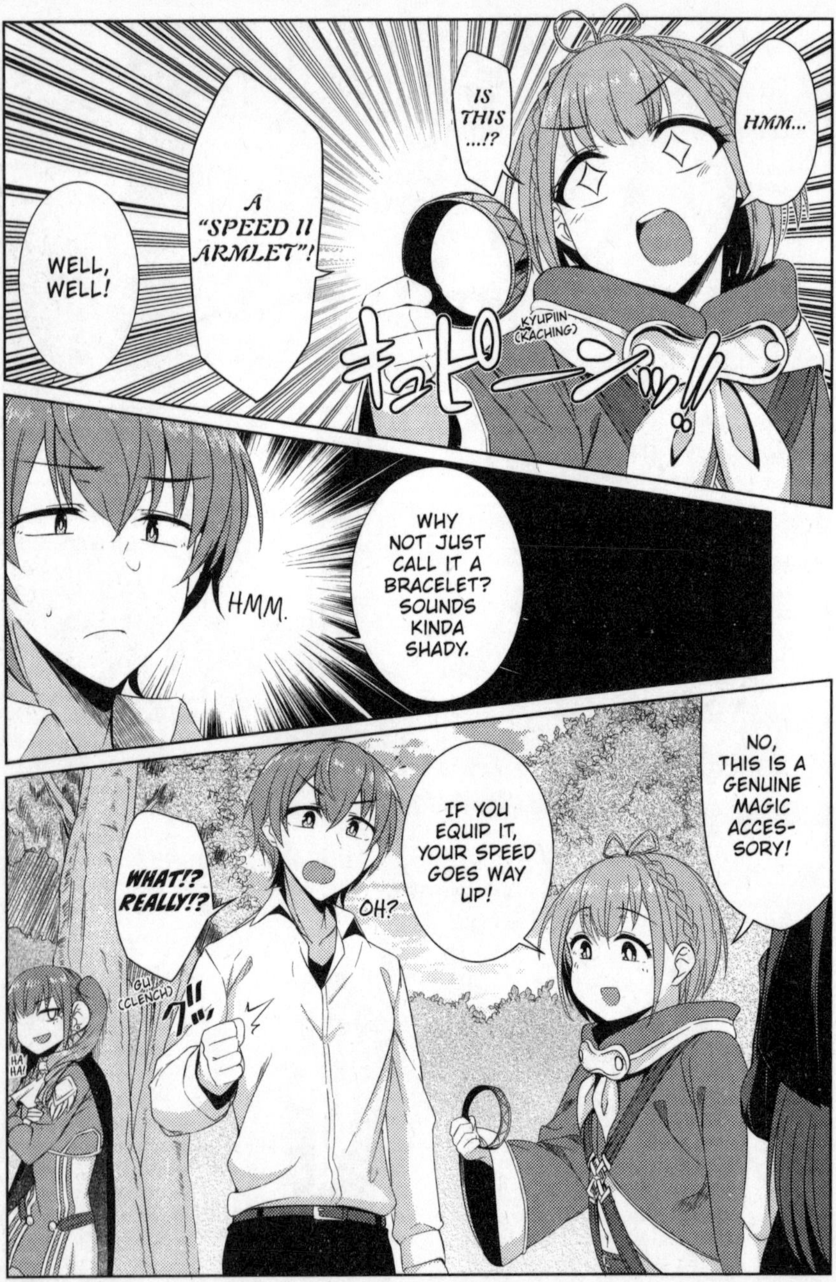
HMM...
IS THIS ...!?
A "SPEED II ARMLET"!
WELL, WELL!
KYUPIIN (KACHING)
WHY NOT JUST CALL IT A BRACELET? SOUNDS KINDA SHADY.
HMM.
NO, THIS IS A GENUINE MAGIC ACCES-SORY!
IF YOU EQUIP IT, YOUR SPEED GOES WAY UP!
OH?
WHAT!? REALLY!?
GU (CLENCH)
HA HA!

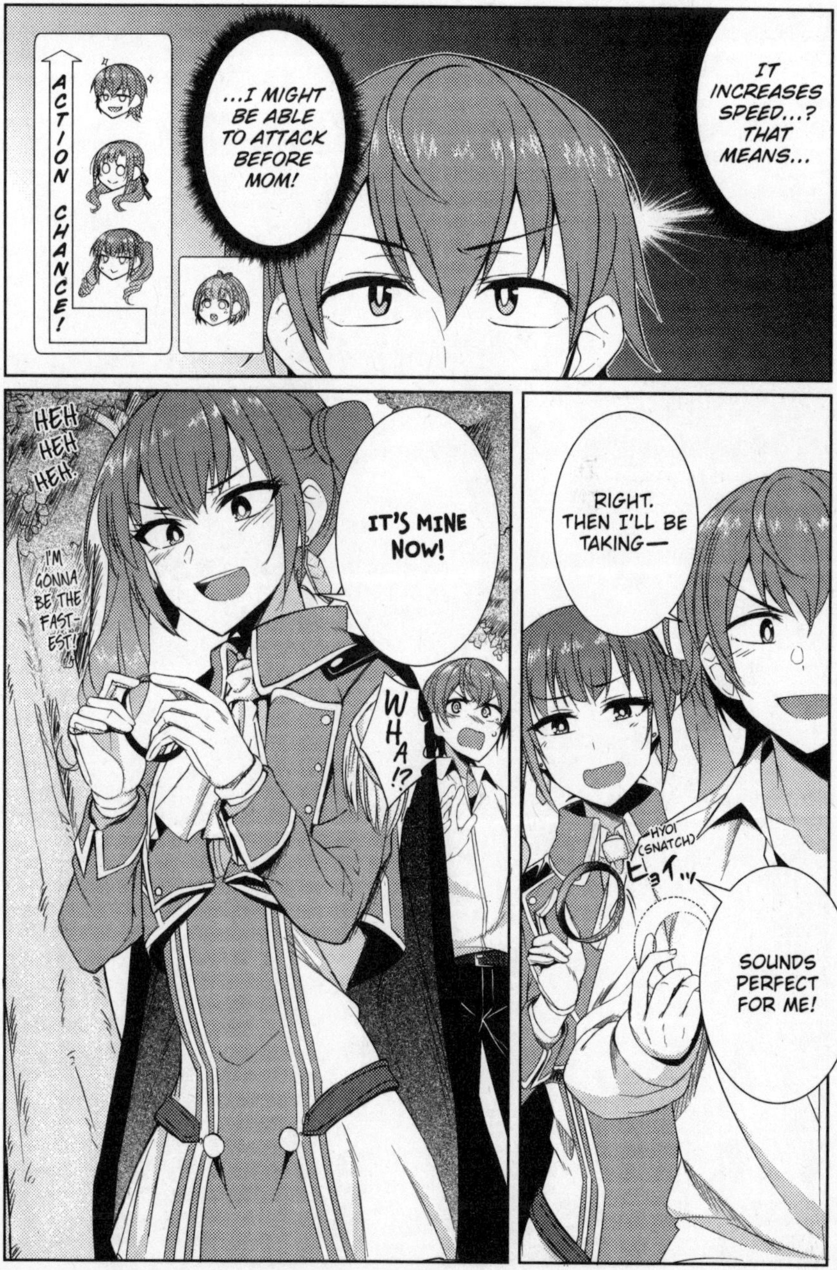
IT INCREASES SPEED...? THAT MEANS...
...I MIGHT BE ABLE TO ATTACK BEFORE MOM!
ACTION CHANCE!
RIGHT. THEN I'LL BE TAKING—
HYOI (SNATCH)
ヒョイッ
SOUNDS PERFECT FOR ME!
IT'S MINE NOW!
WHA!?
HEH HEH HEH
I'M GONNA BE THE FAST-EST!

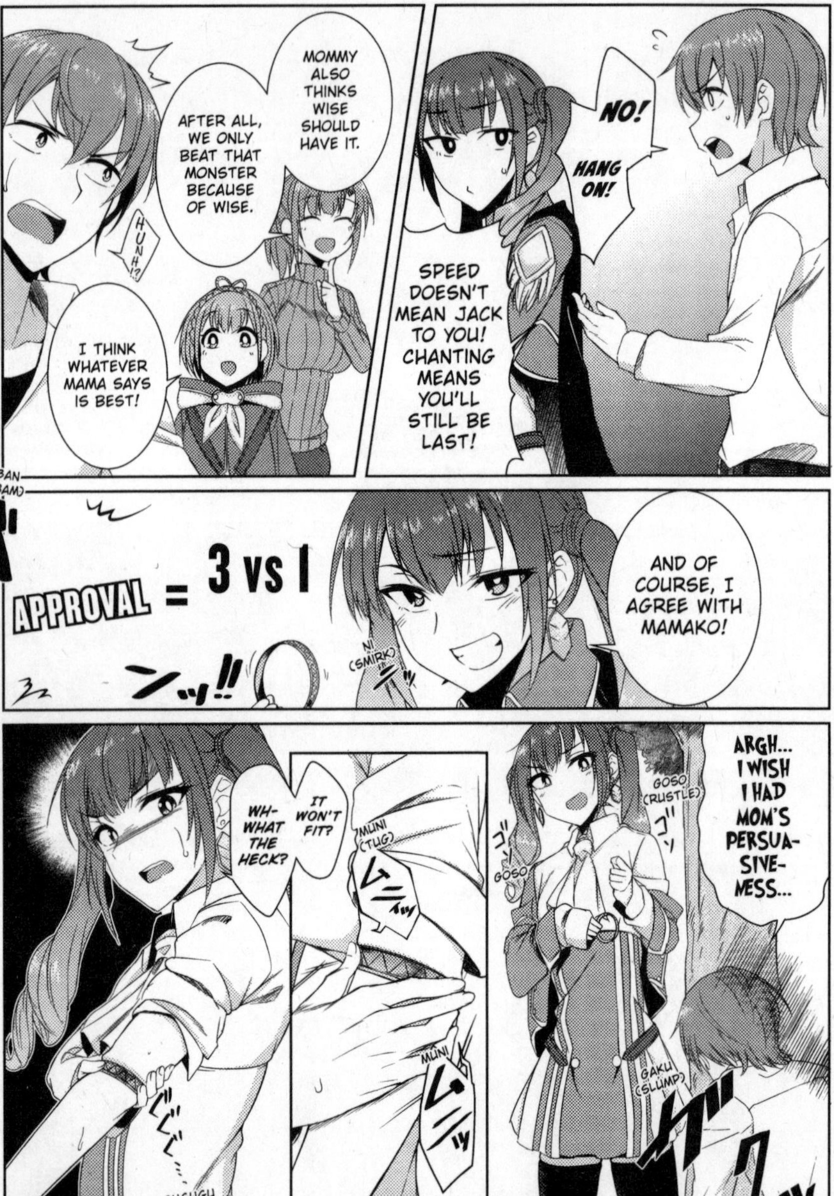
NO!
HANG ON!
SPEED DOESN'T MEAN JACK TO YOU! CHANTING MEANS YOU'LL STILL BE LAST!
MOMMY ALSO THINKS WISE SHOULD HAVE IT.
AFTER ALL, WE ONLY BEAT THAT MONSTER BECAUSE OF WISE.
HUNH!?
I THINK WHATEVER MAMA SAYS IS BEST!
AND OF COURSE, I AGREE WITH MAMAKO!
NI (SMIRK)
APPROVAL = 3 vs 1
BAN (BAM)
ARGH... I WISH I HAD MOM'S PERSUASIVENESS...
GOSO (RUSTLE)
GOSO
GAKU (SLUMP)
IT WON'T FIT?
MUNI (TUG)
MUNI
WH-WHAT THE HECK?
GUGUGU (SHOOOOVE)

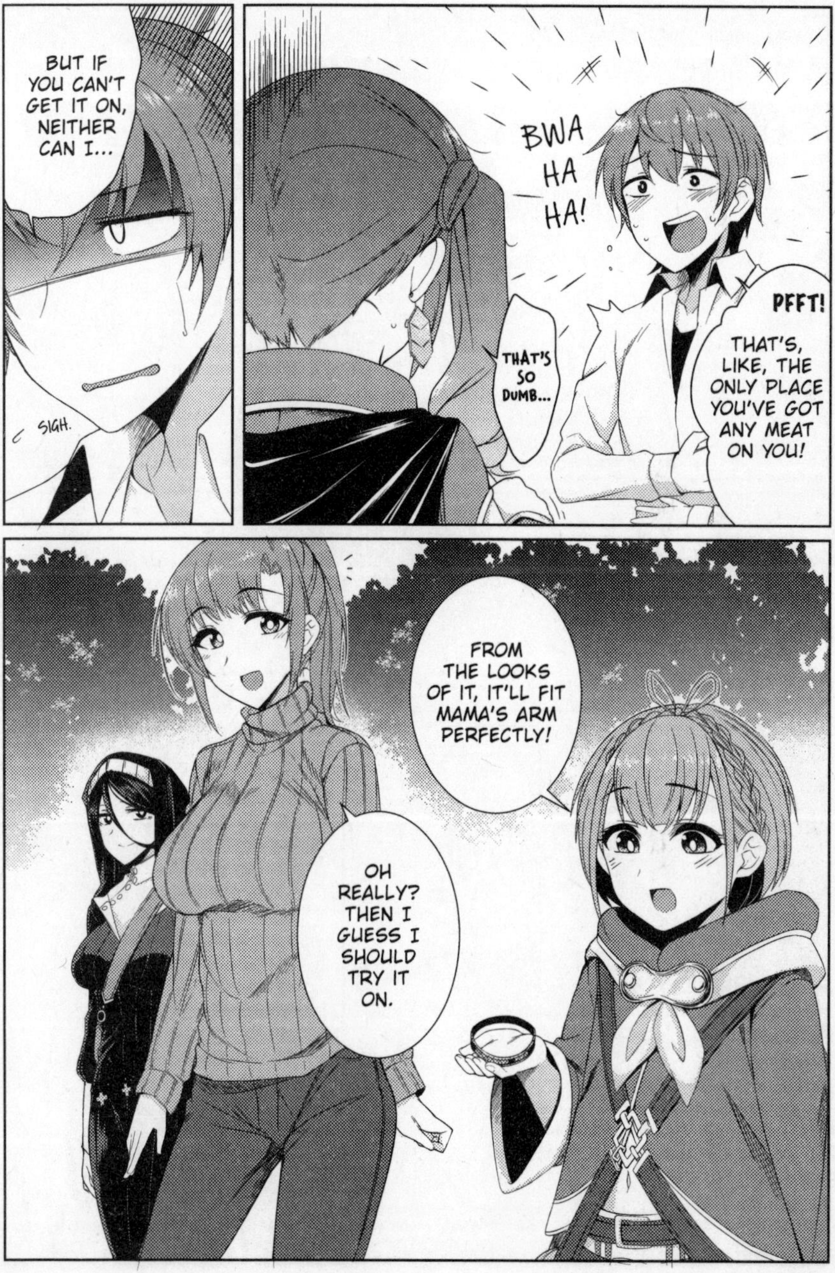

BWA HA HA!
PFFT!
THAT'S, LIKE, THE ONLY PLACE YOU'VE GOT ANY MEAT ON YOU!
THAT'S SO DUMB...
BUT IF YOU CAN'T GET IT ON, NEITHER CAN I...
SIGH.
FROM THE LOOKS OF IT, IT'LL FIT MAMA'S ARM PERFECTLY!
OH REALLY? THEN I GUESS I SHOULD TRY IT ON.

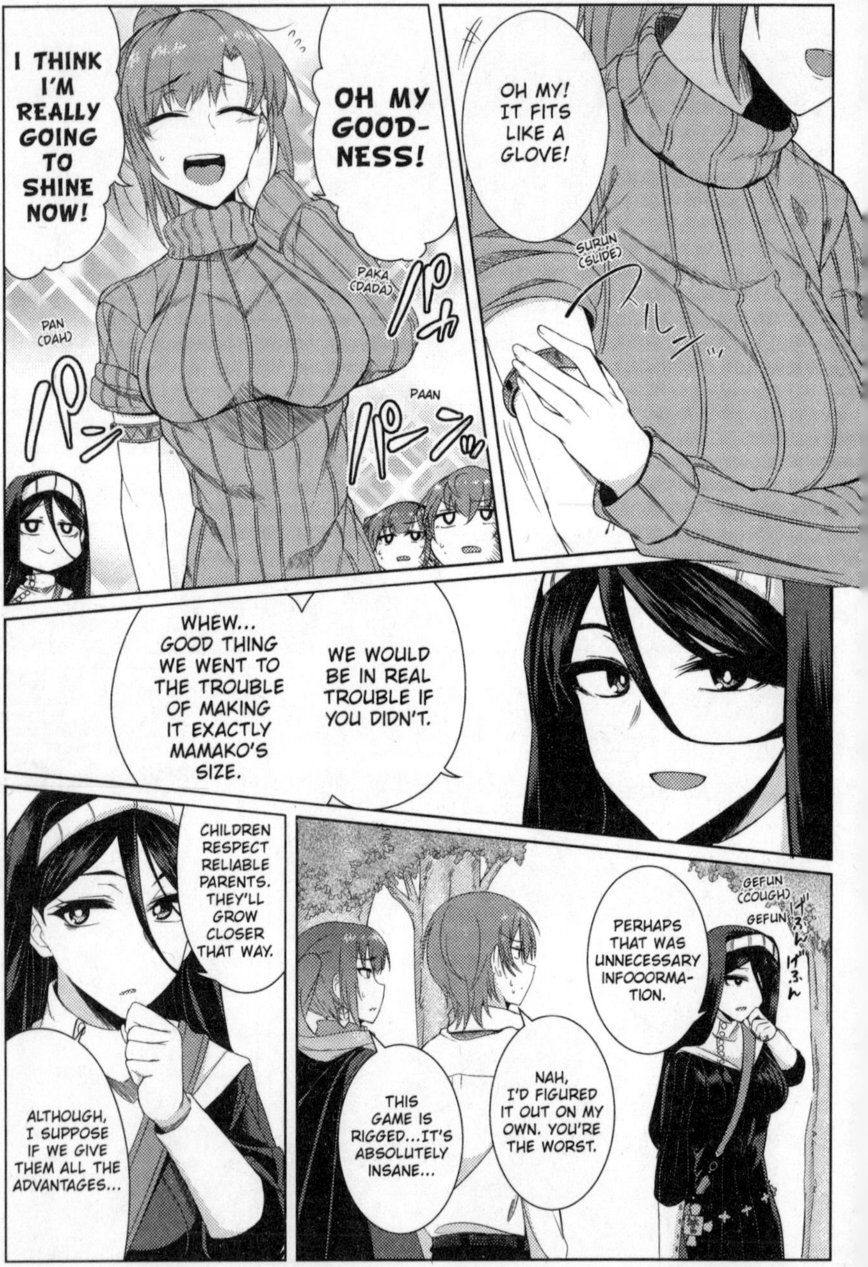

OH MY! IT FITS LIKE A GLOVE!
SURUN (SLIDE)
OH MY GOODNESS!
I THINK I'M REALLY GOING TO SHINE NOW!
PAKA (DADA)
PAAN
PAN (DAH)
WHEW... GOOD THING WE WENT TO THE TROUBLE OF MAKING IT EXACTLY MAMAKO'S SIZE.
WE WOULD BE IN REAL TROUBLE IF YOU DIDN'T.
GEFUN (COUGH) GEFUN
PERHAPS THAT WAS UNNECESSARY INFOOORMA-TION.
NAH, I'D FIGURED IT OUT ON MY OWN. YOU'RE THE WORST.
THIS GAME IS RIGGED...IT'S ABSOLUTELY INSANE...
CHILDREN RESPECT RELIABLE PARENTS. THEY'LL GROW CLOSER THAT WAY.
ALTHOUGH, I SUPPOSE IF WE GIVE THEM ALL THE ADVANTAGES...

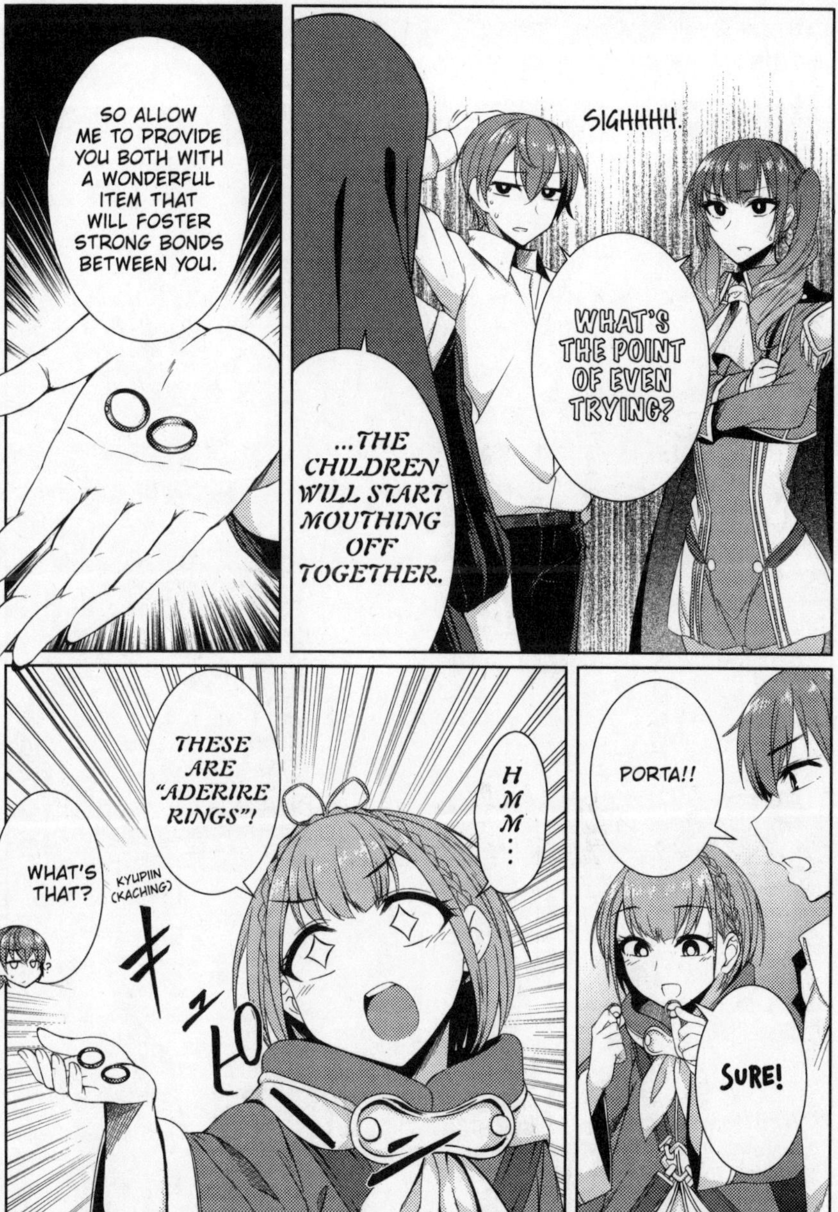
SIGHHHH.
WHAT'S THE POINT OF EVEN TRYING?
...THE CHILDREN WILL START MOUTHING OFF TOGETHER.
SO ALLOW ME TO PROVIDE YOU BOTH WITH A WONDERFUL ITEM THAT WILL FOSTER STRONG BONDS BETWEEN YOU.
PORTA!!
SURE!
HMM...
THESE ARE "ADERIRE RINGS"!
KYUPIIN (KACHING)
WHAT'S THAT?

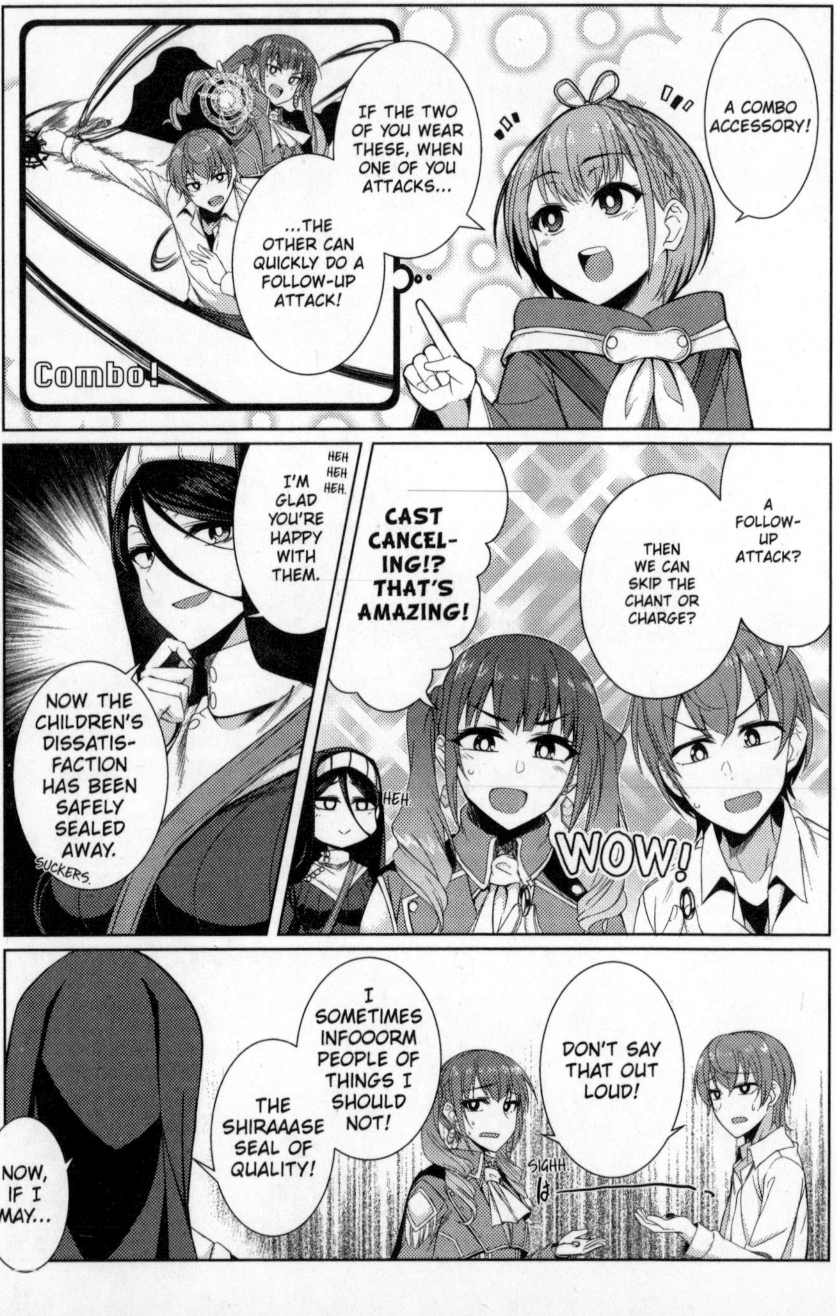
A COMBO ACCESSORY!
IF THE TWO OF YOU WEAR THESE, WHEN ONE OF YOU ATTACKS...
...THE OTHER CAN QUICKLY DO A FOLLOW-UP ATTACK!
Combo!
A FOLLOW-UP ATTACK?
THEN WE CAN SKIP THE CHANT OR CHARGE?
CAST CANCELING!? THAT'S AMAZING!
WOW!
HEH.
HEH HEH HEH.
I'M GLAD YOU'RE HAPPY WITH THEM.
NOW THE CHILDREN'S DISSATISFACTION HAS BEEN SAFELY SEALED AWAY.
SUCKERS.
DON'T SAY THAT OUT LOUD!
SIGHH
I SOMETIMES INFOOORM PEOPLE OF THINGS I SHOULD NOT!
THE SHIRAAASE SEAL OF QUALITY!
NOW, IF I MAY...

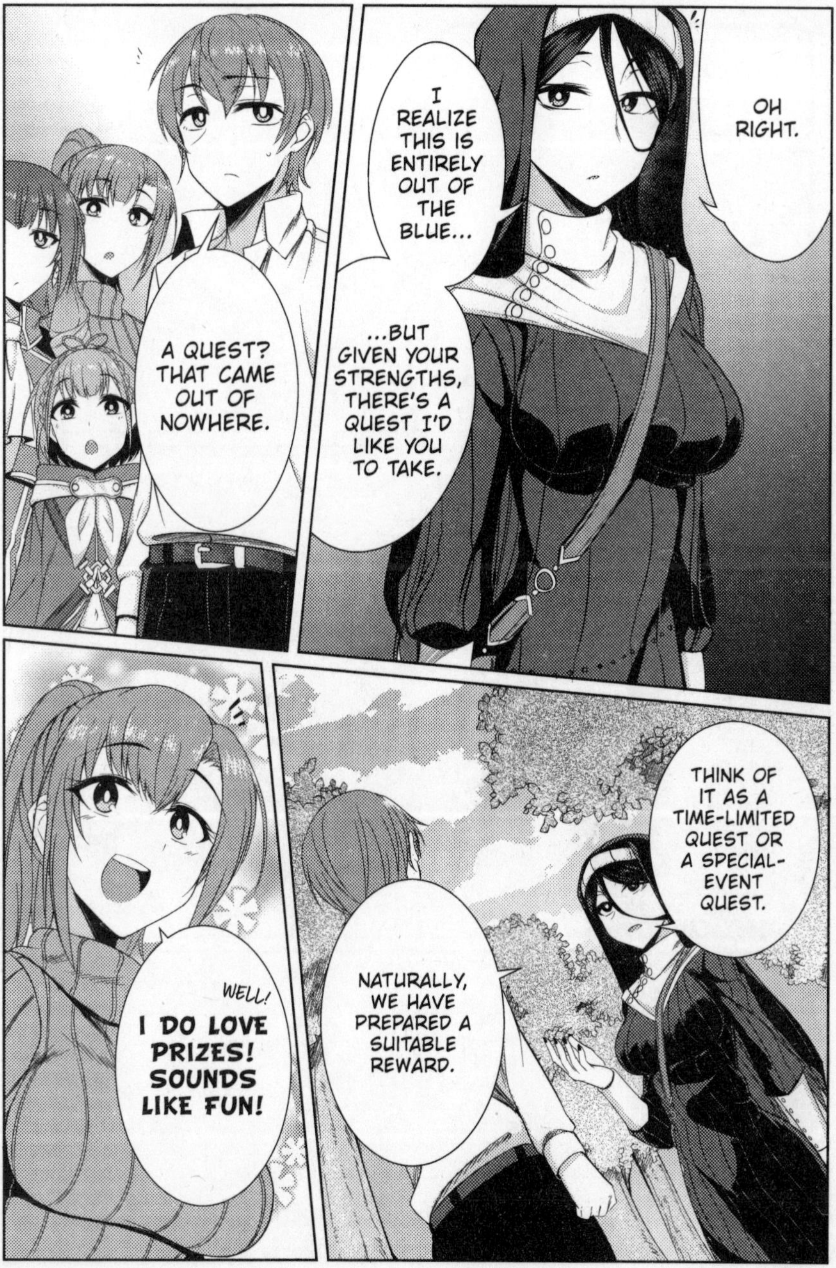
OH RIGHT.
I REALIZE THIS IS ENTIRELY OUT OF THE BLUE...
...BUT GIVEN YOUR STRENGTHS, THERE'S A QUEST I'D LIKE YOU TO TAKE.
A QUEST? THAT CAME OUT OF NOWHERE.
THINK OF IT AS A TIME-LIMITED QUEST OR A SPECIAL-EVENT QUEST.
NATURALLY, WE HAVE PREPARED A SUITABLE REWARD.
WELL! I DO LOVE PRIZES! SOUNDS LIKE FUN!

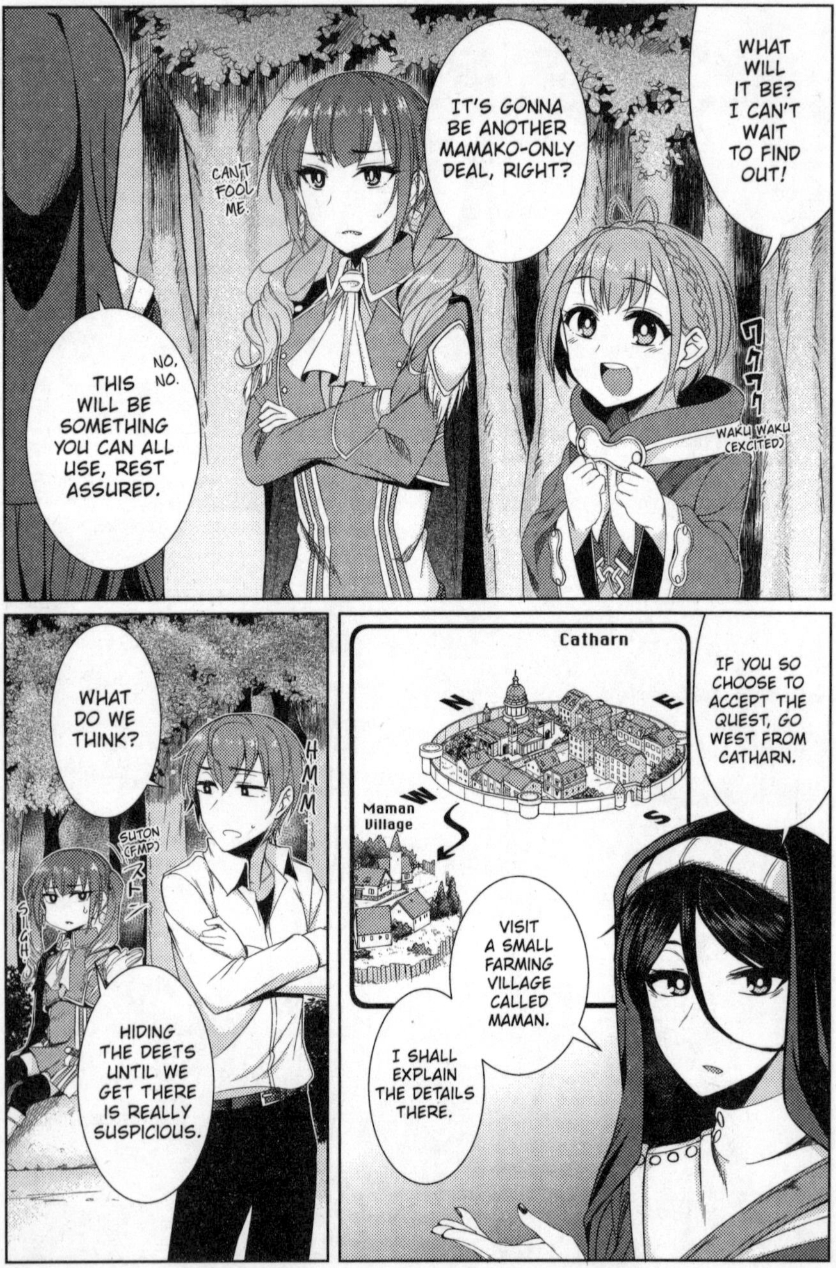
WHAT WILL IT BE? I CAN'T WAIT TO FIND OUT!
WAKU WAKU (EXCITED)
IT'S GONNA BE ANOTHER MAMAKO-ONLY DEAL, RIGHT?
CAN'T FOOL ME.
NO, NO.
THIS WILL BE SOMETHING YOU CAN ALL USE, REST ASSURED.
IF YOU SO CHOOSE TO ACCEPT THE QUEST, GO WEST FROM CATHARN.
Catharn
N
E
W
S
Maman Village
VISIT A SMALL FARMING VILLAGE CALLED MAMAN.
I SHALL EXPLAIN THE DETAILS THERE.
WHAT DO WE THINK?
HMM.
SUTON (FMP)
SIGH
HIDING THE DEETS UNTIL WE GET THERE IS REALLY SUSPICIOUS.

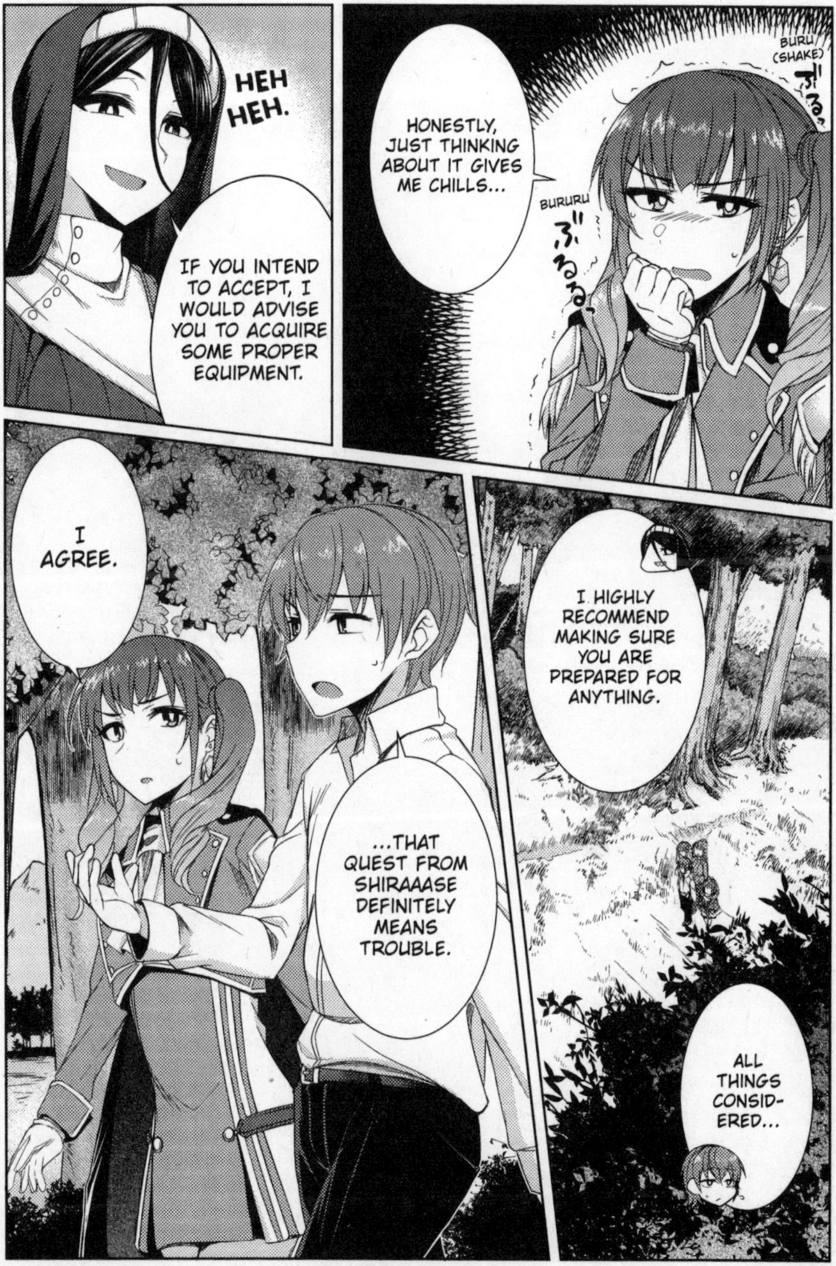
BURU (SHAKE)
HONESTLY, JUST THINKING ABOUT IT GIVES ME CHILLS...
BURURU
HEH HEH.
IF YOU INTEND TO ACCEPT, I WOULD ADVISE YOU TO ACQUIRE SOME PROPER EQUIPMENT.
I HIGHLY RECOMMEND MAKING SURE YOU ARE PREPARED FOR ANYTHING.
ALL THINGS CONSID-ERED...
...THAT QUEST FROM SHIRAAASE DEFINITELY MEANS TROUBLE.
I AGREE.

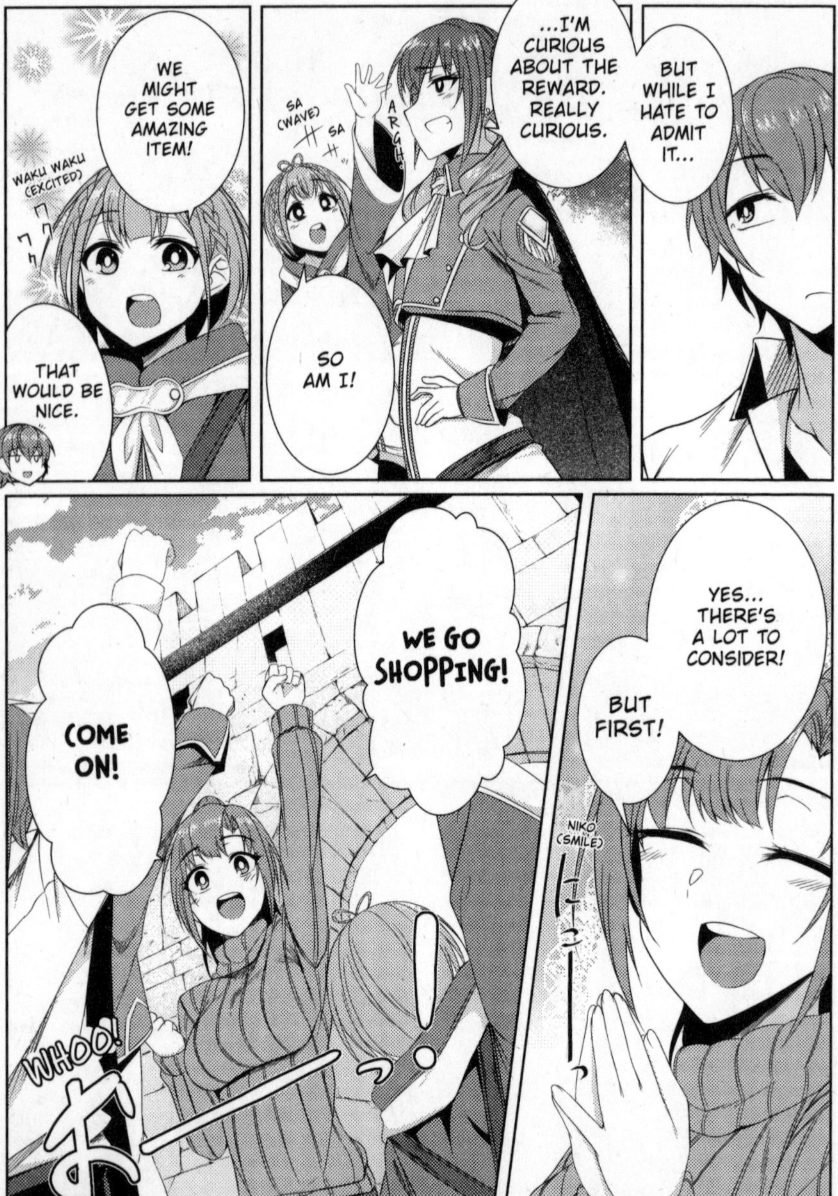
BUT WHILE I HATE TO ADMIT IT...
...I'M CURIOUS ABOUT THE REWARD. REALLY CURIOUS.
ARGH
SA (WAVE) SA
SO AM I!
WE MIGHT GET SOME AMAZING ITEM!
WAKU WAKU (EXCITED)
THAT WOULD BE NICE.
YES... THERE'S A LOT TO CONSIDER!
BUT FIRST!
NIKO (SMILE)
WE GO SHOPPING!
COME ON!
WHOO!

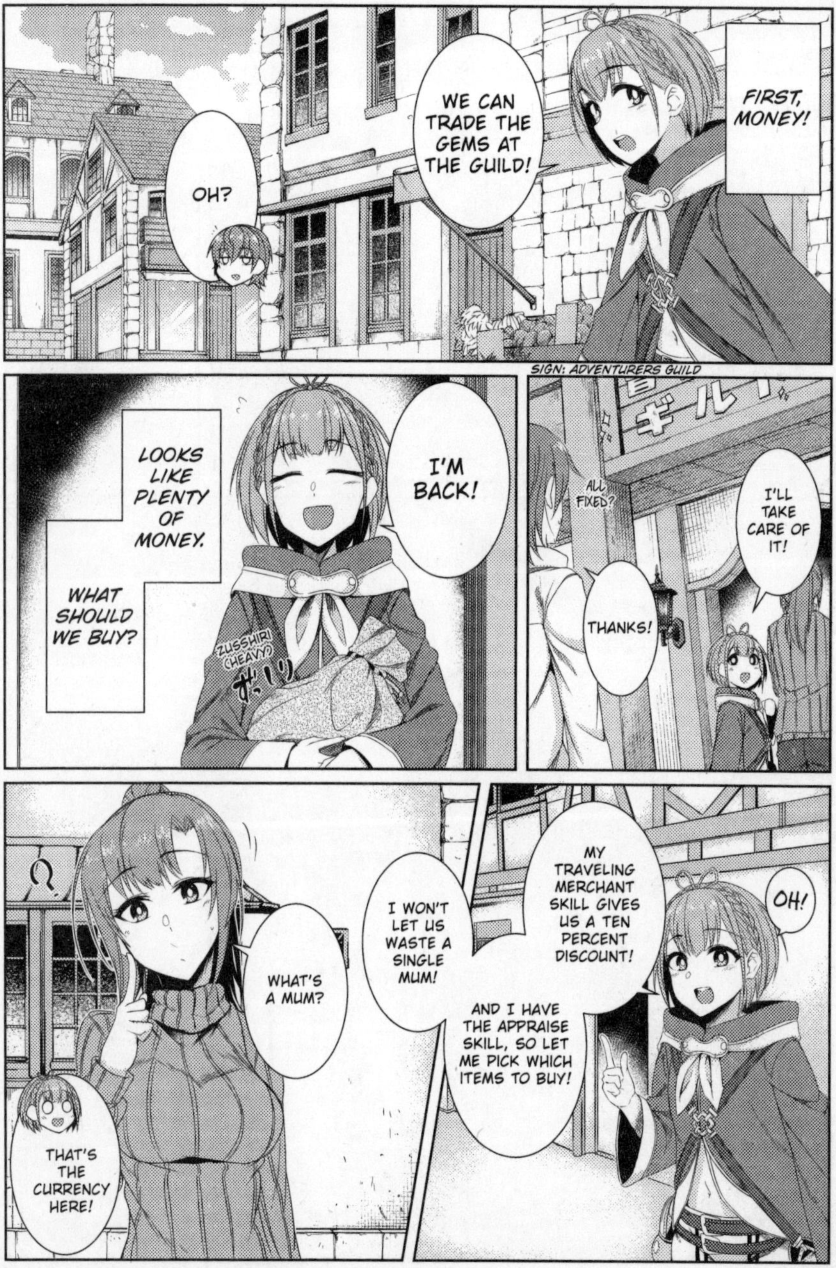
FIRST, MONEY!
WE CAN TRADE THE GEMS AT THE GUILD!
OH?
SIGN: ADVENTURERS GUILD
I'LL TAKE CARE OF IT!
ALL FIXED?
THANKS!
I'M BACK!
LOOKS LIKE PLENTY OF MONEY.
WHAT SHOULD WE BUY?
ZUSSHIRI (HEAVY)
OH!
MY TRAVELING MERCHANT SKILL GIVES US A TEN PERCENT DISCOUNT!
I WON'T LET US WASTE A SINGLE MUM!
AND I HAVE THE APPRAISE SKILL, SO LET ME PICK WHICH ITEMS TO BUY!
WHAT'S A MUM?
THAT'S THE CURRENCY HERE!

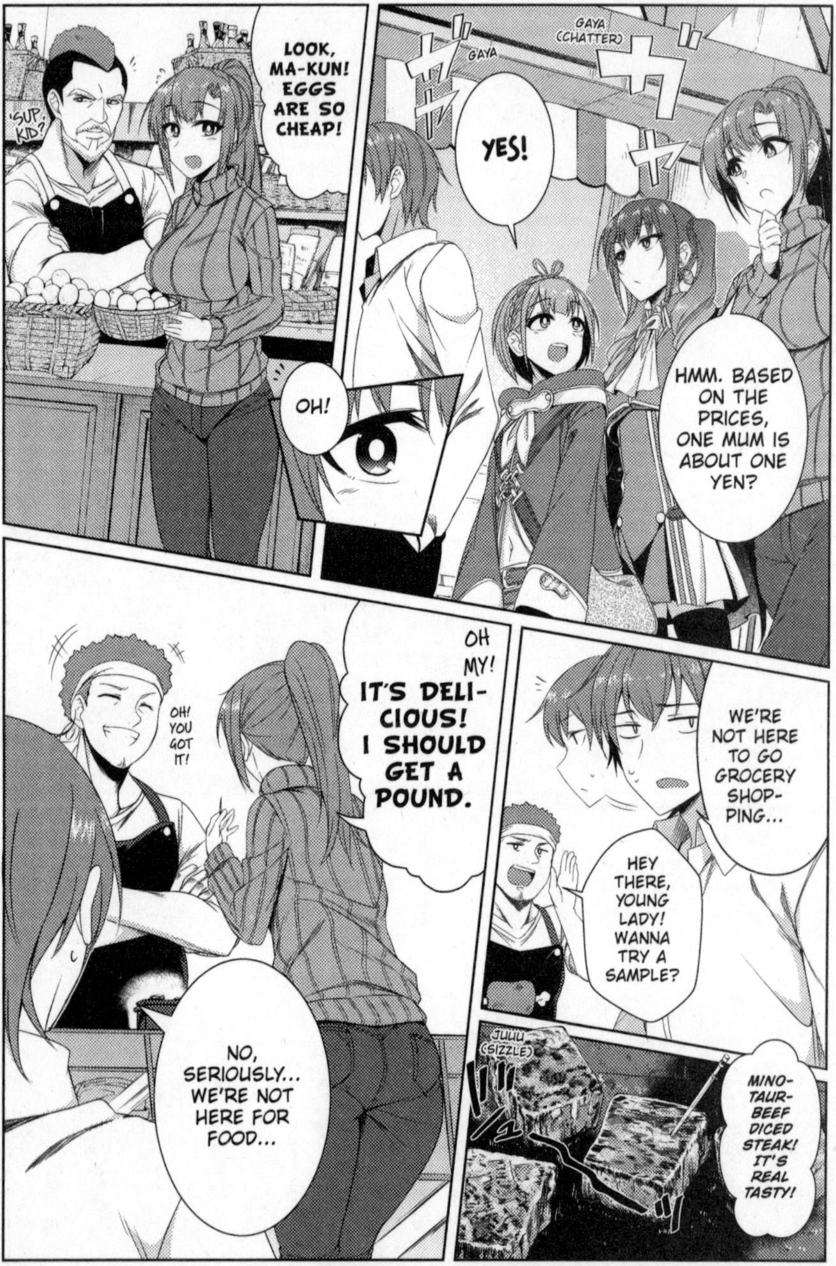
GAYA (CHATTER)
GAYA
YES!
HMM. BASED ON THE PRICES, ONE MUM IS ABOUT ONE YEN?
OH!
LOOK, MA-KUN! EGGS ARE SO CHEAP!
'SUP, KID?
WE'RE NOT HERE TO GO GROCERY SHOP-PING...
HEY THERE, YOUNG LADY! WANNA TRY A SAMPLE?
JUUU (SIZZLE)
MINO-TAUR-BEEF DICED STEAK! IT'S REAL TASTY!
OH MY!
IT'S DELI-CIOUS! I SHOULD GET A POUND.
OH! YOU GOT IT!
NO, SERIOUSLY... WE'RE NOT HERE FOR FOOD...

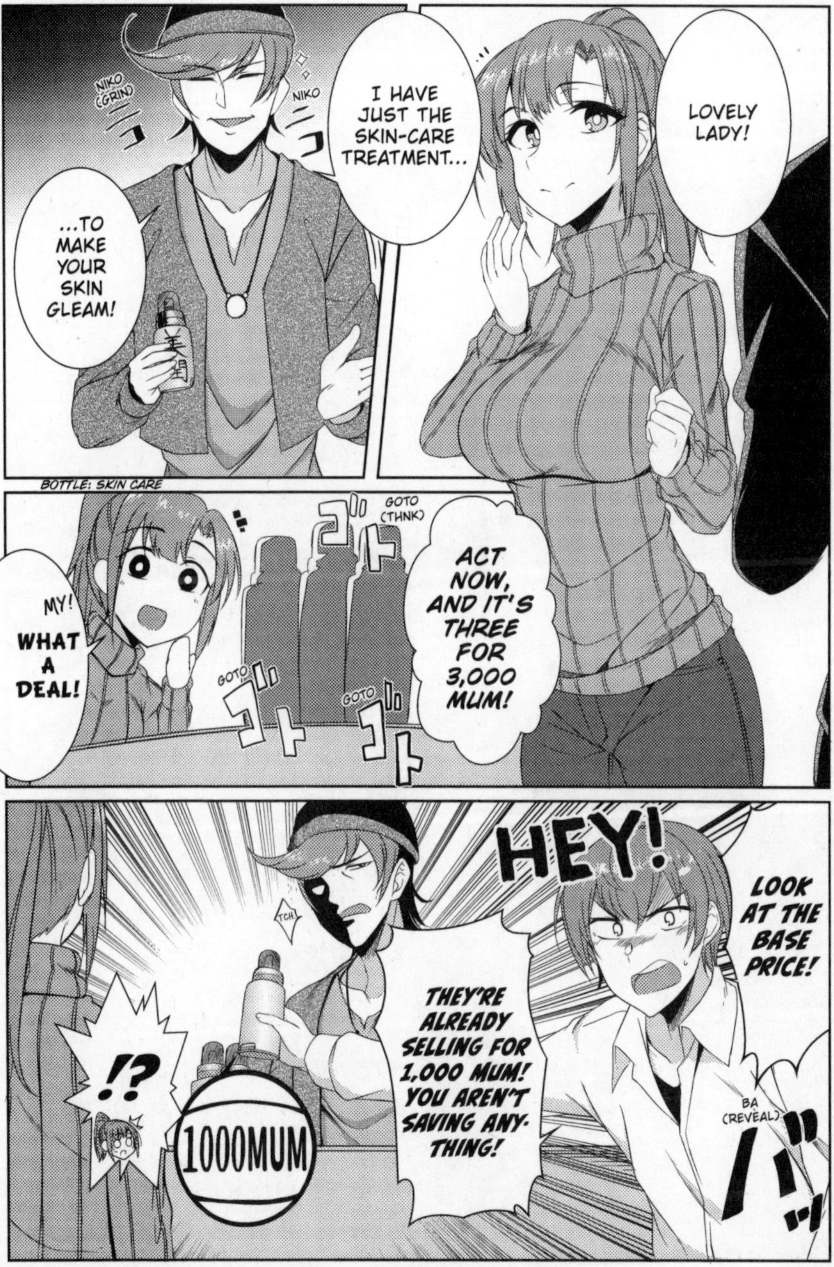
LOVELY LADY!
I HAVE JUST THE SKIN-CARE TREATMENT...
NIKO
NIKO (GRIN)
...TO MAKE YOUR SKIN GLEAM!
BOTTLE: SKIN CARE
GOTO (THNK)
ACT NOW, AND IT'S THREE FOR 3,000 MUM!
GOTO
GOTO
MY! WHAT A DEAL!
LOOK AT THE BASE PRICE!
HEY!
BA (REVEAL)
THEY'RE ALREADY SELLING FOR 1,000 MUM! YOU AREN'T SAVING ANY-THING!
TCH!
1000MUM
!?

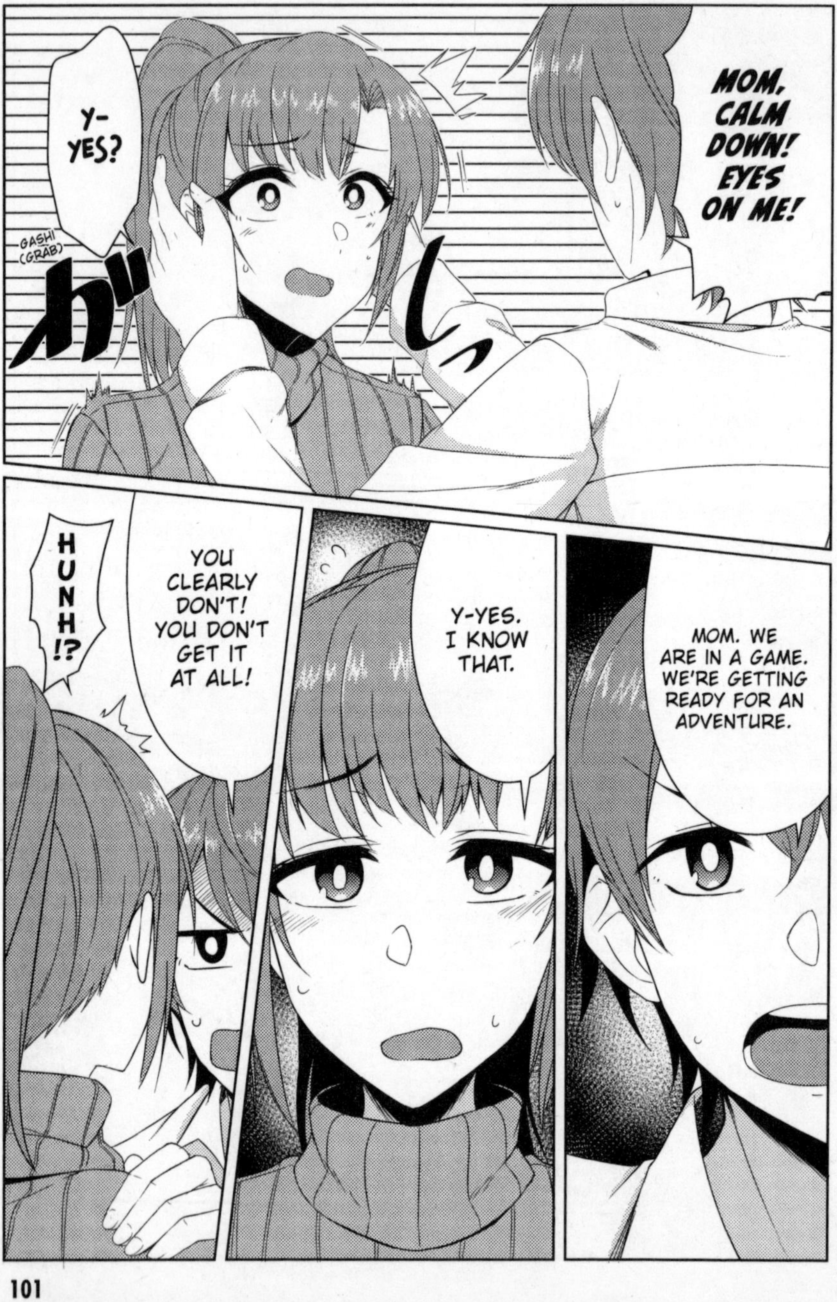
MOM, CALM DOWN! EYES ON ME!
GASHI (GRAB)
Y-YES?
MOM. WE ARE IN A GAME. WE'RE GETTING READY FOR AN ADVENTURE.
Y-YES. I KNOW THAT.
YOU CLEARLY DON'T! YOU DON'T GET IT AT ALL!
HUNH!?

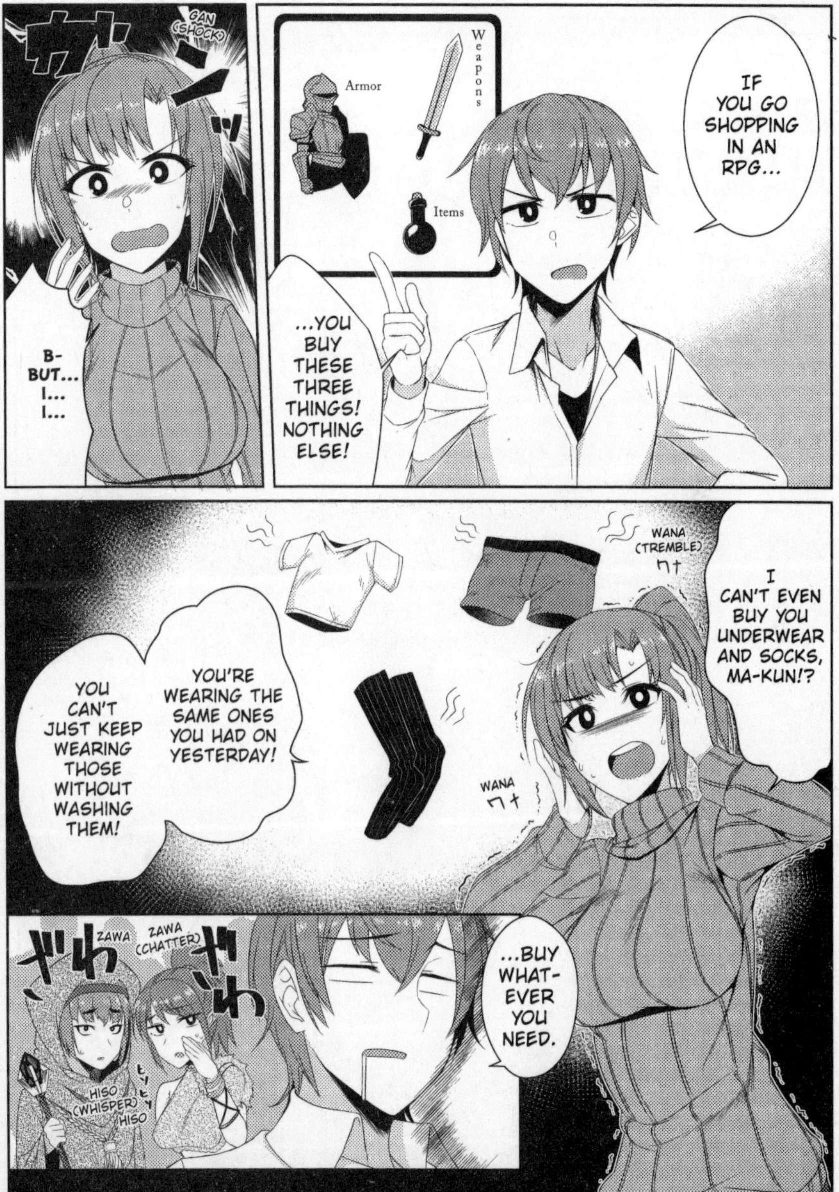
IF YOU GO SHOPPING IN AN RPG...
Weapons
Armor
Items
...YOU BUY THESE THREE THINGS! NOTHING ELSE!
GAN (SHOCK)
B-BUT... I... I...
I CAN'T EVEN BUY YOU UNDERWEAR AND SOCKS, MA-KUN!?
WANA (TREMBLE)
WANA
YOU'RE WEARING THE SAME ONES YOU HAD ON YESTERDAY!
YOU CAN'T JUST KEEP WEARING THOSE WITHOUT WASHING THEM!
...BUY WHAT-EVER YOU NEED.
ZAWA (CHATTER)
ZAWA
HISO (WHISPER) HISO

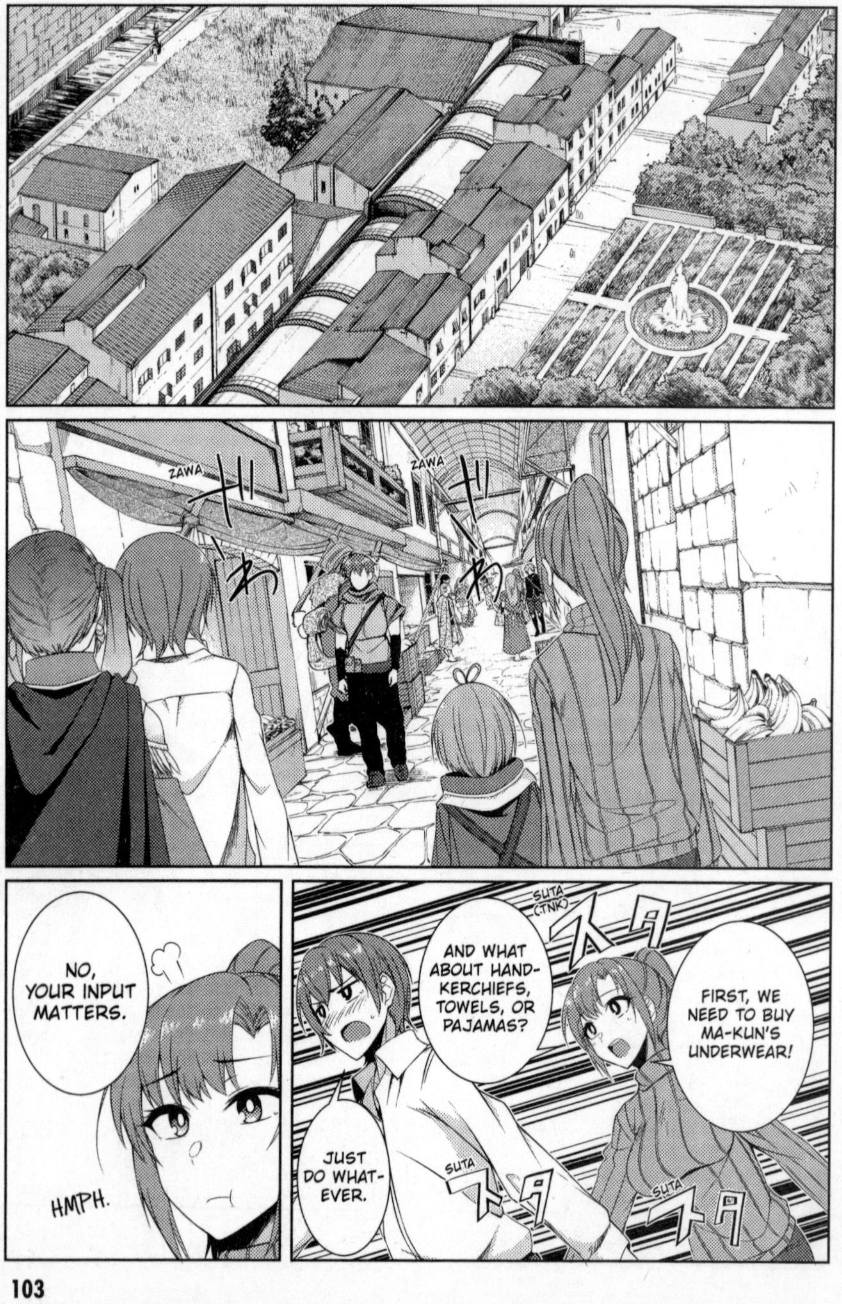
ZAWA
ZAWA
SUTA (TNK)
FIRST, WE NEED TO BUY MA-KUN'S UNDERWEAR!
AND WHAT ABOUT HAND-KERCHIEFS, TOWELS, OR PAJAMAS?
SUTA
JUST DO WHAT-EVER.
SUTA
NO, YOUR INPUT MATTERS.
HMPH.

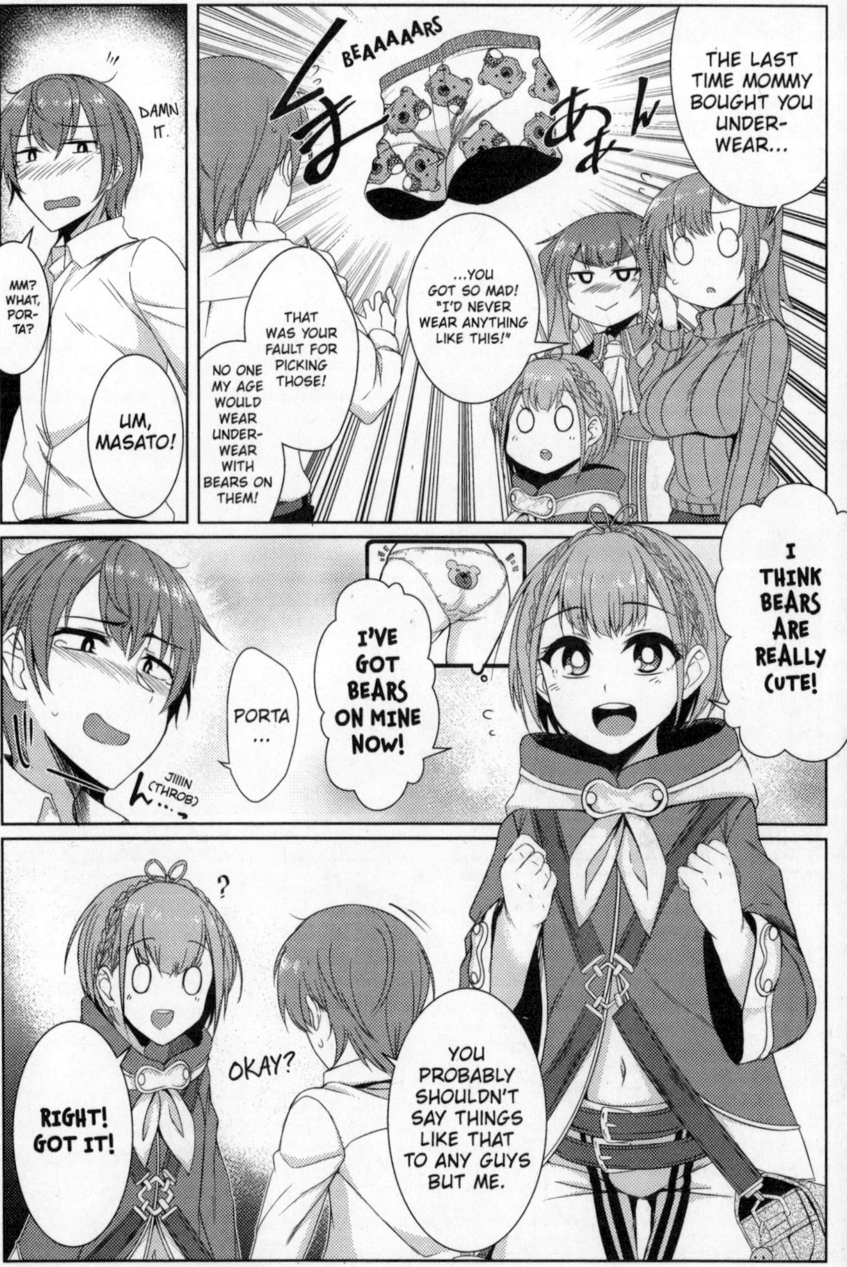
THE LAST TIME MOMMY BOUGHT YOU UNDER-WEAR...
BEAAAAARS
...YOU GOT SO MAD! "I'D NEVER WEAR ANYTHING LIKE THIS!"
THAT WAS YOUR FAULT FOR PICKING THOSE!
NO ONE MY AGE WOULD WEAR UNDER-WEAR WITH BEARS ON THEM!
DAMN IT.
UM, MASATO!
MM? WHAT, PORTA?
I THINK BEARS ARE REALLY CUTE!
I'VE GOT BEARS ON MINE NOW!
PORTA ...
JIIIIN (THROB)
YOU PROBABLY SHOULDN'T SAY THINGS LIKE THAT TO ANY GUYS BUT ME.
OKAY?
?
RIGHT! GOT IT!

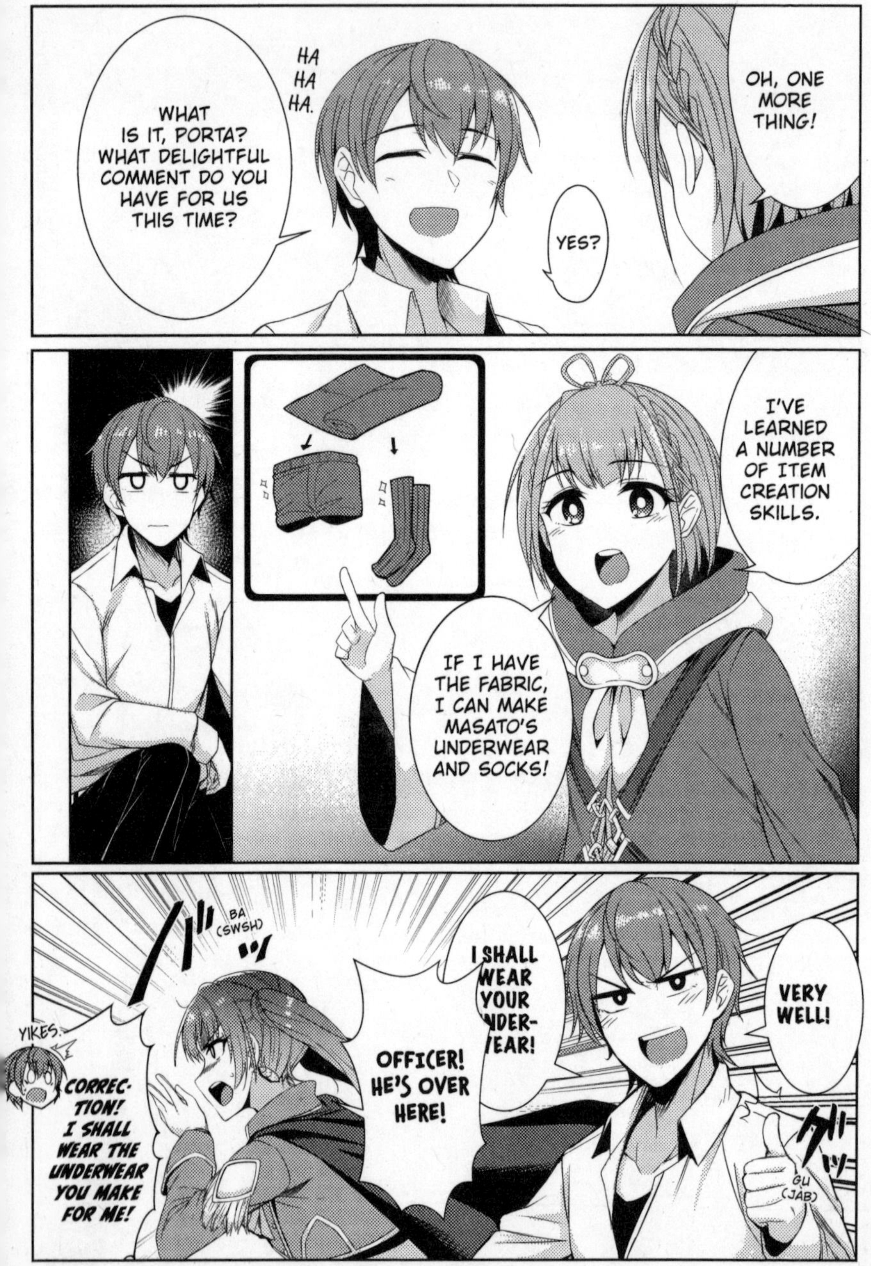
OH, ONE MORE THING!
YES?
HA HA HA.
WHAT IS IT, PORTA? WHAT DELIGHTFUL COMMENT DO YOU HAVE FOR US THIS TIME?
I'VE LEARNED A NUMBER OF ITEM CREATION SKILLS.
IF I HAVE THE FABRIC, I CAN MAKE MASATO'S UNDERWEAR AND SOCKS!
VERY WELL!
GU (JAB)
I SHALL WEAR YOUR UNDER-WEAR!
OFFICER! HE'S OVER HERE!
BA (SWSH)
YIKES.
CORREC-TION! I SHALL WEAR THE UNDERWEAR YOU MAKE FOR ME!

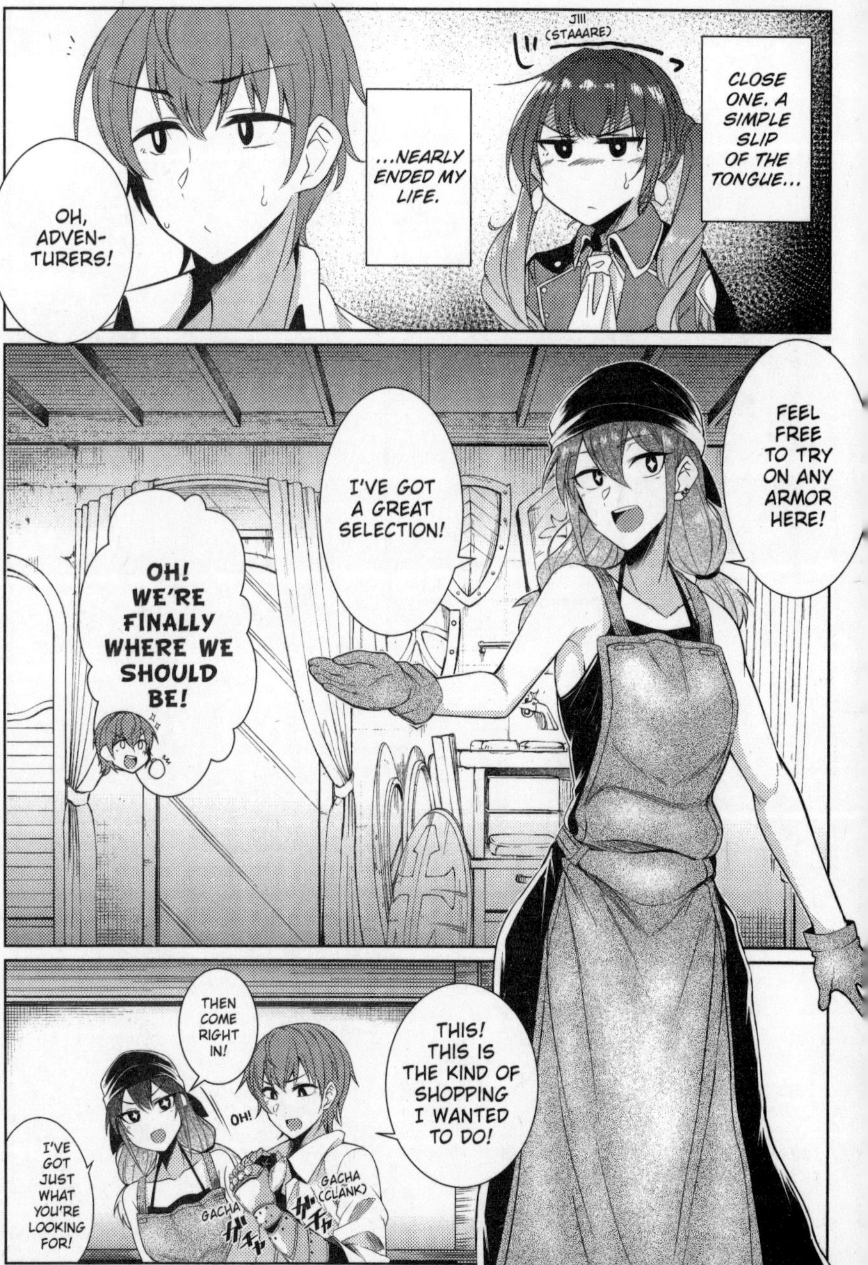
CLOSE ONE. A SIMPLE SLIP OF THE TONGUE...
JIII (STAAARE)
...NEARLY ENDED MY LIFE.
OH, ADVENTURERS!
FEEL FREE TO TRY ON ANY ARMOR HERE!
I'VE GOT A GREAT SELECTION!
OH! WE'RE FINALLY WHERE WE SHOULD BE!
THIS! THIS IS THE KIND OF SHOPPING I WANTED TO DO!
THEN COME RIGHT IN!
OH!
GACHA (CLANK)
GACHA
I'VE GOT JUST WHAT YOU'RE LOOKING FOR!

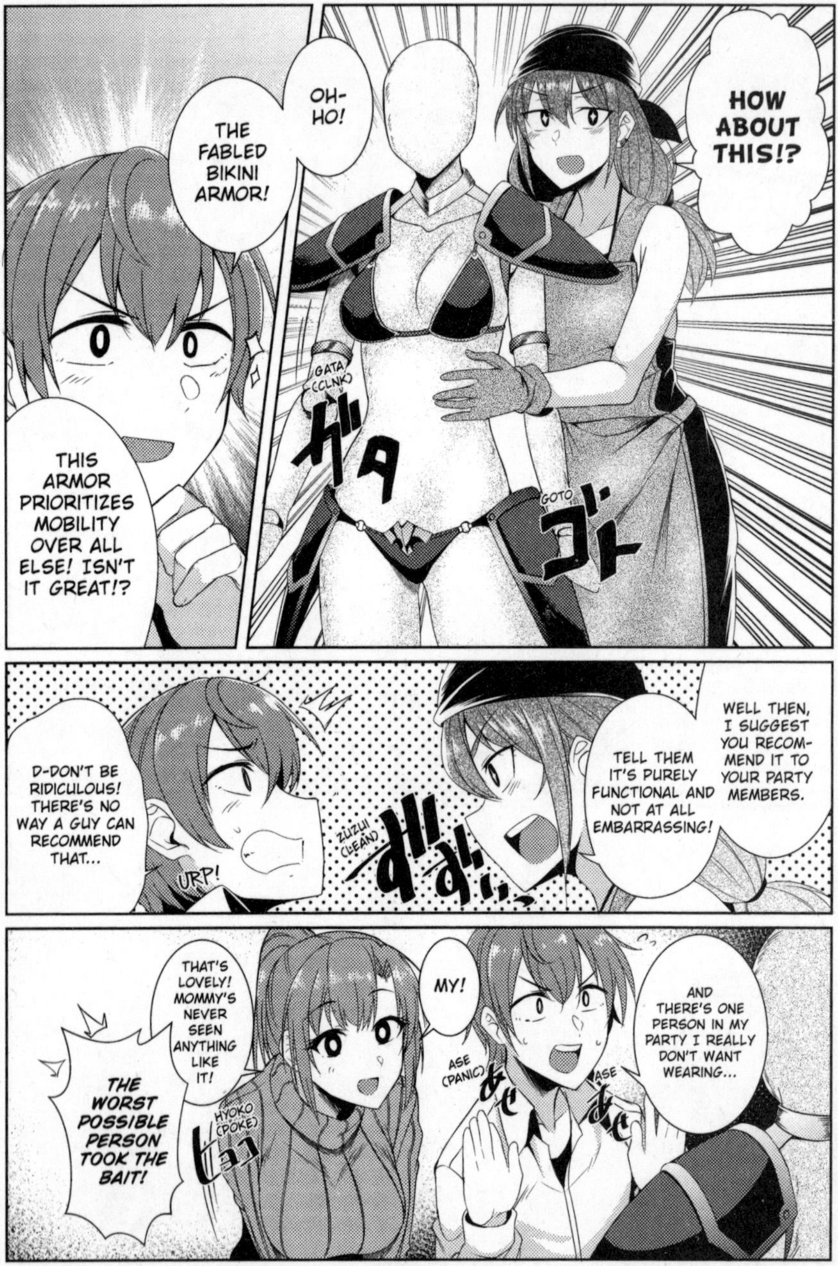
HOW ABOUT THIS!?
GOTO
GATA (CLNK)
OH-HO!
THE FABLED BIKINI ARMOR!
THIS ARMOR PRIORITIZES MOBILITY OVER ALL ELSE! ISN'T IT GREAT!?
WELL THEN, I SUGGEST YOU RECOMMEND IT TO YOUR PARTY MEMBERS.
TELL THEM IT'S PURELY FUNCTIONAL AND NOT AT ALL EMBARRASSING!
ZUZUI (LEAN)
D-DON'T BE RIDICULOUS! THERE'S NO WAY A GUY CAN RECOMMEND THAT...
URP!
AND THERE'S ONE PERSON IN MY PARTY I REALLY DON'T WANT WEARING...
ASE
ASE (PANIC)
MY!
THAT'S LOVELY! MOMMY'S NEVER SEEN ANYTHING LIKE IT!
HYOKO (POKE)
THE WORST POSSIBLE PERSON TOOK THE BAIT!

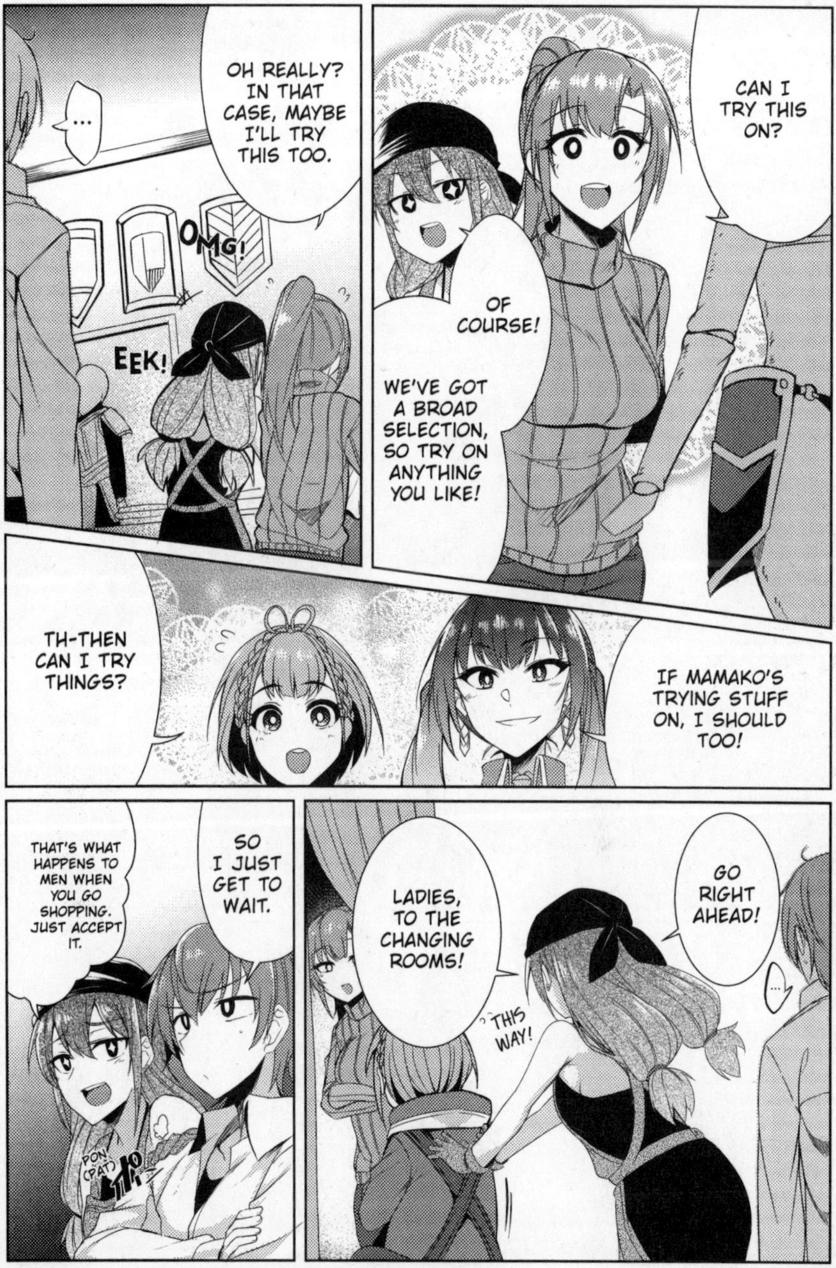
CAN I TRY THIS ON?
OF COURSE!
WE'VE GOT A BROAD SELECTION, SO TRY ON ANYTHING YOU LIKE!
OH REALLY? IN THAT CASE, MAYBE I'LL TRY THIS TOO.
...
OMG!
EEK!
IF MAMAKO'S TRYING STUFF ON, I SHOULD TOO!
TH-THEN CAN I TRY THINGS?
GO RIGHT AHEAD!
...
LADIES, TO THE CHANGING ROOMS!
THIS WAY!
SO I JUST GET TO WAIT.
THAT'S WHAT HAPPENS TO MEN WHEN YOU GO SHOPPING. JUST ACCEPT IT.
PON (PAT)

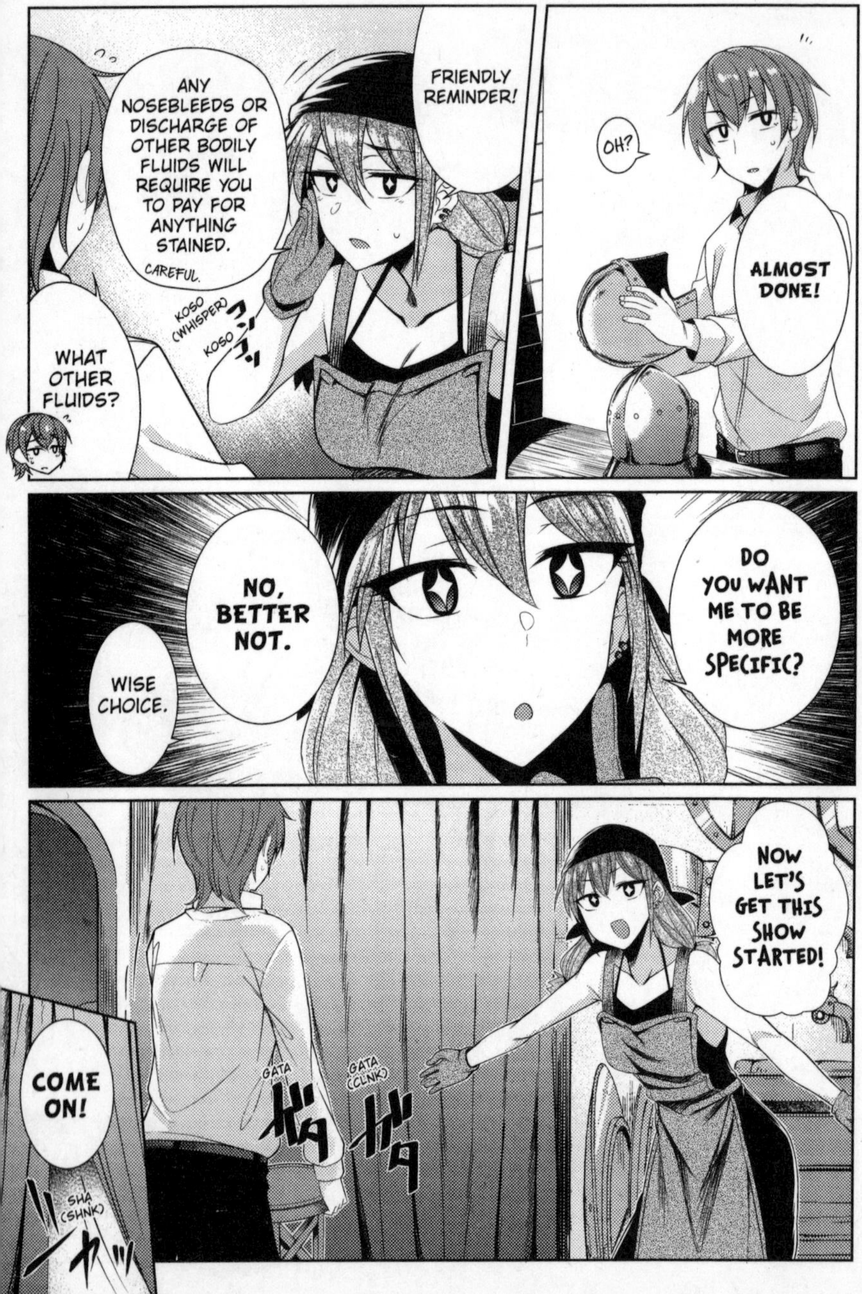

OH?
ALMOST DONE!
FRIENDLY REMINDER!
ANY NOSEBLEEDS OR DISCHARGE OF OTHER BODILY FLUIDS WILL REQUIRE YOU TO PAY FOR ANYTHING STAINED.
CAREFUL.
KOSO (WHISPER) KOSO
WHAT OTHER FLUIDS?
DO YOU WANT ME TO BE MORE SPECIFIC?
NO, BETTER NOT.
WISE CHOICE.
NOW LET'S GET THIS SHOW STARTED!
GATA (CLNK)
GATA
COME ON!
SHA (SHNK)

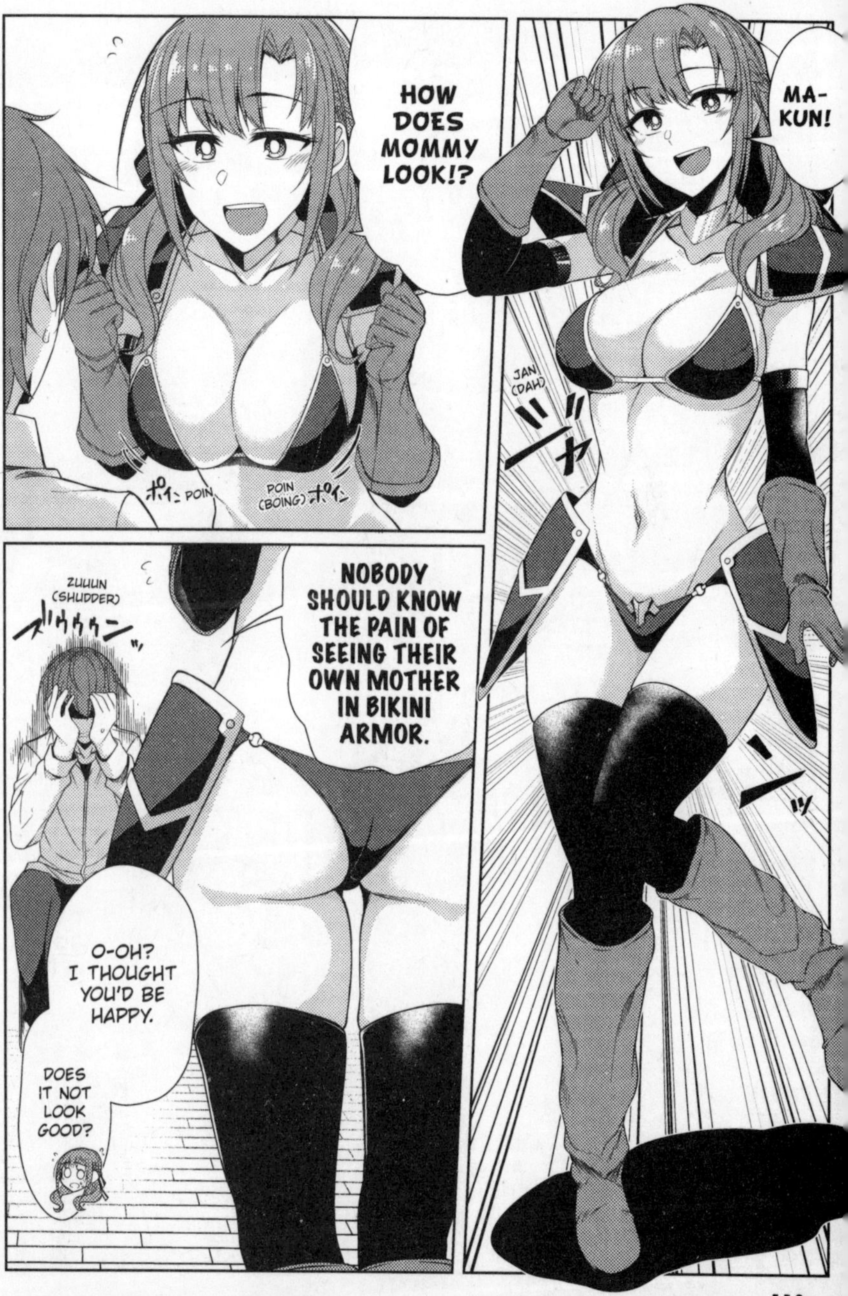
MA-KUN!
JAN (DAH)
HOW DOES MOMMY LOOK!?
POIN (BOING)
POIN
NOBODY SHOULD KNOW THE PAIN OF SEEING THEIR OWN MOTHER IN BIKINI ARMOR.
ZUUUN (SHUDDER)
O-OH? I THOUGHT YOU'D BE HAPPY.
DOES IT NOT LOOK GOOD?

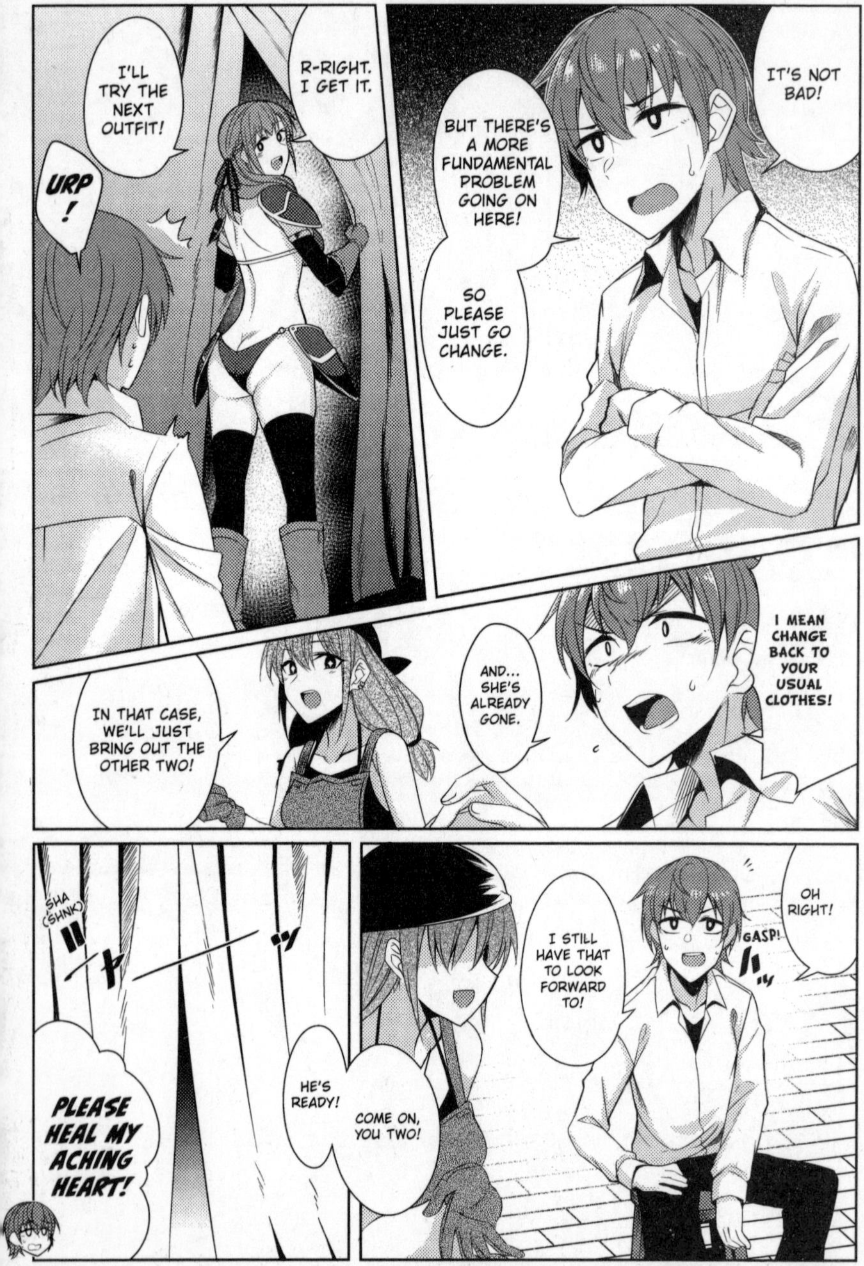
IT'S NOT BAD!
BUT THERE'S A MORE FUNDAMENTAL PROBLEM GOING ON HERE!
SO PLEASE JUST GO CHANGE.
R-RIGHT. I GET IT.
I'LL TRY THE NEXT OUTFIT!
URP!
I MEAN CHANGE BACK TO YOUR USUAL CLOTHES!
AND... SHE'S ALREADY GONE.
IN THAT CASE, WE'LL JUST BRING OUT THE OTHER TWO!
OH RIGHT!
GASP!
I STILL HAVE THAT TO LOOK FORWARD TO!
HE'S READY!
COME ON, YOU TWO!
SHA (SHNK)
PLEASE HEAL MY ACHING HEART!

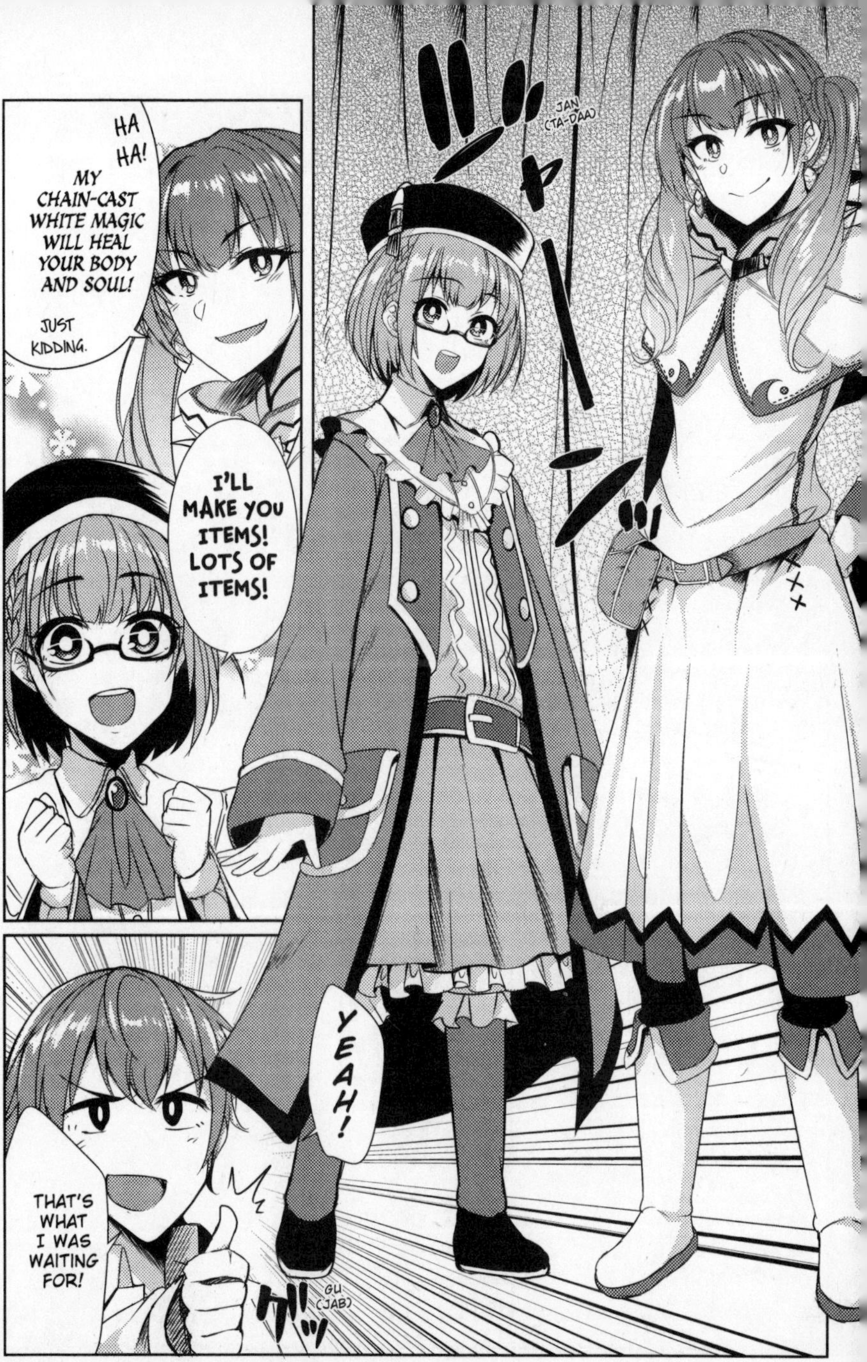
JAN (TA-DAA)
HA HA! MY CHAIN-CAST WHITE MAGIC WILL HEAL YOUR BODY AND SOUL!
JUST KIDDING.
I'LL MAKE YOU ITEMS! LOTS OF ITEMS!
YEAH!
THAT'S WHAT I WAS WAITING FOR!
GU (JAB)

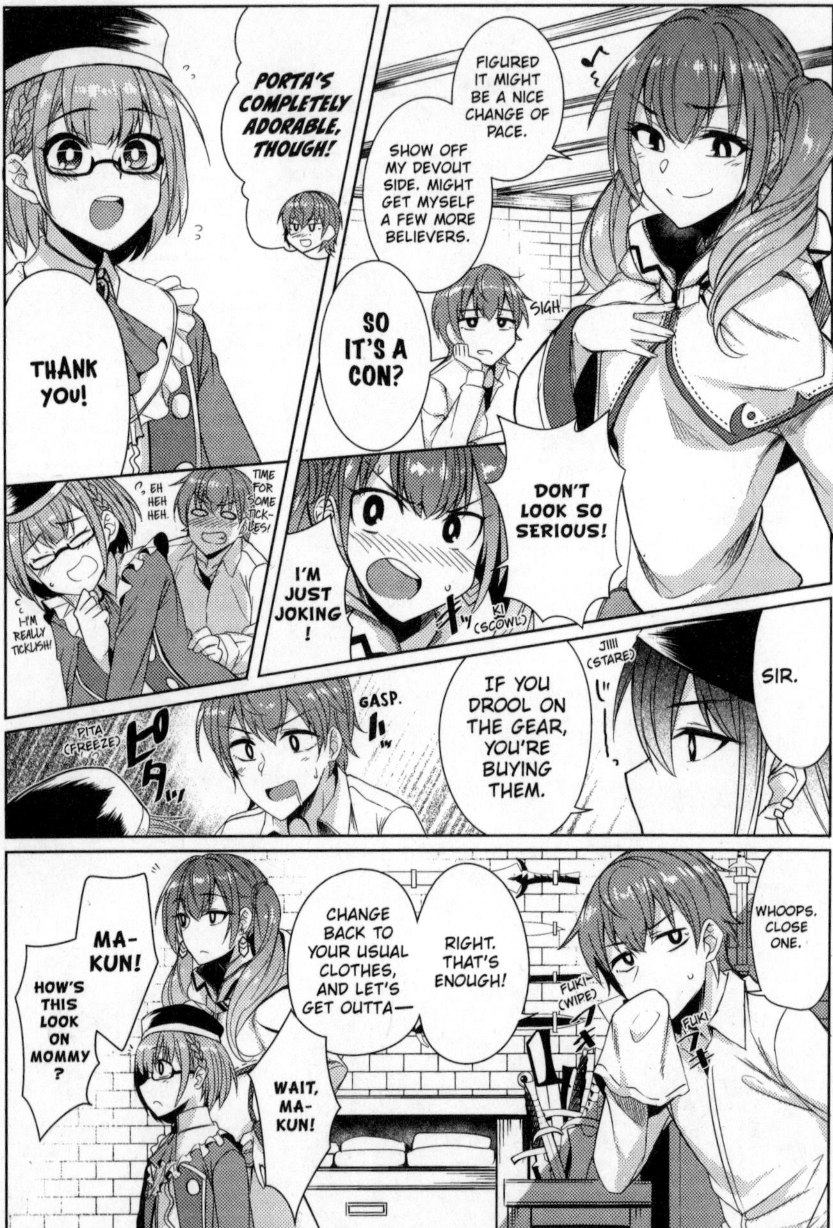
FIGURED IT MIGHT BE A NICE CHANGE OF PACE.
SHOW OFF MY DEVOUT SIDE. MIGHT GET MYSELF A FEW MORE BELIEVERS.
SIGH.
SO IT'S A CON?
DON'T LOOK SO SERIOUS!
PORTA'S COMPLETELY ADORABLE, THOUGH!
THANK YOU!
KI (SCOWL)
I'M JUST JOKING!
TIME FOR SOME TICK-LES!
EH HEH HEH.
I'M REALLY TICKLISH!
SIR.
JIIII (STARE)
IF YOU DROOL ON THE GEAR, YOU'RE BUYING THEM.
GASP.
PITA (FREEZE)
WHOOPS. CLOSE ONE.
FUKI (WIPE)
FUKI
RIGHT. THAT'S ENOUGH!
CHANGE BACK TO YOUR USUAL CLOTHES, AND LET'S GET OUTTA—
WAIT, MA-KUN!
MA-KUN!
HOW'S THIS LOOK ON MOMMY?

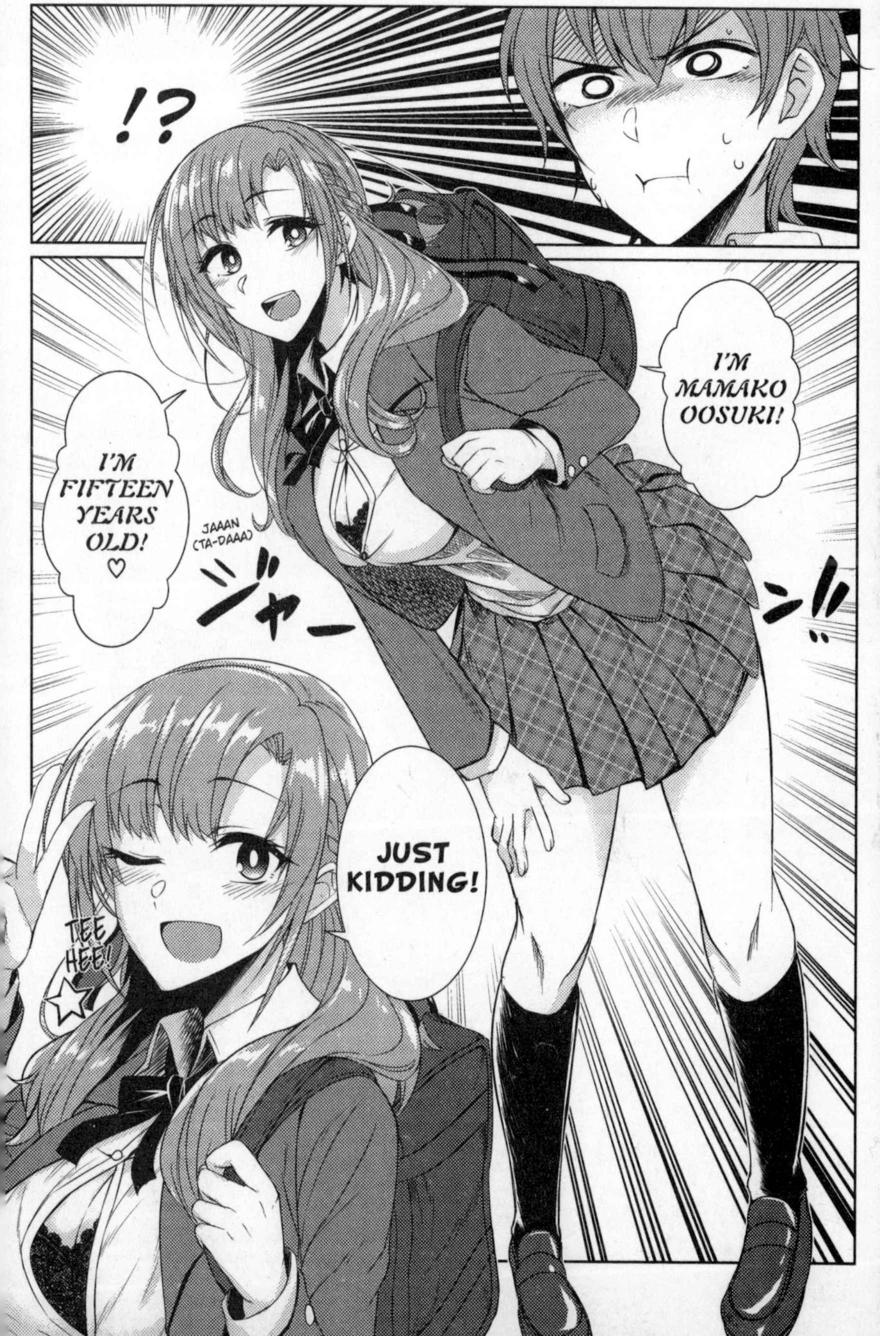
!?
I'M MAMAKO OOSUKI!
I'M FIFTEEN YEARS OLD! ♡
JAAAN (TA-DAAA)
ジャーン!!
JUST KIDDING!
TEE HEE! ☆

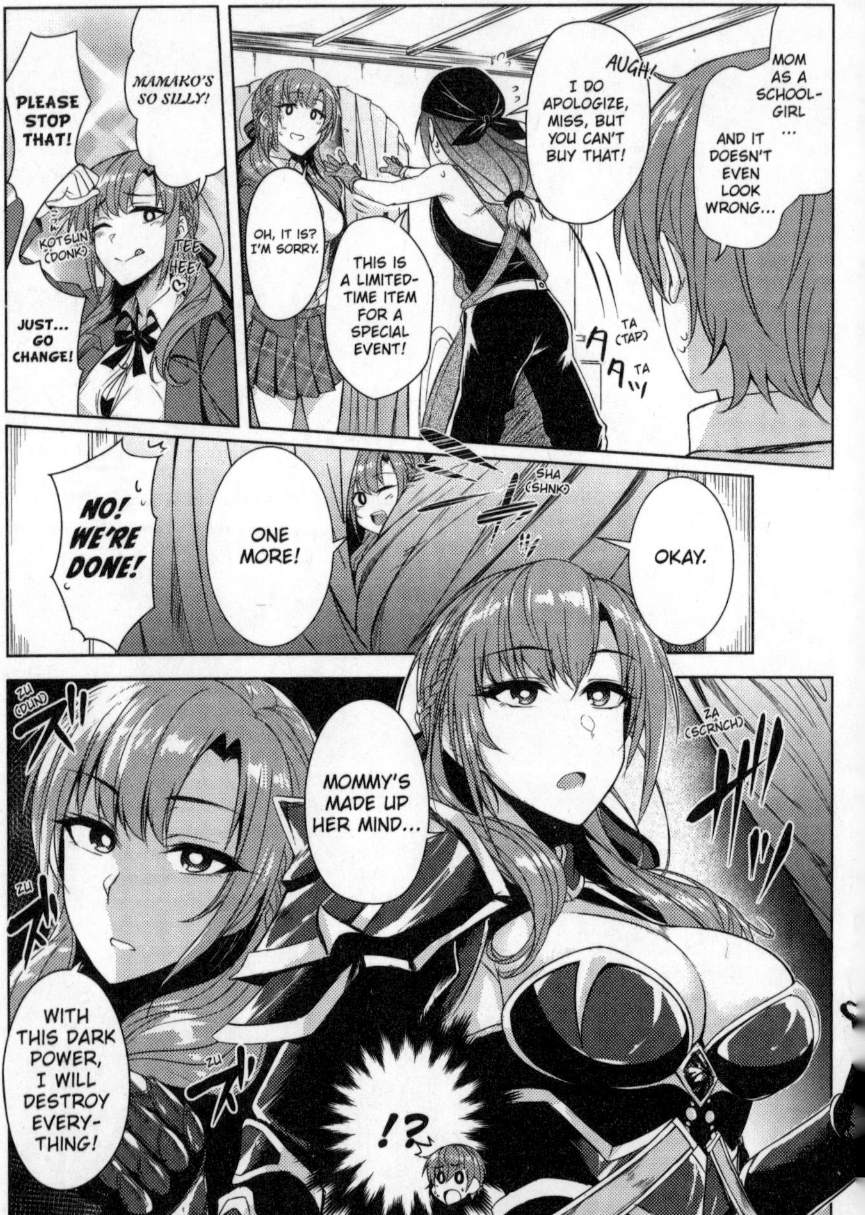
MOM AS A SCHOOL-GIRL...
AND IT DOESN'T EVEN LOOK WRONG...
AUGH!
I DO APOLOGIZE, MISS, BUT YOU CAN'T BUY THAT!
OH, IT IS? I'M SORRY.
THIS IS A LIMITED-TIME ITEM FOR A SPECIAL EVENT!
TA (TAP) TA
MAMAKO'S SO SILLY!
PLEASE STOP THAT!
KOTSUN (DONK)
TEE HEE!
JUST... GO CHANGE!
OKAY.
SHA (SHNK)
ONE MORE!
NO! WE'RE DONE!
ZA (SCRNCH)
MOMMY'S MADE UP HER MIND...
ZU (DUN)
ZU
WITH THIS DARK POWER, I WILL DESTROY EVERY-THING!
ZU
!?

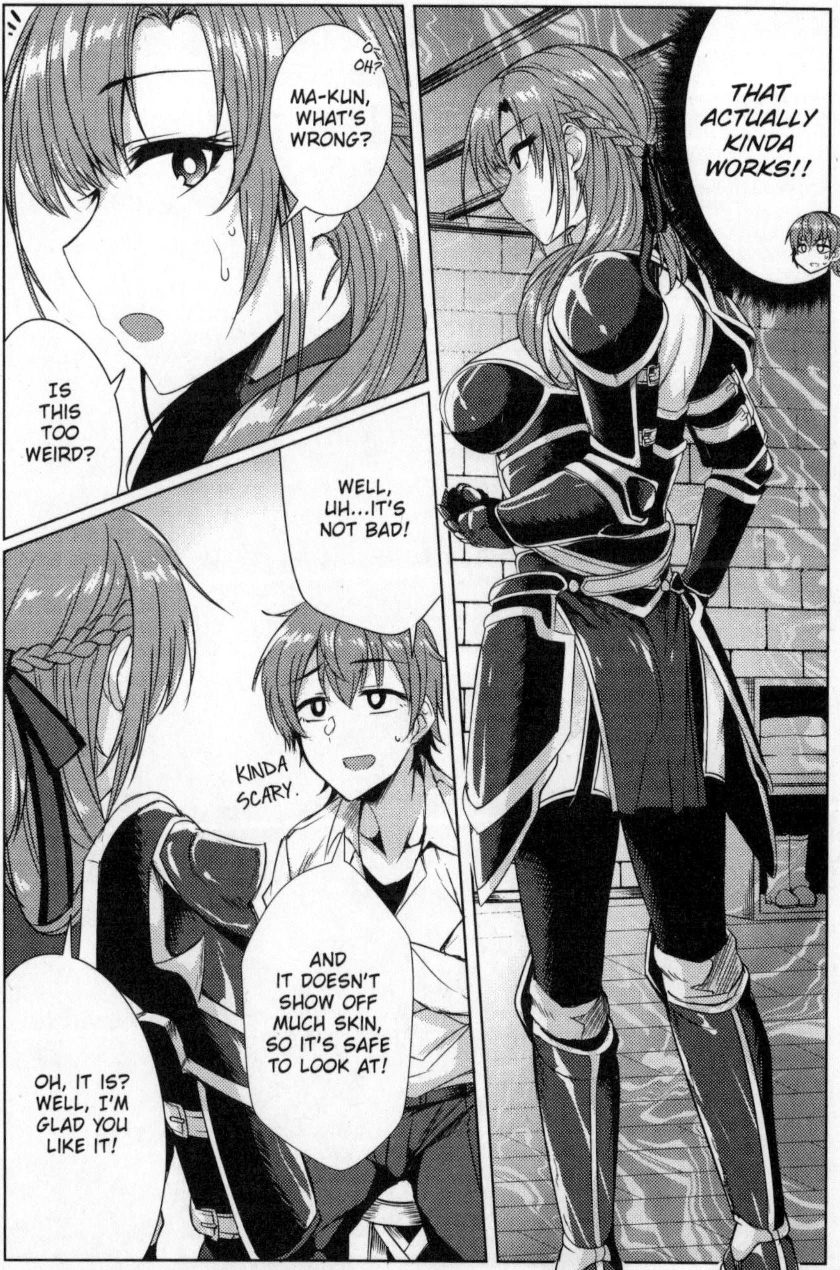
THAT ACTUALLY KINDA WORKS!!
O- OH?
MA-KUN, WHAT'S WRONG?
IS THIS TOO WEIRD?
WELL, UH...IT'S NOT BAD!
KINDA SCARY.
AND IT DOESN'T SHOW OFF MUCH SKIN, SO IT'S SAFE TO LOOK AT!
OH, IT IS? WELL, I'M GLAD YOU LIKE IT!

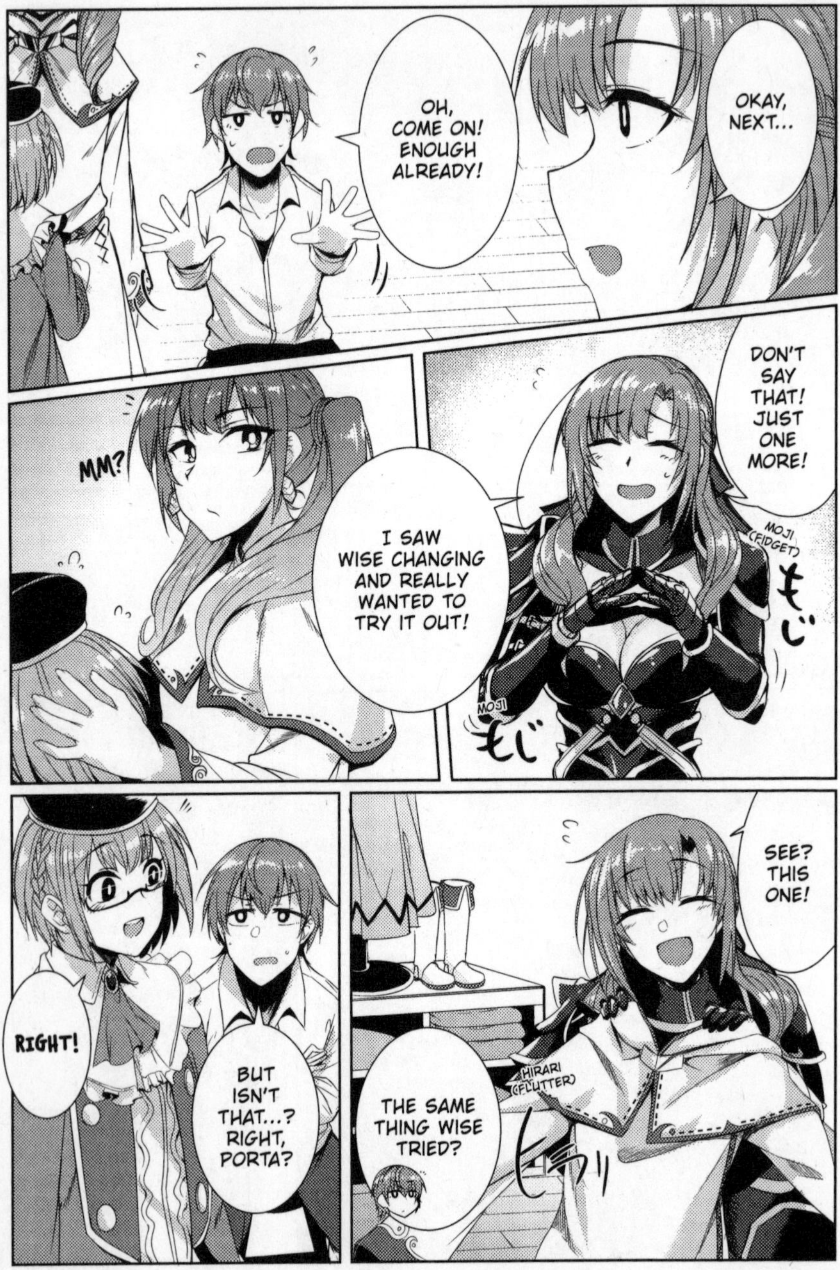
OKAY, NEXT...
OH, COME ON! ENOUGH ALREADY!
DON'T SAY THAT! JUST ONE MORE!
MOJI (FIDGET)
MOJI
I SAW WISE CHANGING AND REALLY WANTED TO TRY IT OUT!
MM?
SEE? THIS ONE!
HIRARI (FLUTTER)
THE SAME THING WISE TRIED?
BUT ISN'T THAT...? RIGHT, PORTA?
RIGHT!

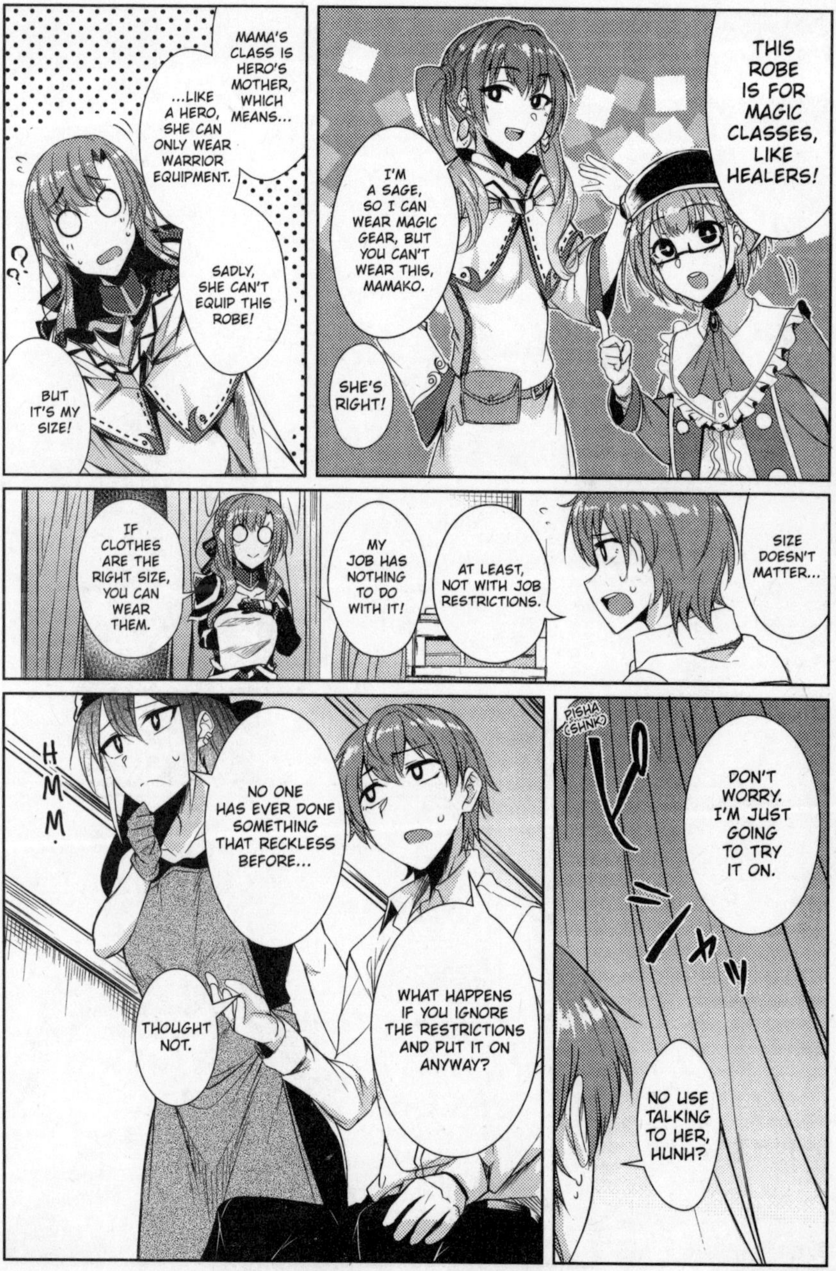
THIS ROBE IS FOR MAGIC CLASSES, LIKE HEALERS!
I'M A SAGE, SO I CAN WEAR MAGIC GEAR, BUT YOU CAN'T WEAR THIS, MAMAKO.
SHE'S RIGHT!
MAMA'S CLASS IS HERO'S MOTHER, WHICH MEANS...
...LIKE A HERO, SHE CAN ONLY WEAR WARRIOR EQUIPMENT.
SADLY, SHE CAN'T EQUIP THIS ROBE!
BUT IT'S MY SIZE!
SIZE DOESN'T MATTER...
AT LEAST, NOT WITH JOB RESTRICTIONS.
MY JOB HAS NOTHING TO DO WITH IT!
IF CLOTHES ARE THE RIGHT SIZE, YOU CAN WEAR THEM.
PISHA (SHNK)
DON'T WORRY. I'M JUST GOING TO TRY IT ON.
NO USE TALKING TO HER, HUNH?
NO ONE HAS EVER DONE SOMETHING THAT RECKLESS BEFORE...
HMM
WHAT HAPPENS IF YOU IGNORE THE RESTRICTIONS AND PUT IT ON ANYWAY?
THOUGHT NOT.

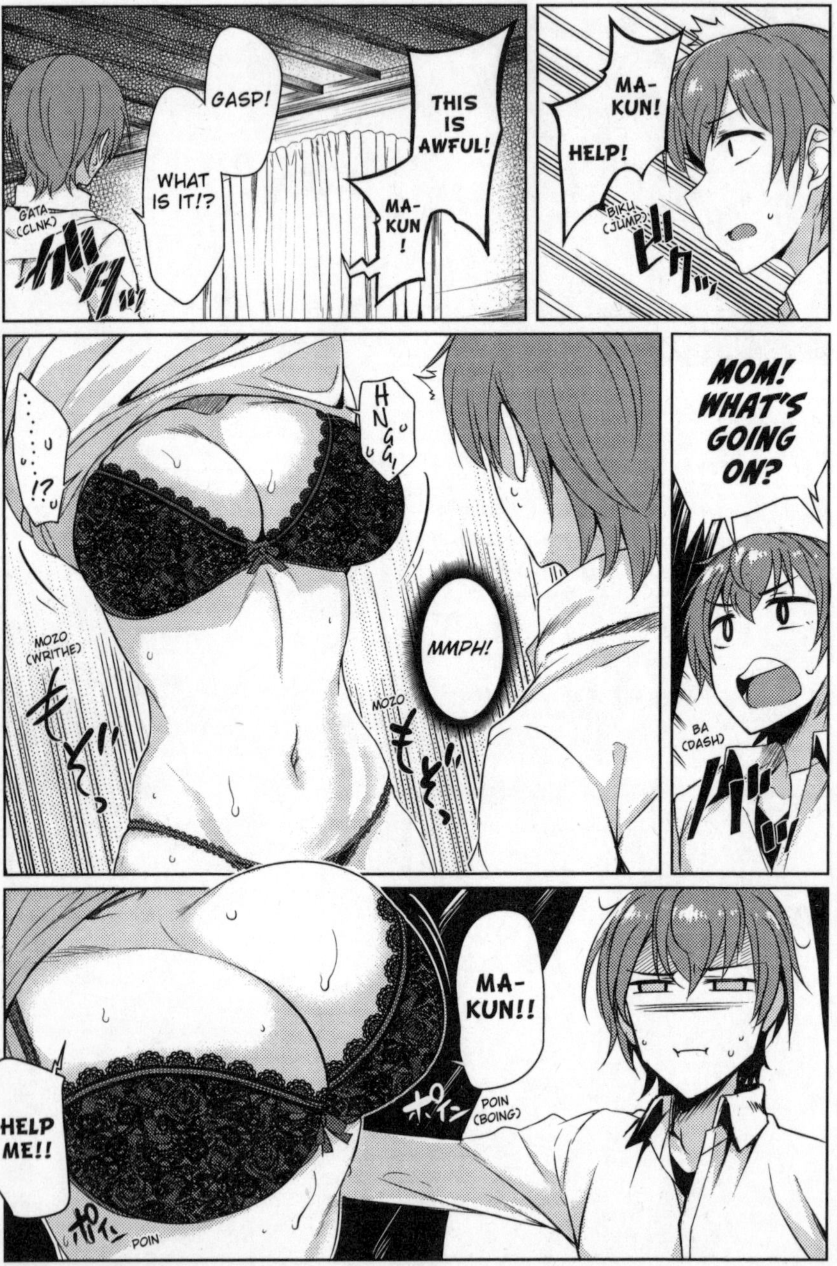
MA-KUN!
HELP!
BIKU (JUMP)
THIS IS AWFUL!
GASP!
MA-KUN!
WHAT IS IT!?
GATA (CLNK)
MOM! WHAT'S GOING ON?
BA (DASH)
HNGG!
MMPH!
...!?
MOZO
MOZO (WRITHE)
MA-KUN!!
POIN (BOING)
HELP ME!!
POIN

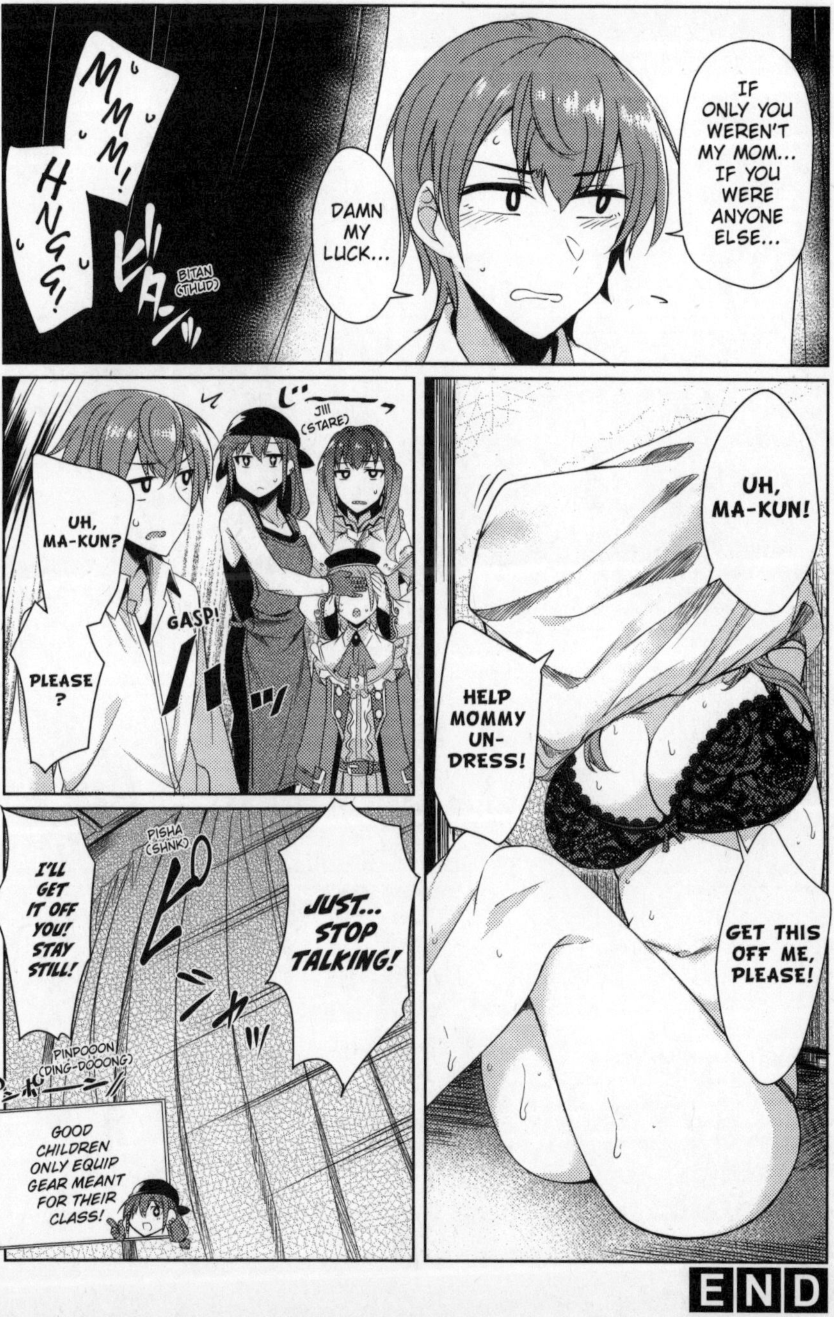
IF ONLY YOU WEREN'T MY MOM... IF YOU WERE ANYONE ELSE...
DAMN MY LUCK...
BITAN (THUD)
MMM!
HNGG!
UH, MA-KUN!
HELP MOMMY UN-DRESS!
GET THIS OFF ME, PLEASE!
JIII (STARE)
UH, MA-KUN?
GASP!
PLEASE?
PISHA (SHNK)
JUST... STOP TALKING!
I'LL GET IT OFF YOU! STAY STILL!
PINPOOON (DING-DOOONG)
GOOD CHILDREN ONLY EQUIP GEAR MEANT FOR THEIR CLASS!

END

Chapter 3:

UNDERWEAR IS ARMOR. MAKE SURE IT'S HIGH IN DEFENSE. OTHERWISE, MY SON MIGHT DIE! ④

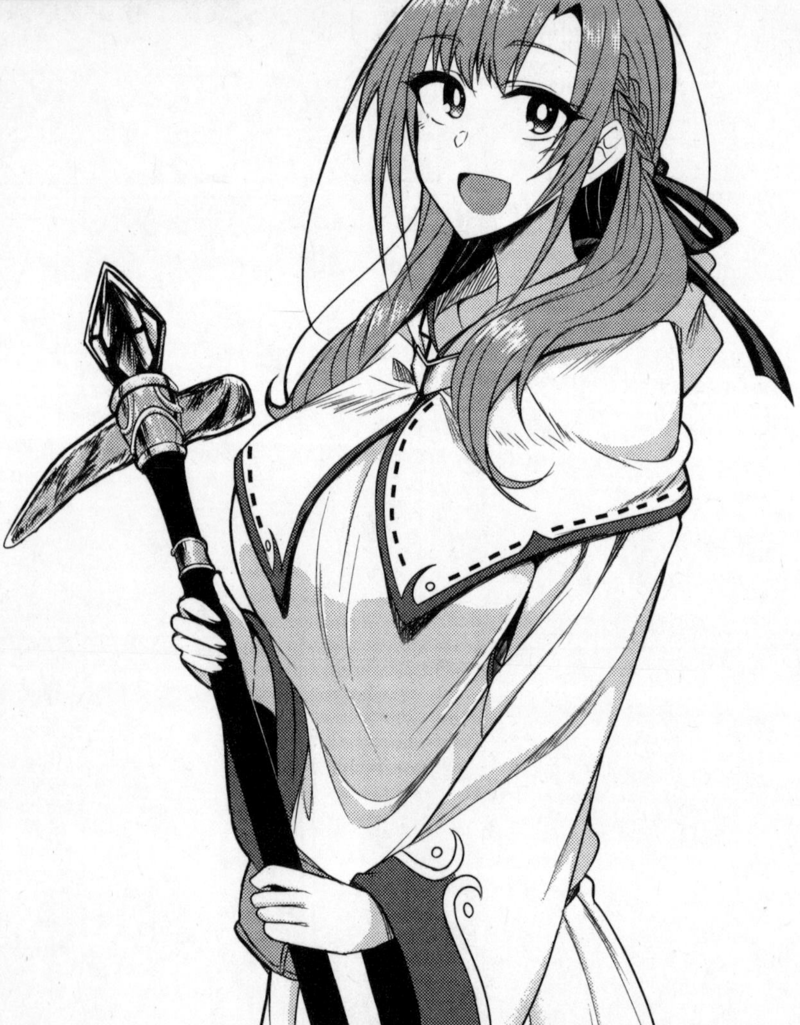

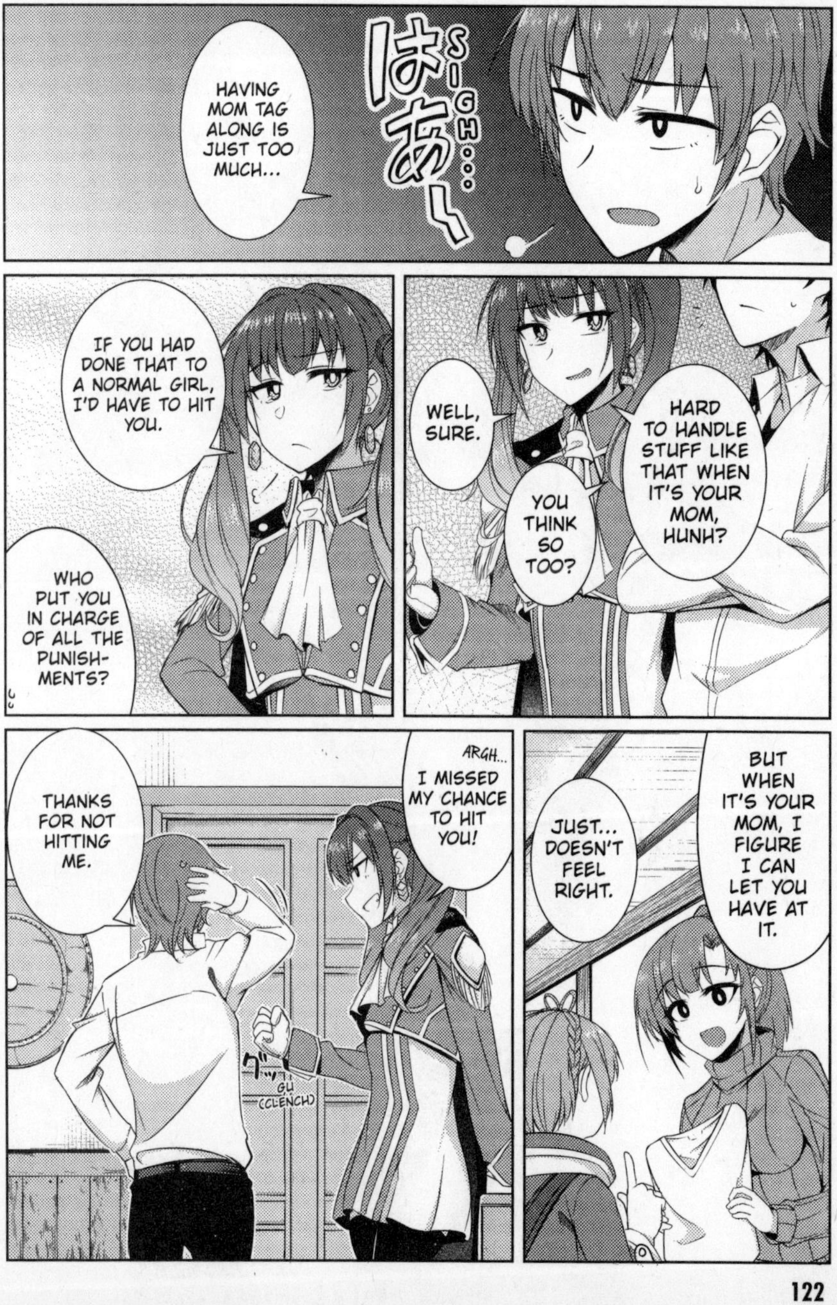
はあ~ SIGH...
HAVING MOM TAG ALONG IS JUST TOO MUCH...
HARD TO HANDLE STUFF LIKE THAT WHEN IT'S YOUR MOM, HUNH?
WELL, SURE.
YOU THINK SO TOO?
IF YOU HAD DONE THAT TO A NORMAL GIRL, I'D HAVE TO HIT YOU.
WHO PUT YOU IN CHARGE OF ALL THE PUNISH-MENTS?
BUT WHEN IT'S YOUR MOM, I FIGURE I CAN LET YOU HAVE AT IT.
JUST... DOESN'T FEEL RIGHT.
ARGH... I MISSED MY CHANCE TO HIT YOU!
グッ GU (CLENCH)
THANKS FOR NOT HITTING ME.

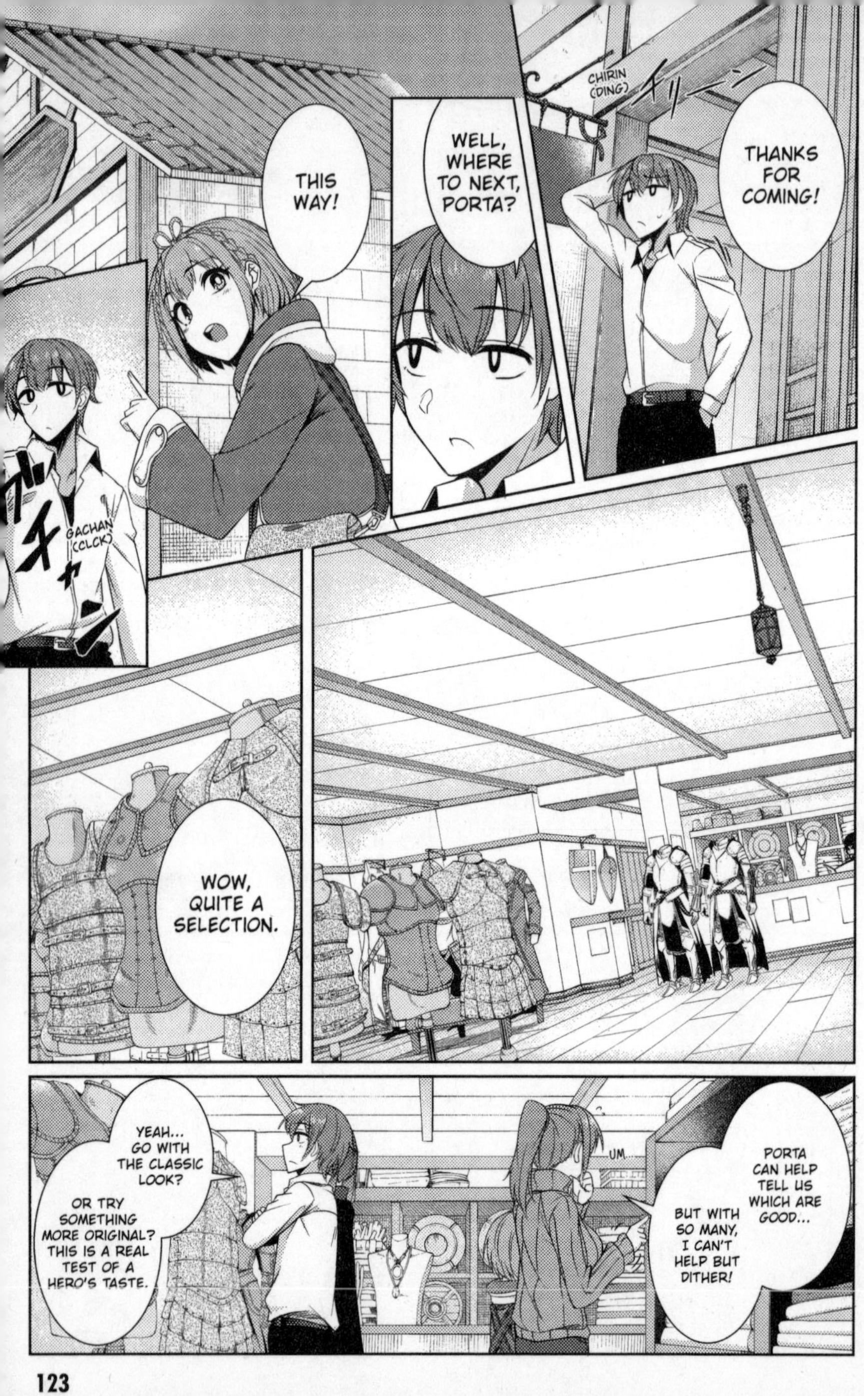
CHIRIN (DING)
THANKS FOR COMING!
WELL, WHERE TO NEXT, PORTA?
THIS WAY!
GACHAN (CLCK)
WOW, QUITE A SELECTION.
PORTA CAN HELP TELL US WHICH ARE GOOD...
BUT WITH SO MANY, I CAN'T HELP BUT DITHER!
UM...
YEAH... GO WITH THE CLASSIC LOOK?
OR TRY SOMETHING MORE ORIGINAL? THIS IS A REAL TEST OF A HERO'S TASTE.

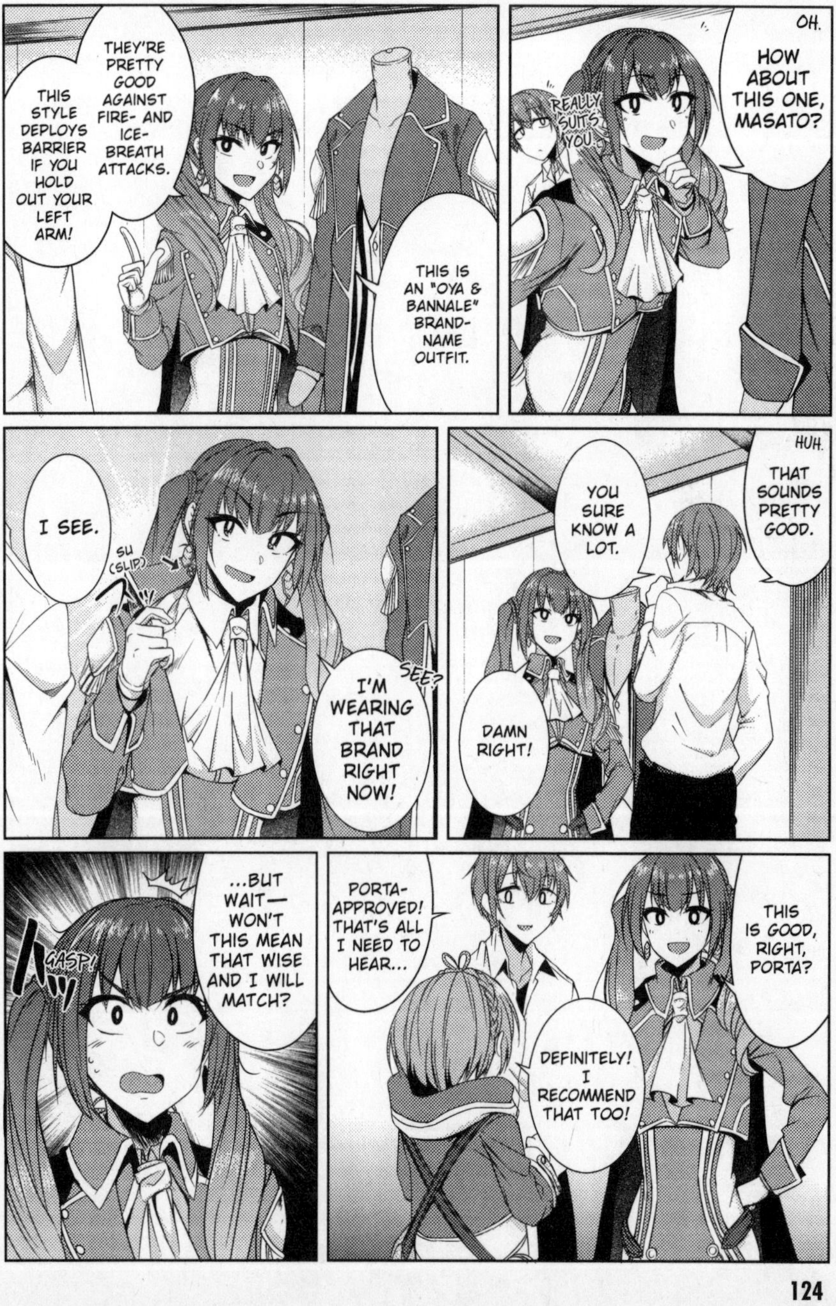
OH.
HOW ABOUT THIS ONE, MASATO?
REALLY SUITS YOU.
THIS IS AN "OYA & BANNALE" BRAND-NAME OUTFIT.
THEY'RE PRETTY GOOD AGAINST FIRE- AND ICE-BREATH ATTACKS.
THIS STYLE DEPLOYS BARRIER IF YOU HOLD OUT YOUR LEFT ARM!
HUH.
THAT SOUNDS PRETTY GOOD.
YOU SURE KNOW A LOT.
DAMN RIGHT!
SEE?
I'M WEARING THAT BRAND RIGHT NOW!
SU (SLIP)
I SEE.
THIS IS GOOD, RIGHT, PORTA?
DEFINITELY! I RECOMMEND THAT TOO!
PORTA-APPROVED! THAT'S ALL I NEED TO HEAR...
GASP!
...BUT WAIT—WON'T THIS MEAN THAT WISE AND I WILL MATCH?

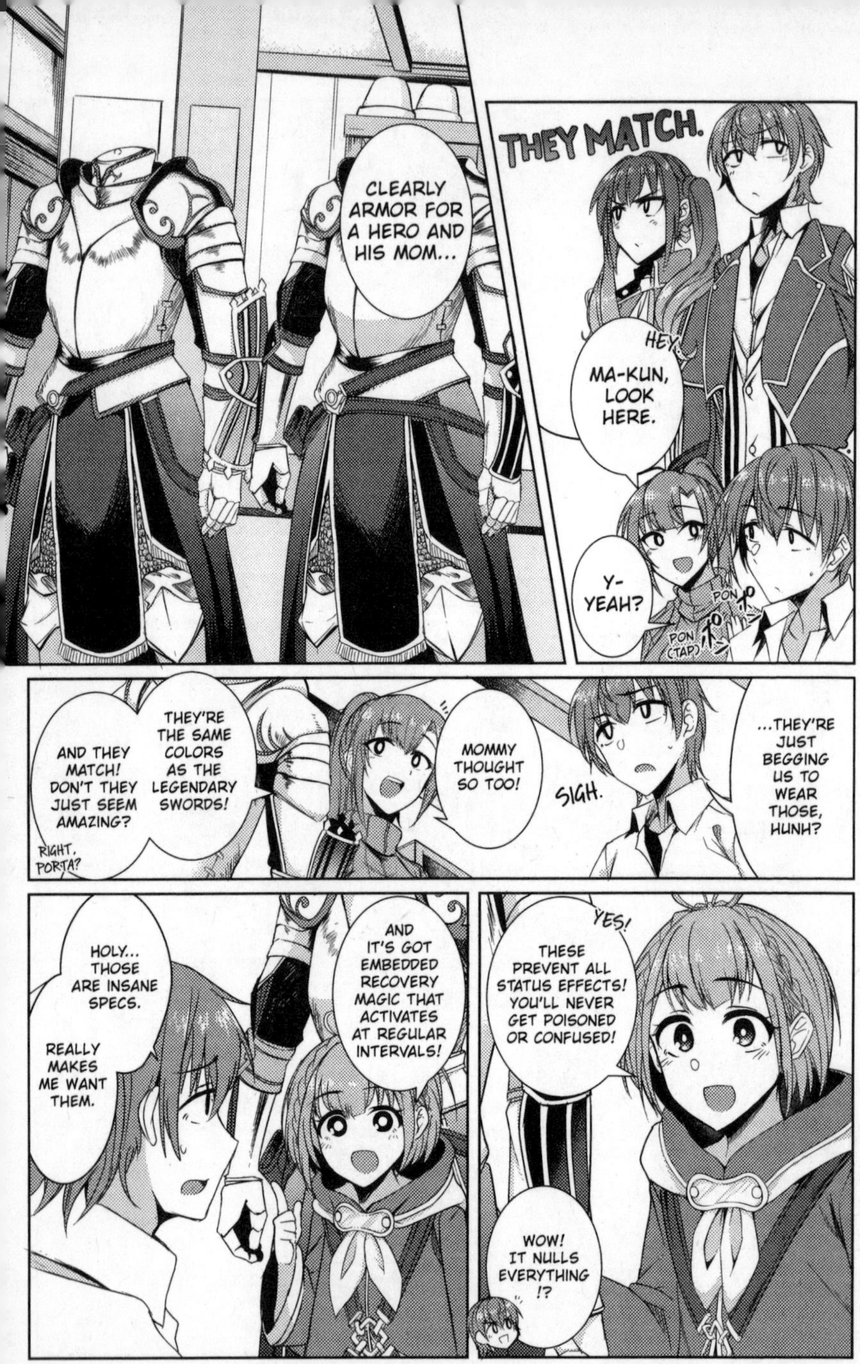
THEY MATCH.
HEY, MA-KUN, LOOK HERE.
Y-YEAH?
PON PON (TAP)
CLEARLY ARMOR FOR A HERO AND HIS MOM...
...THEY'RE JUST BEGGING US TO WEAR THOSE, HUNH?
SIGH.
MOMMY THOUGHT SO TOO!
THEY'RE THE SAME COLORS AS THE LEGENDARY SWORDS!
AND THEY MATCH! DON'T THEY JUST SEEM AMAZING?
RIGHT, PORTA?
YES!
THESE PREVENT ALL STATUS EFFECTS! YOU'LL NEVER GET POISONED OR CONFUSED!
WOW! IT NULLS EVERYTHING!?
AND IT'S GOT EMBEDDED RECOVERY MAGIC THAT ACTIVATES AT REGULAR INTERVALS!
HOLY... THOSE ARE INSANE SPECS.
REALLY MAKES ME WANT THEM.

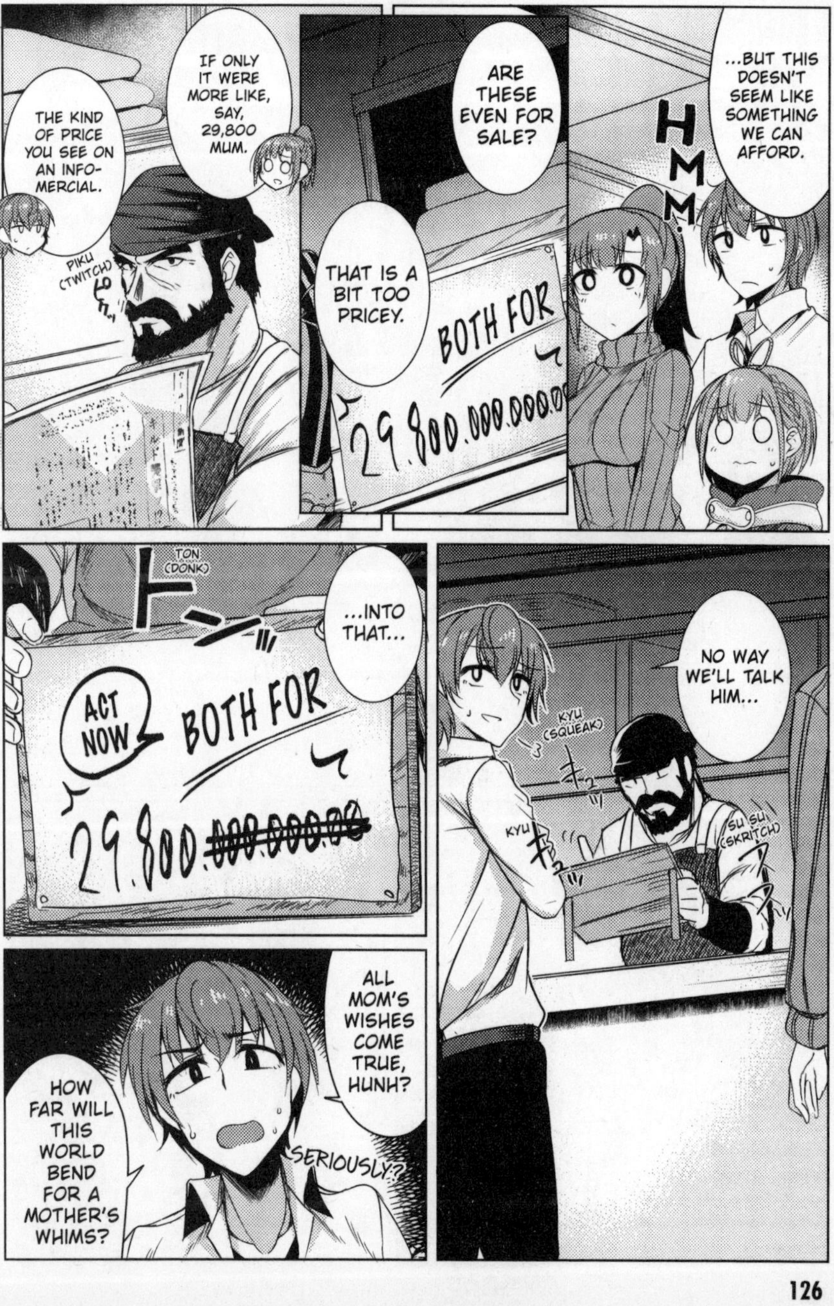
...BUT THIS DOESN'T SEEM LIKE SOMETHING WE CAN AFFORD.
HMM
ARE THESE EVEN FOR SALE?
THAT IS A BIT TOO PRICEY.
BOTH FOR
29.800.000.000.00
IF ONLY IT WERE MORE LIKE, SAY, 29,800 MUM.
THE KIND OF PRICE YOU SEE ON AN INFO-MERCIAL.
PIKU (TWITCH)
NO WAY WE'LL TALK HIM...
KYU (SQUEAK)
KYU
SU SU (SKRITCH)
TON (DONK)
...INTO THAT...
ACT NOW
BOTH FOR
29.800.000.000.00
ALL MOM'S WISHES COME TRUE, HUNH?
HOW FAR WILL THIS WORLD BEND FOR A MOTHER'S WHIMS?
SERIOUSLY?

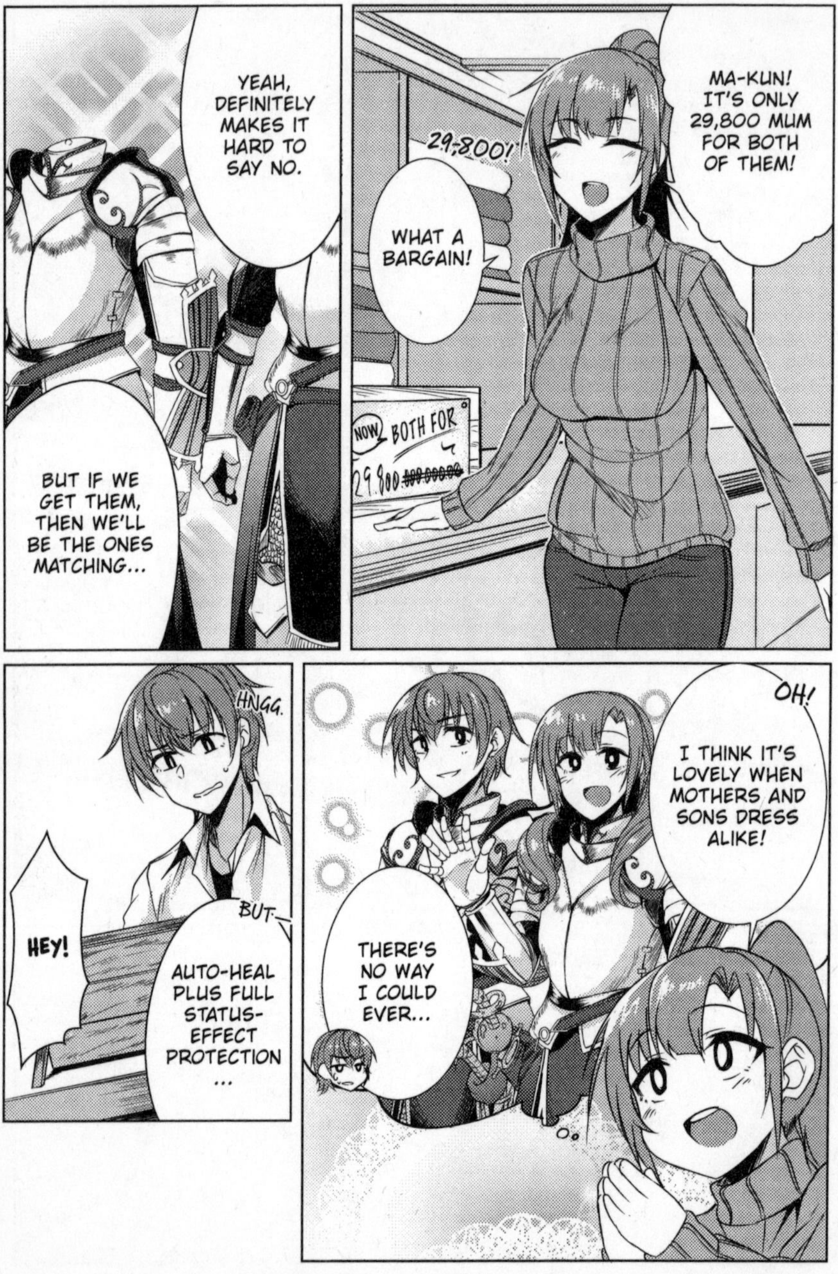
MA-KUN! IT'S ONLY 29,800 MUM FOR BOTH OF THEM!
29,800!
WHAT A BARGAIN!
NOW
BOTH FOR
29,800
YEAH, DEFINITELY MAKES IT HARD TO SAY NO.
BUT IF WE GET THEM, THEN WE'LL BE THE ONES MATCHING...
OH!
I THINK IT'S LOVELY WHEN MOTHERS AND SONS DRESS ALIKE!
THERE'S NO WAY I COULD EVER...
HNGG.
BUT—
AUTO-HEAL PLUS FULL STATUS-EFFECT PROTECTION ...
HEY!

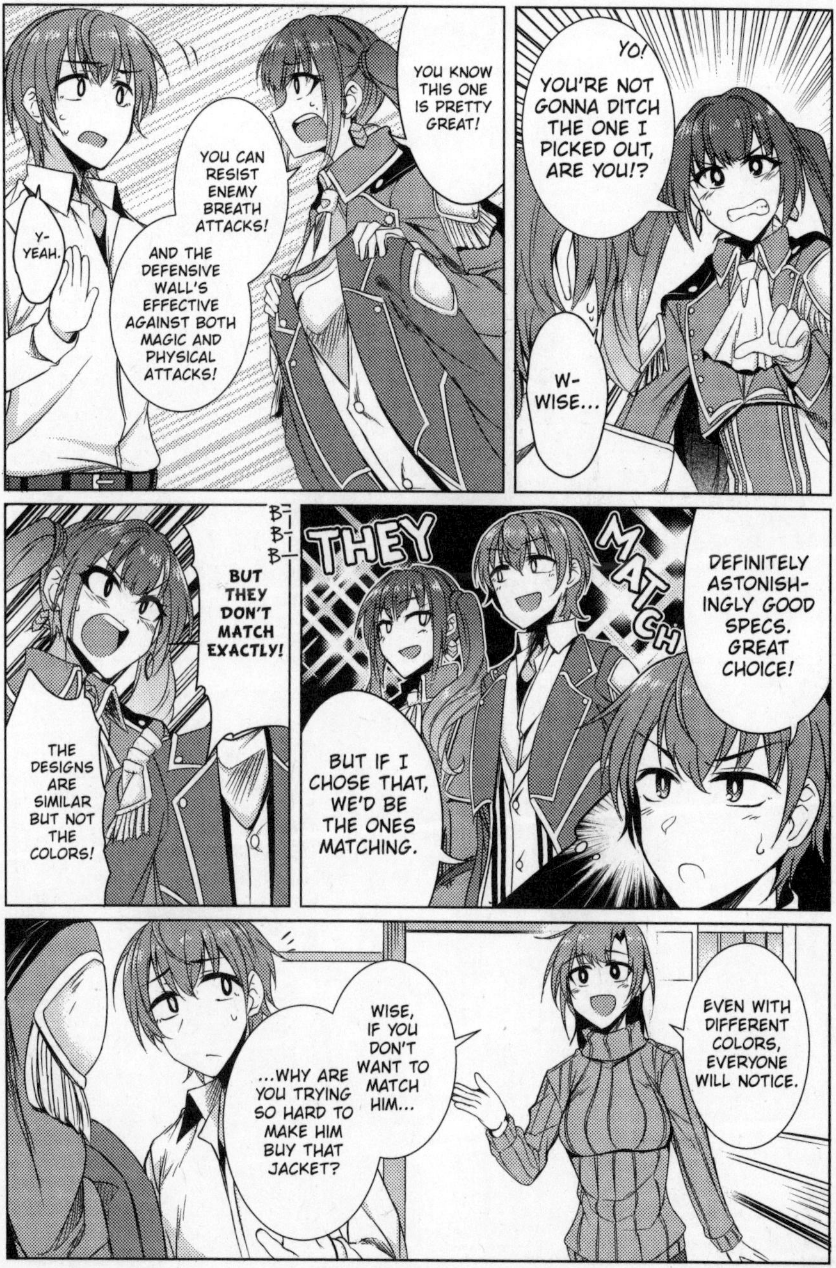
YO! YOU'RE NOT GONNA DITCH THE ONE I PICKED OUT, ARE YOU!?
W-WISE...
YOU KNOW THIS ONE IS PRETTY GREAT!
YOU CAN RESIST ENEMY BREATH ATTACKS!
AND THE DEFENSIVE WALL'S EFFECTIVE AGAINST BOTH MAGIC AND PHYSICAL ATTACKS!
Y-YEAH.
DEFINITELY ASTONISHINGLY GOOD SPECS. GREAT CHOICE!
THEY MATCH
BUT IF I CHOSE THAT, WE'D BE THE ONES MATCHING.
B-B-B-
BUT THEY DON'T MATCH EXACTLY!
THE DESIGNS ARE SIMILAR BUT NOT THE COLORS!
EVEN WITH DIFFERENT COLORS, EVERYONE WILL NOTICE.
WISE, IF YOU DON'T WANT TO MATCH HIM...
...WHY ARE YOU TRYING SO HARD TO MAKE HIM BUY THAT JACKET?

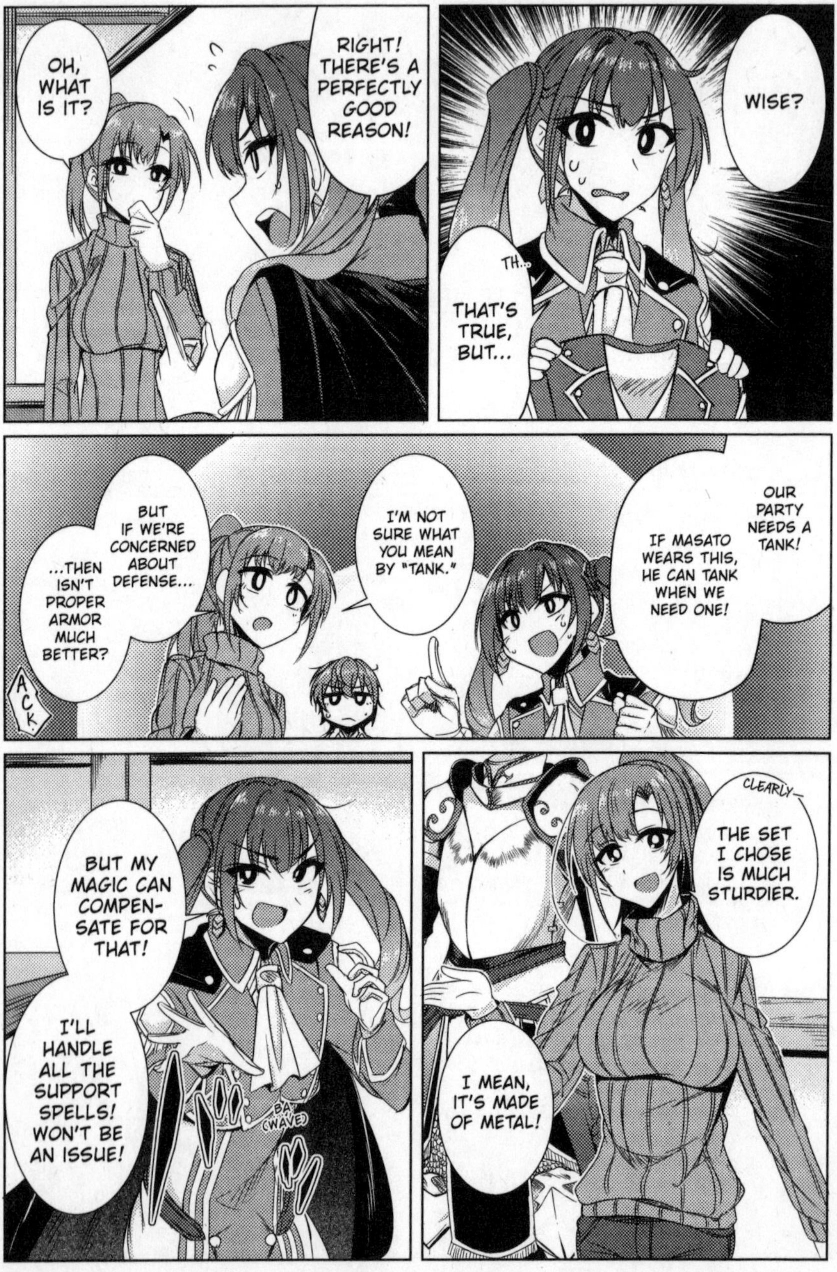
WISE?
TH...
THAT'S TRUE, BUT...
RIGHT! THERE'S A PERFECTLY GOOD REASON!
OH, WHAT IS IT?
OUR PARTY NEEDS A TANK!
IF MASATO WEARS THIS, HE CAN TANK WHEN WE NEED ONE!
I'M NOT SURE WHAT YOU MEAN BY "TANK."
BUT IF WE'RE CONCERNED ABOUT DEFENSE...
...THEN ISN'T PROPER ARMOR MUCH BETTER?
ACK.
CLEARLY—
THE SET I CHOSE IS MUCH STURDIER.
I MEAN, IT'S MADE OF METAL!
BUT MY MAGIC CAN COMPENSATE FOR THAT!
BA (WAVE)
I'LL HANDLE ALL THE SUPPORT SPELLS! WON'T BE AN ISSUE!

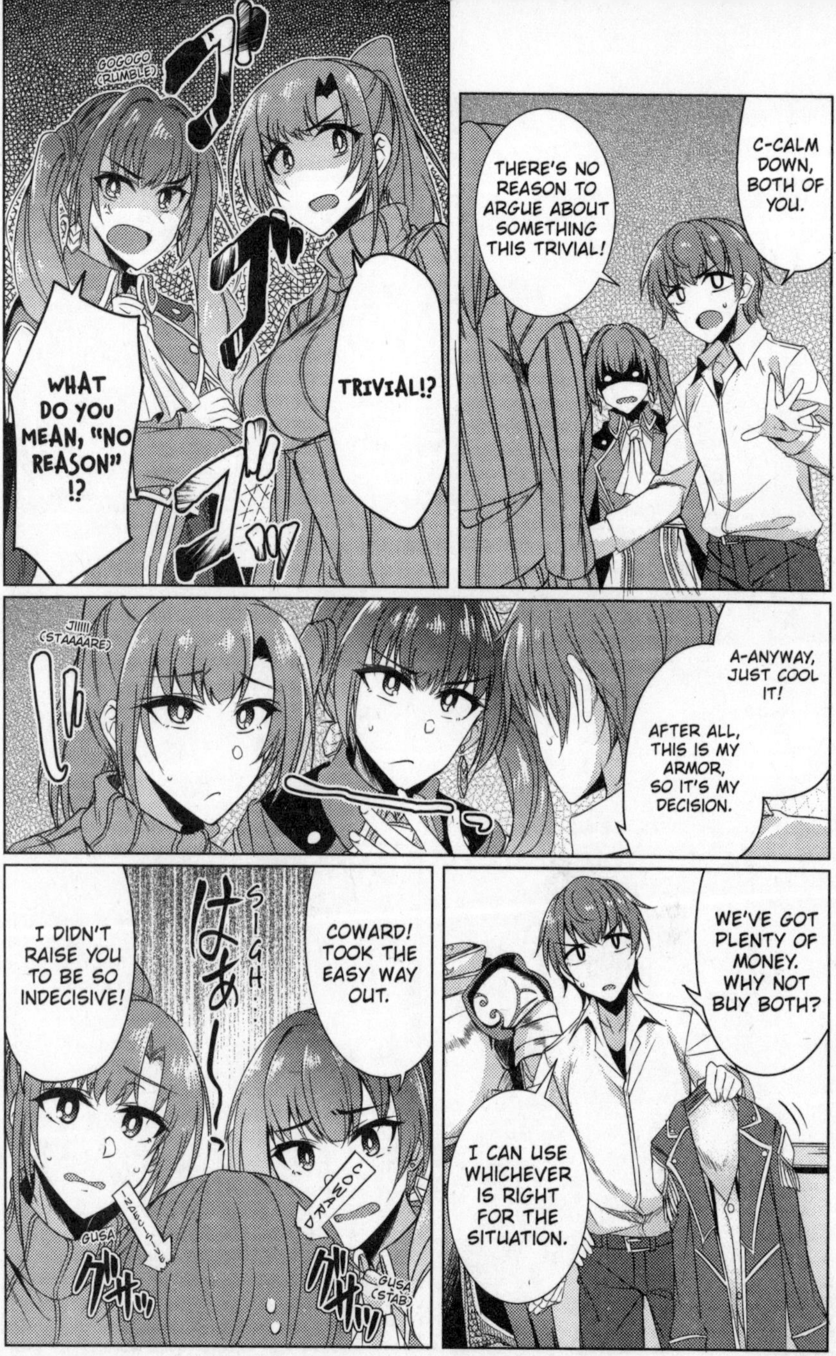
C-CALM DOWN, BOTH OF YOU.
THERE'S NO REASON TO ARGUE ABOUT SOMETHING THIS TRIVIAL!
GOGOGO (RUMBLE)
TRIVIAL!?
WHAT DO YOU MEAN, "NO REASON" !?
A-ANYWAY, JUST COOL IT!
AFTER ALL, THIS IS MY ARMOR, SO IT'S MY DECISION.
JIIIII (STAAAARE)
WE'VE GOT PLENTY OF MONEY. WHY NOT BUY BOTH?
I CAN USE WHICHEVER IS RIGHT FOR THE SITUATION.
SIGH...
COWARD! TOOK THE EASY WAY OUT.
I DIDN'T RAISE YOU TO BE SO INDECISIVE!
COWARD
GUSA (STAB)
GUSA

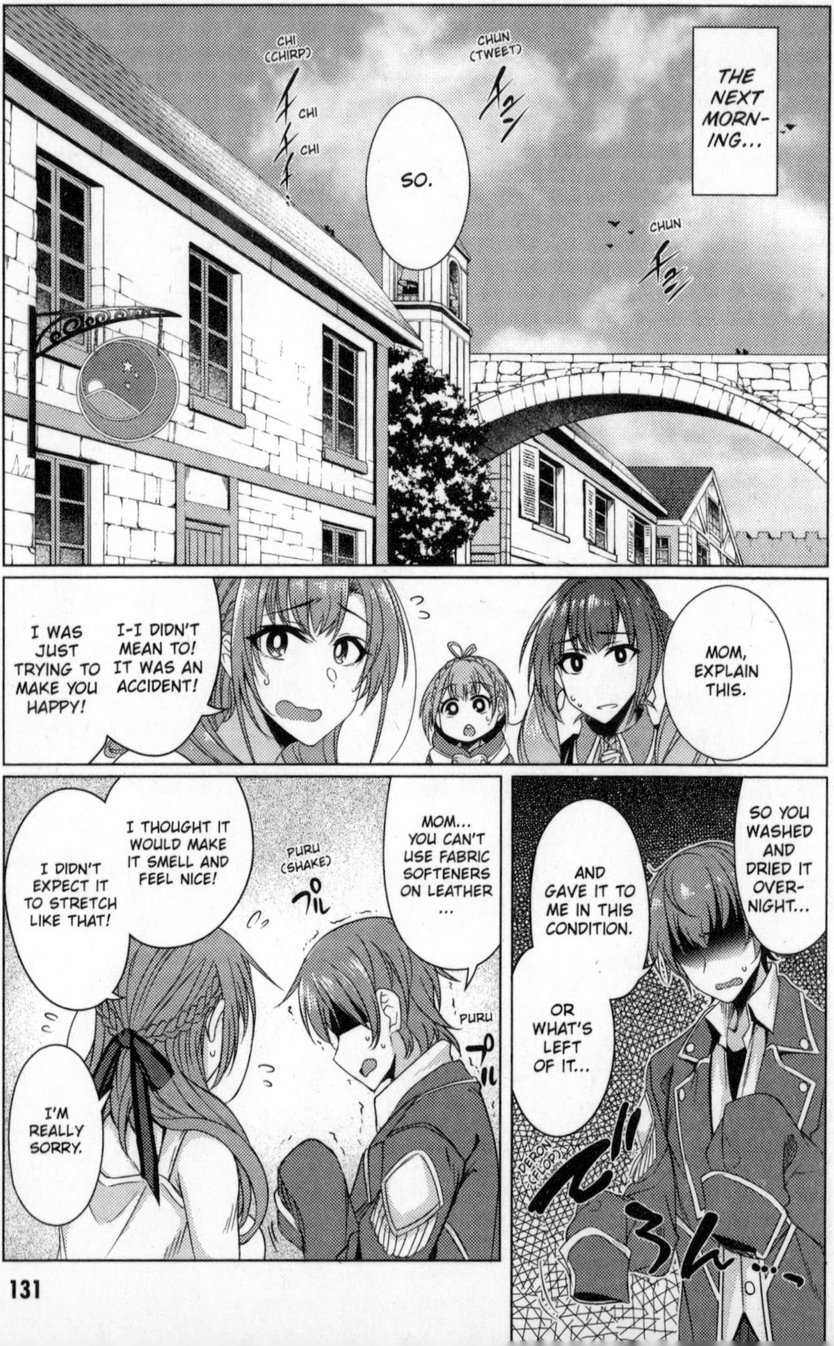
THE NEXT MORNING...
CHUN (TWEET)
CHI (CHIRP)
CHI
CHI
CHUN
SO.
MOM, EXPLAIN THIS.
I-I DIDN'T MEAN TO! IT WAS AN ACCIDENT!
I WAS JUST TRYING TO MAKE YOU HAPPY!
SO YOU WASHED AND DRIED IT OVERNIGHT...
AND GAVE IT TO ME IN THIS CONDITION.
OR WHAT'S LEFT OF IT...
DERON (FLOP)
MOM... YOU CAN'T USE FABRIC SOFTENERS ON LEATHER ...
PURU (SHAKE)
PURU
I THOUGHT IT WOULD MAKE IT SMELL AND FEEL NICE!
I DIDN'T EXPECT IT TO STRETCH LIKE THAT!
I'M REALLY SORRY.

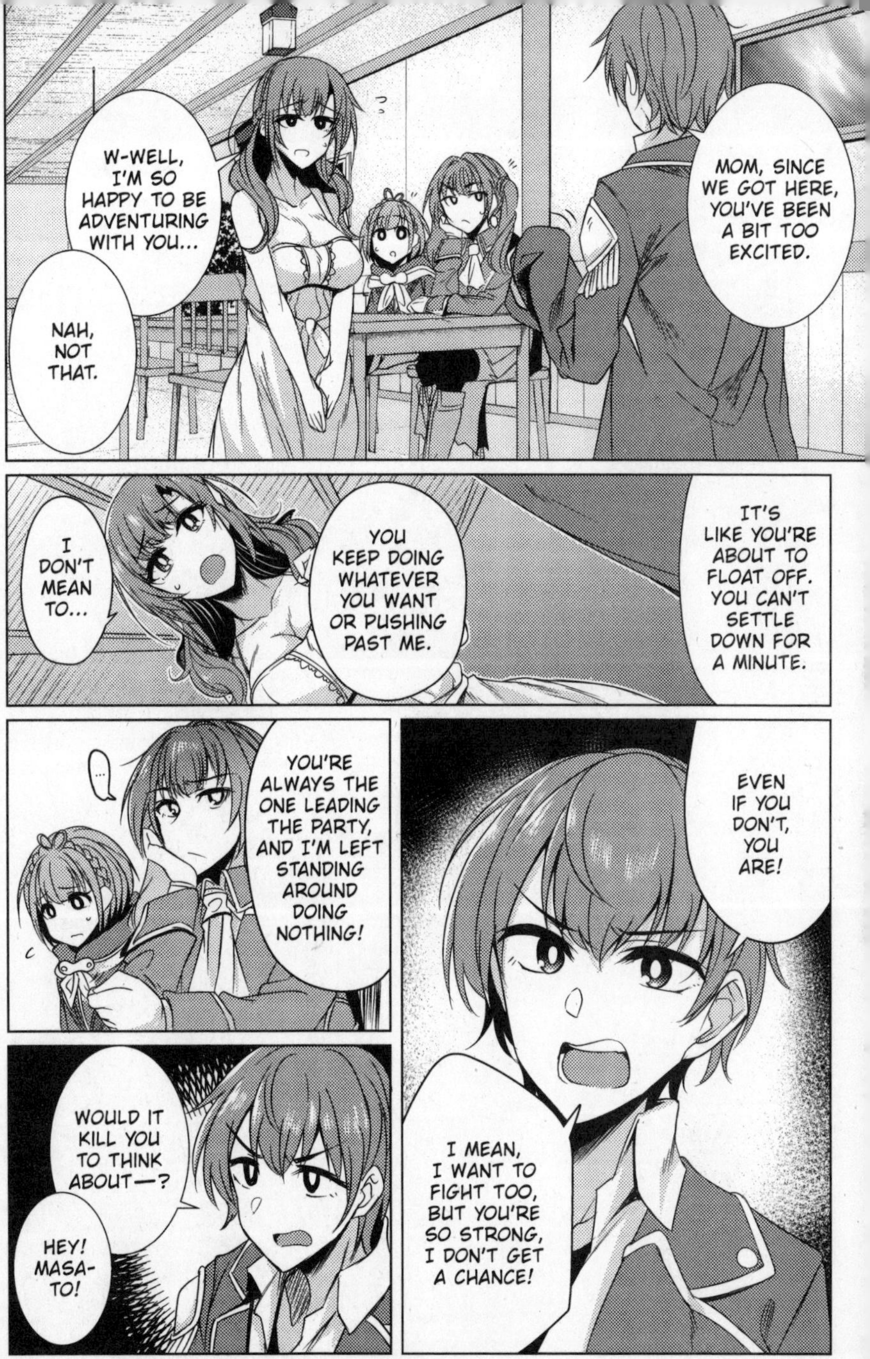
MOM, SINCE WE GOT HERE, YOU'VE BEEN A BIT TOO EXCITED.
W-WELL, I'M SO HAPPY TO BE ADVENTURING WITH YOU...
NAH, NOT THAT.
IT'S LIKE YOU'RE ABOUT TO FLOAT OFF. YOU CAN'T SETTLE DOWN FOR A MINUTE.
YOU KEEP DOING WHATEVER YOU WANT OR PUSHING PAST ME.
I DON'T MEAN TO...
EVEN IF YOU DON'T, YOU ARE!
I MEAN, I WANT TO FIGHT TOO, BUT YOU'RE SO STRONG, I DON'T GET A CHANCE!
...
YOU'RE ALWAYS THE ONE LEADING THE PARTY, AND I'M LEFT STANDING AROUND DOING NOTHING!
WOULD IT KILL YOU TO THINK ABOUT—?
HEY! MASA-TO!

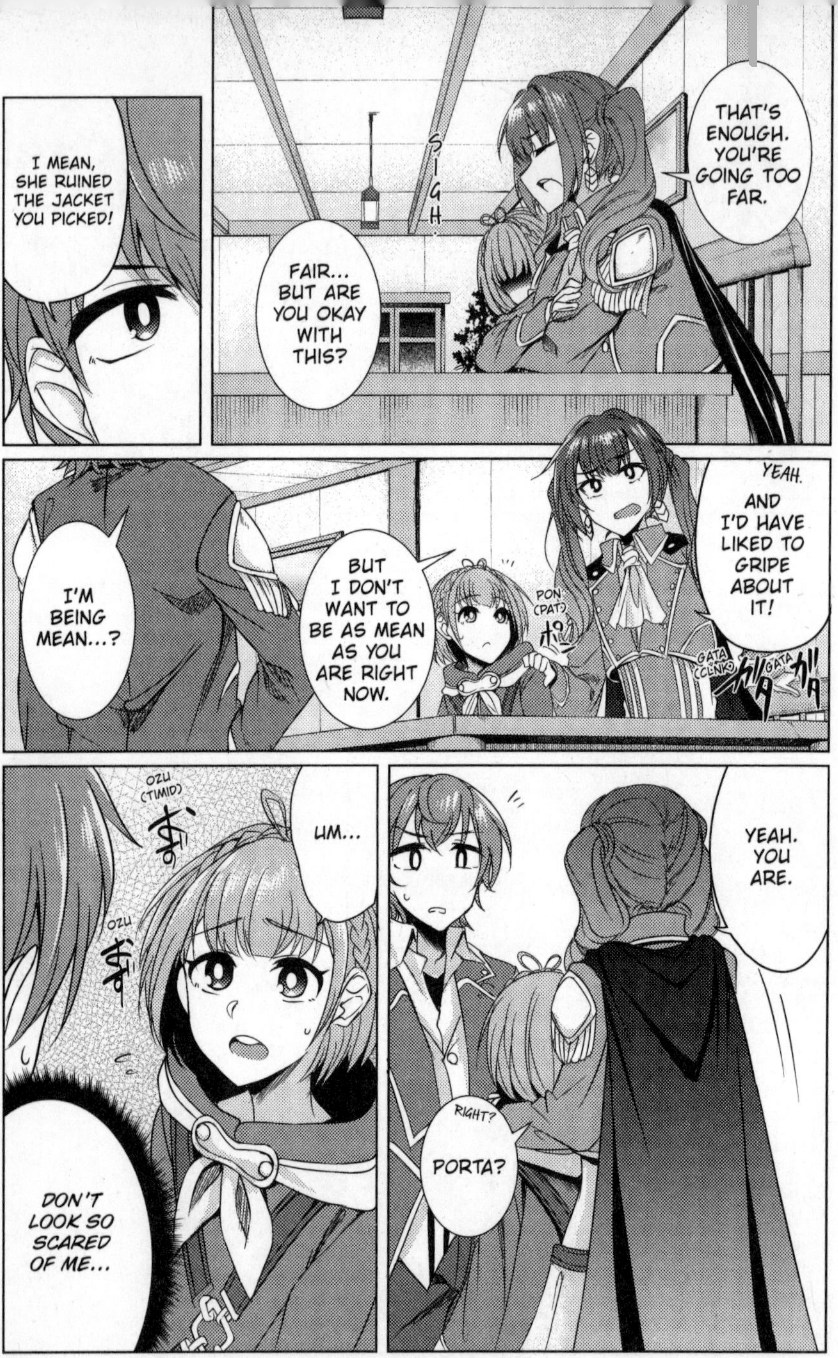
SIGH
THAT'S ENOUGH. YOU'RE GOING TOO FAR.
FAIR... BUT ARE YOU OKAY WITH THIS?
I MEAN, SHE RUINED THE JACKET YOU PICKED!
YEAH.
AND I'D HAVE LIKED TO GRIPE ABOUT IT!
GATA (CLNK)
GATA
PON (PAT)
BUT I DON'T WANT TO BE AS MEAN AS YOU ARE RIGHT NOW.
I'M BEING MEAN...?
YEAH. YOU ARE.
RIGHT?
PORTA?
UM...
OZU (TIMID)
OZU
DON'T LOOK SO SCARED OF ME...

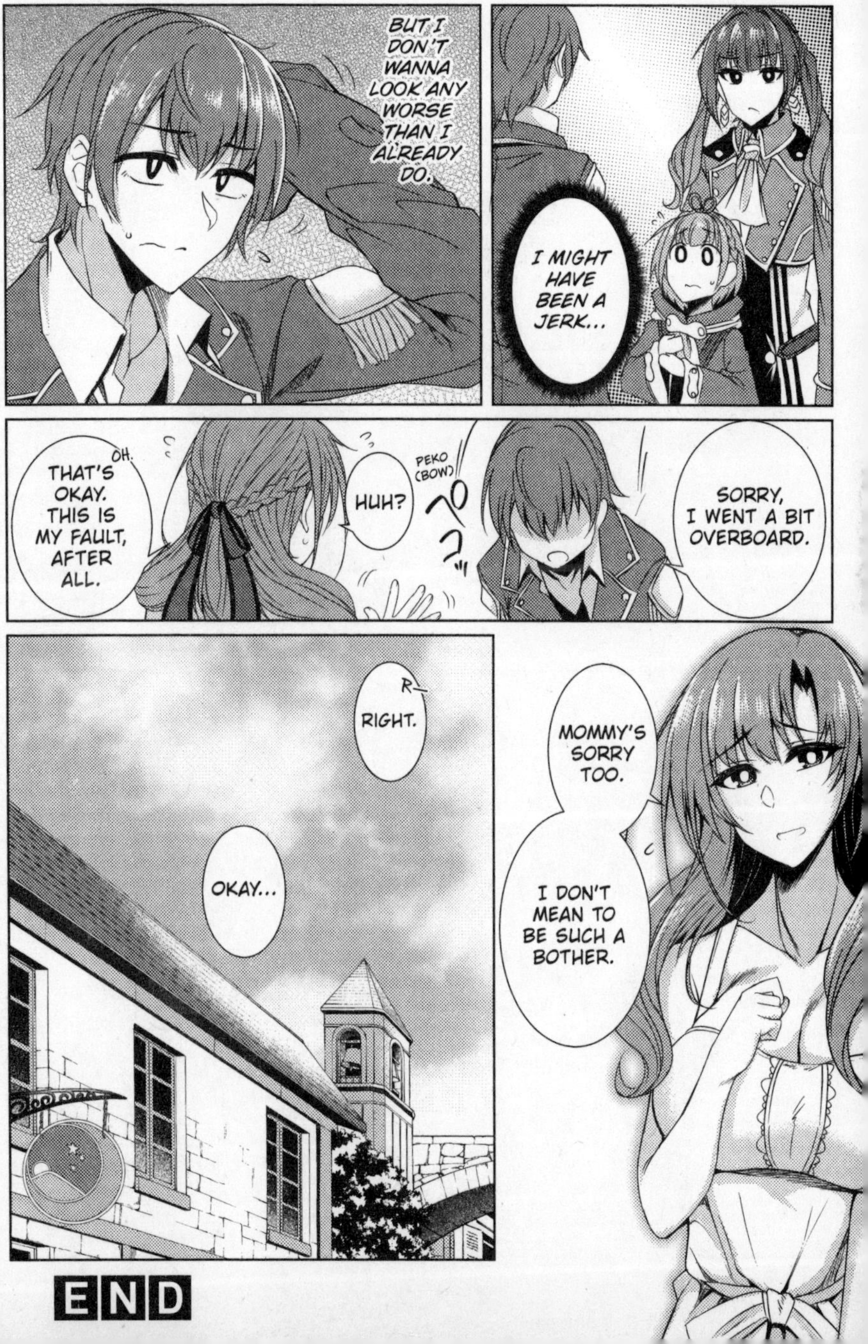
I MIGHT HAVE BEEN A JERK...
BUT I DON'T WANNA LOOK ANY WORSE THAN I ALREADY DO.
SORRY, I WENT A BIT OVERBOARD.
PEKO (BOW)
HUH?
OH.
THAT'S OKAY. THIS IS MY FAULT, AFTER ALL.
MOMMY'S SORRY TOO.
I DON'T MEAN TO BE SUCH A BOTHER.
R— RIGHT.
OKAY...
END

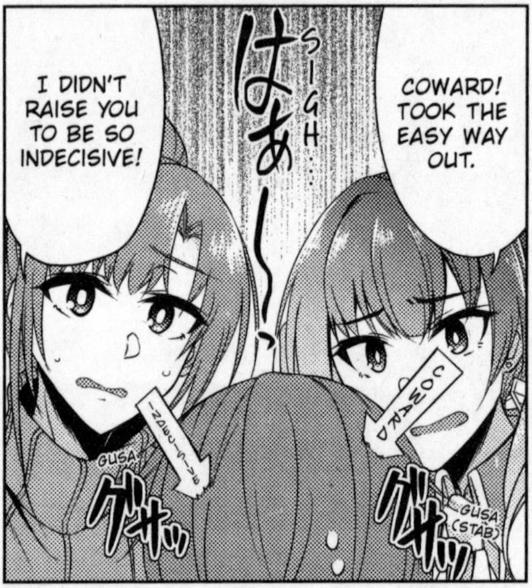
COWARD! TOOK THE EASY WAY OUT.
SIGH
はぁ～
I DIDN'T RAISE YOU TO BE SO INDECISIVE!
COWARD
GUSA (STAB)
INDECISIVE!
GUSA

Do You Love Your Mom and Her Two-Hit Multi-Target Attacks?

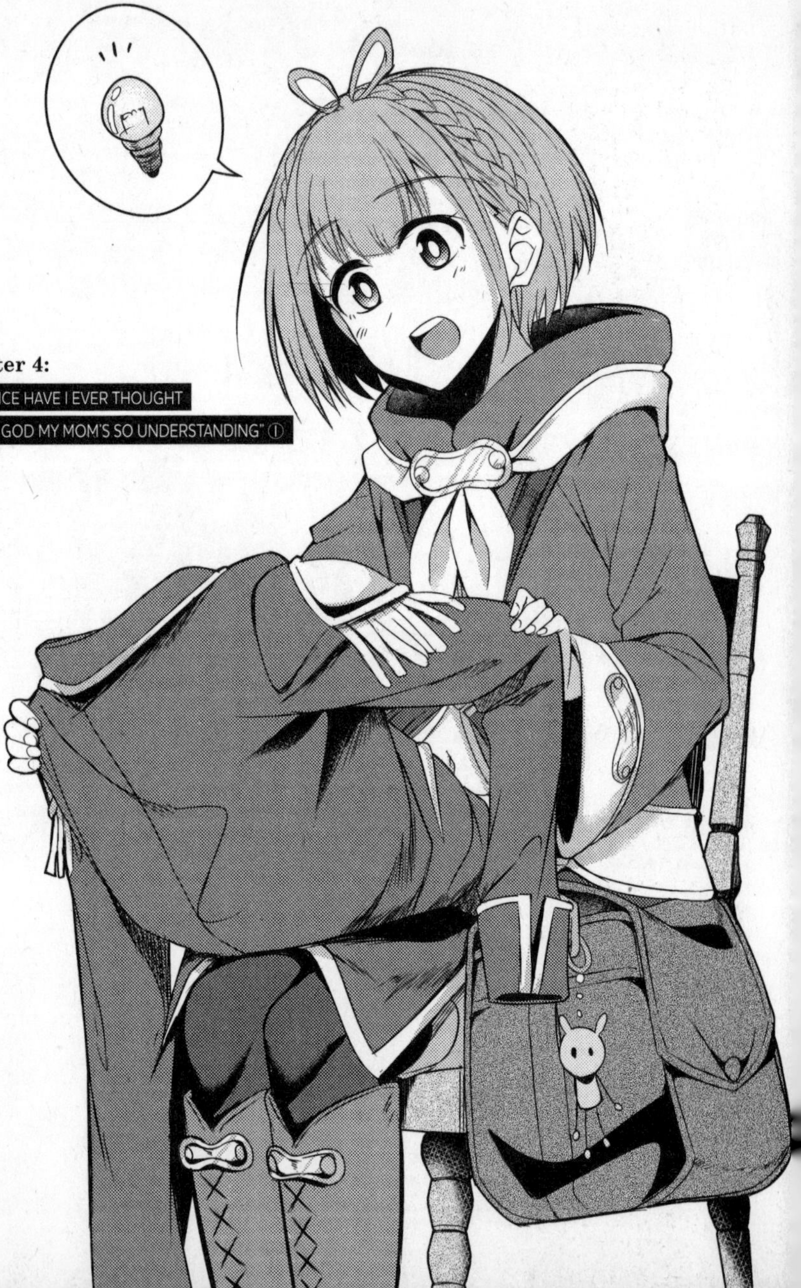

Chapter 4:

NOT ONCE HAVE I EVER THOUGHT "THANK GOD MY MOM'S SO UNDERSTANDING" ①

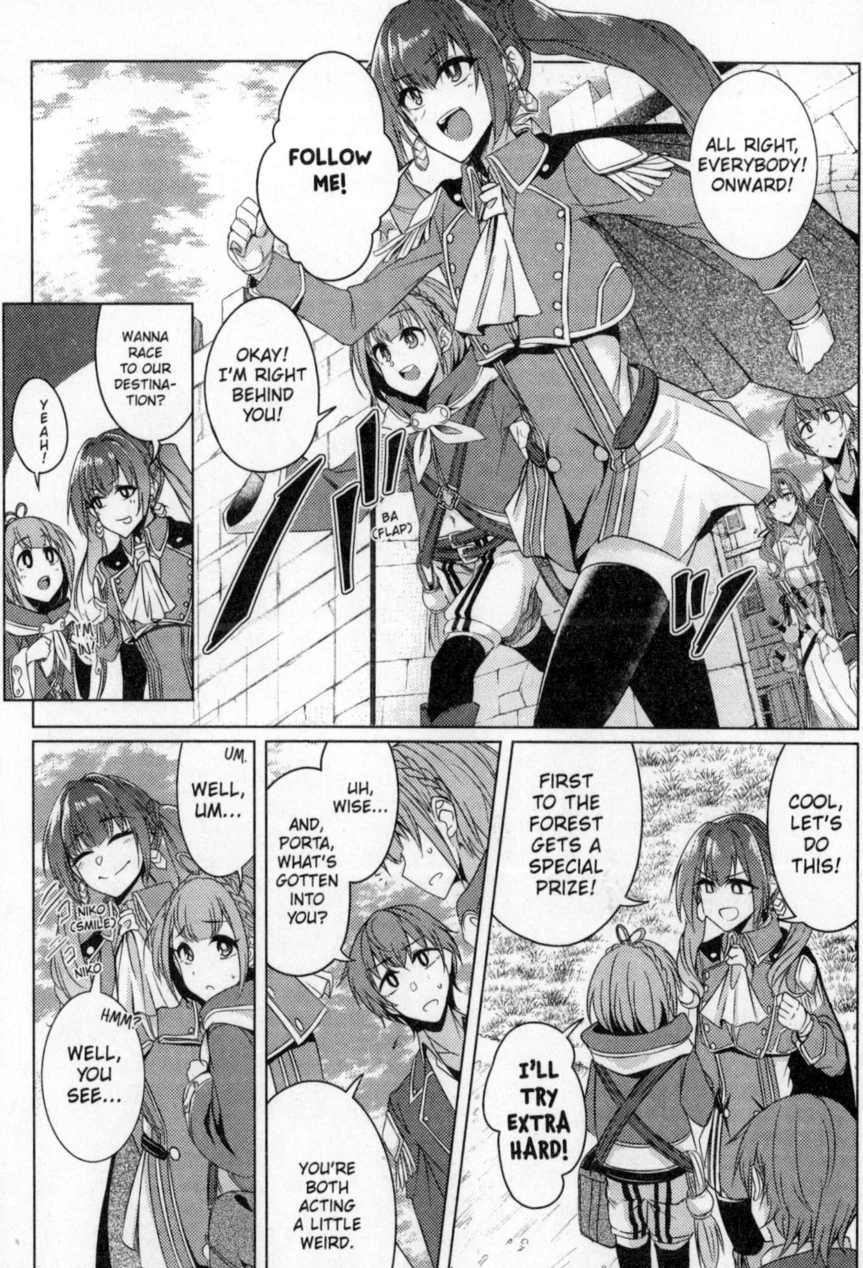
ALL RIGHT, EVERYBODY! ONWARD!
FOLLOW ME!
OKAY! I'M RIGHT BEHIND YOU!
BA (FLAP)
WANNA RACE TO OUR DESTINATION?
YEAH!
I'M IN!
COOL, LET'S DO THIS!
FIRST TO THE FOREST GETS A SPECIAL PRIZE!
I'LL TRY EXTRA HARD!
UH, WISE... AND, PORTA, WHAT'S GOTTEN INTO YOU?
YOU'RE BOTH ACTING A LITTLE WEIRD.
UM.
WELL, UM...
NIKO (SMILE)
NIKO
HMM?
WELL, YOU SEE...

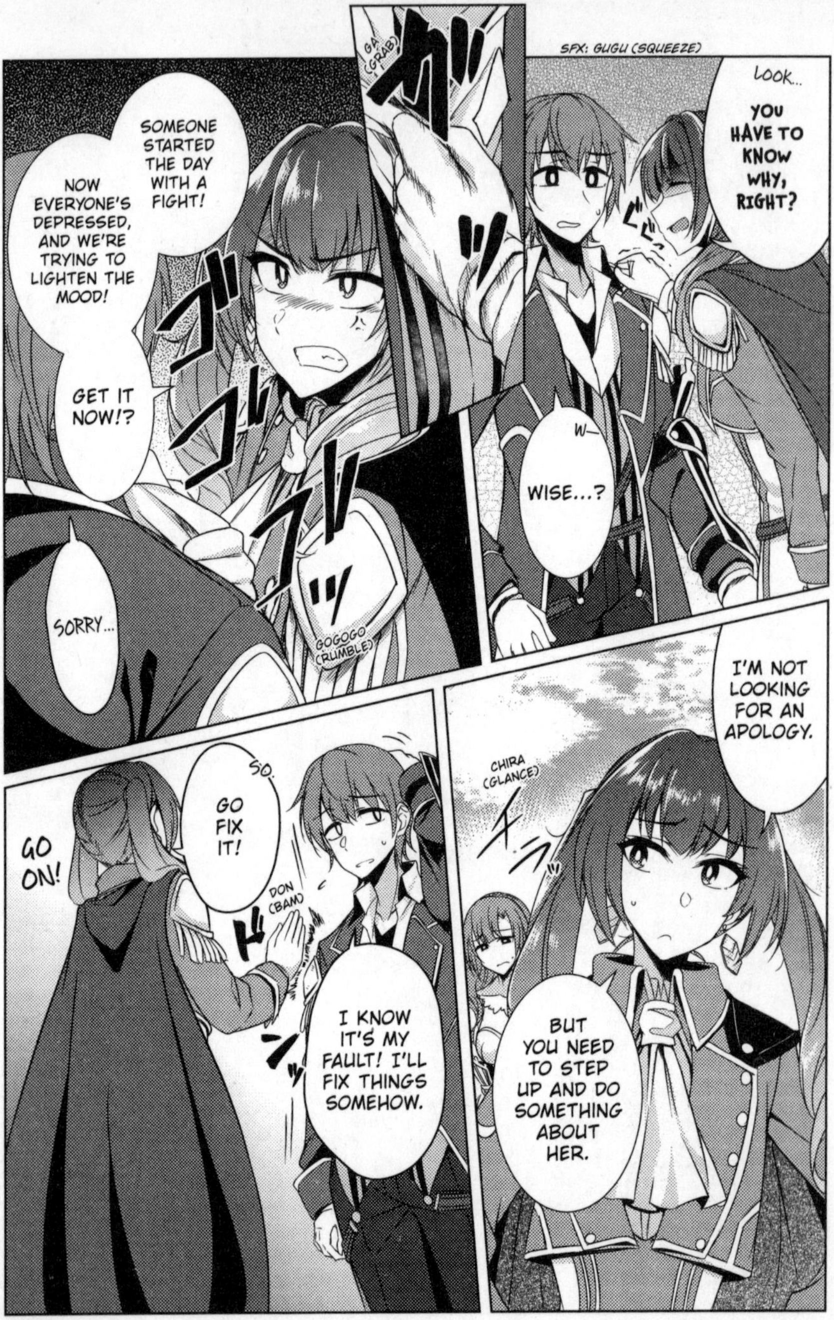
SFX: GUGU (SQUEEZE)
LOOK...
YOU HAVE TO KNOW WHY, RIGHT?
W—
WISE...?
GA (GRAB)
SOMEONE STARTED THE DAY WITH A FIGHT!
NOW EVERYONE'S DEPRESSED, AND WE'RE TRYING TO LIGHTEN THE MOOD!
GET IT NOW!?
GOGOGO (RUMBLE)
SORRY...
I'M NOT LOOKING FOR AN APOLOGY.
CHIRA (GLANCE)
BUT YOU NEED TO STEP UP AND DO SOMETHING ABOUT HER.
SO.
GO FIX IT!
GO ON!
DON (BAM)
I KNOW IT'S MY FAULT! I'LL FIX THINGS SOMEHOW.

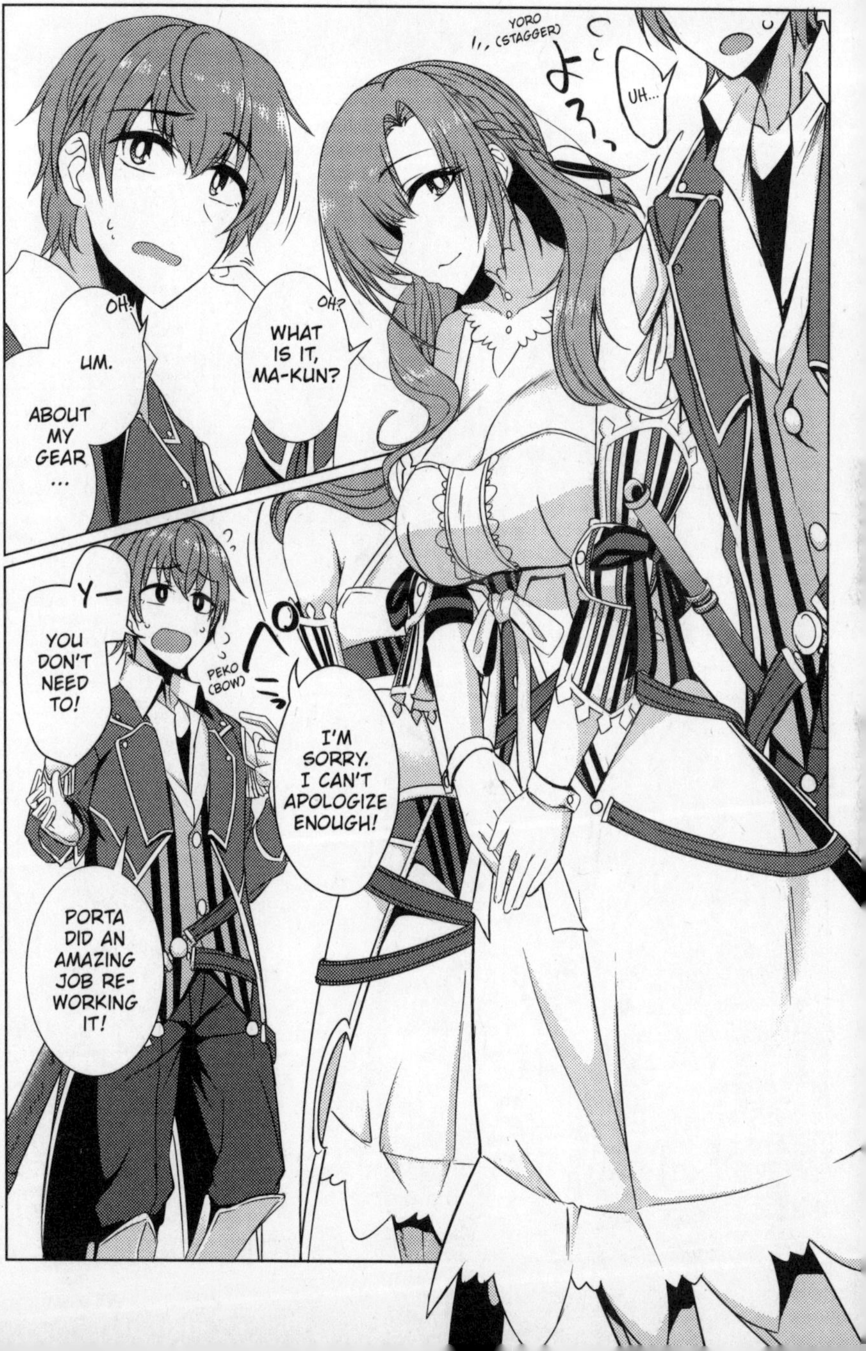
YORO (STAGGER)
UH...
OH? WHAT IS IT, MA-KUN?
OH! UM. ABOUT MY GEAR...
PEKO (BOW)
I'M SORRY. I CAN'T APOLOGIZE ENOUGH!
Y— YOU DON'T NEED TO!
PORTA DID AN AMAZING JOB RE-WORKING IT!

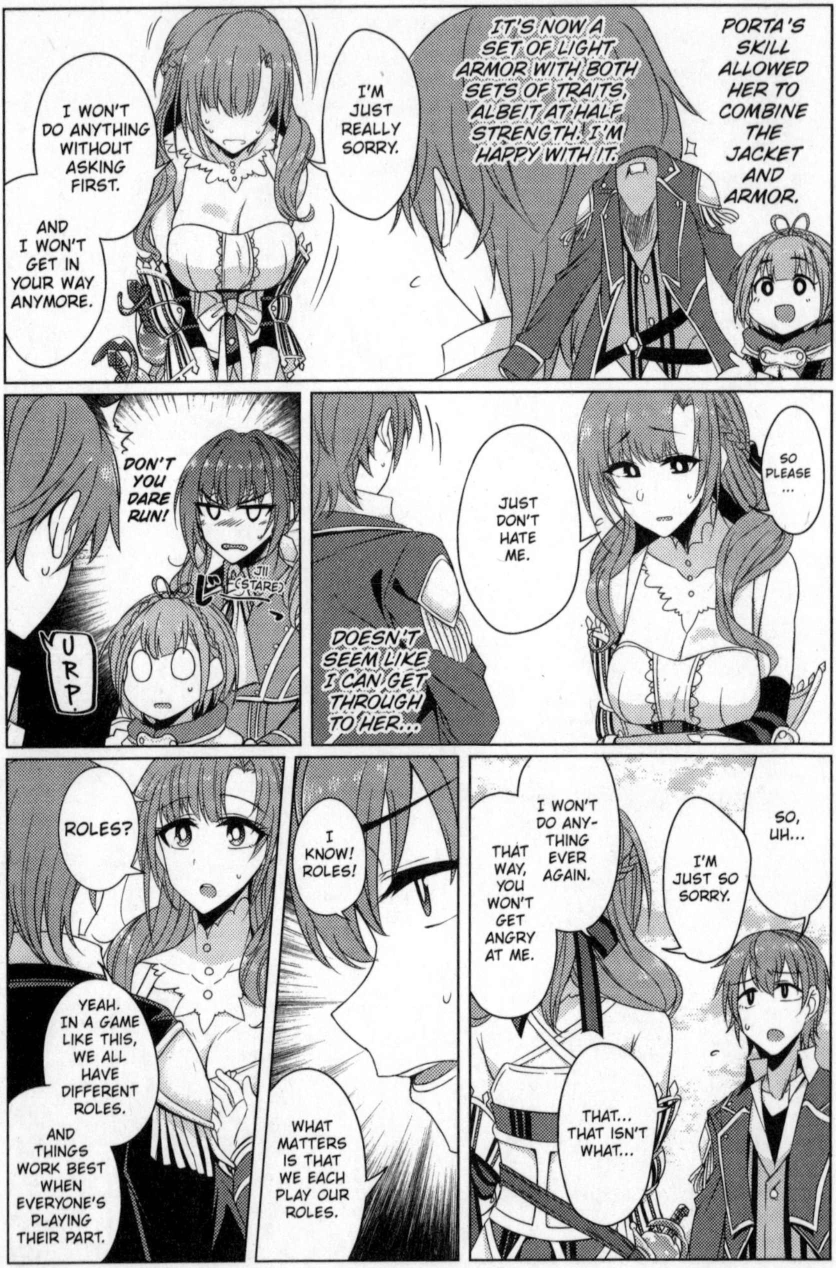
PORTA'S SKILL ALLOWED HER TO COMBINE THE JACKET AND ARMOR.
IT'S NOW A SET OF LIGHT ARMOR WITH BOTH SETS OF TRAITS, ALBEIT AT HALF STRENGTH. I'M HAPPY WITH IT.
I'M JUST REALLY SORRY.
I WON'T DO ANYTHING WITHOUT ASKING FIRST.
AND I WON'T GET IN YOUR WAY ANYMORE.
SO PLEASE ...
JUST DON'T HATE ME.
DOESN'T SEEM LIKE I CAN GET THROUGH TO HER...
DON'T YOU DARE RUN!
JII (STARE)
URP.
SO, UH...
I'M JUST SO SORRY.
I WON'T DO ANY-THING EVER AGAIN.
THAT WAY, YOU WON'T GET ANGRY AT ME.
THAT... THAT ISN'T WHAT...
I KNOW! ROLES!
WHAT MATTERS IS THAT WE EACH PLAY OUR ROLES.
ROLES?
YEAH. IN A GAME LIKE THIS, WE ALL HAVE DIFFERENT ROLES.
AND THINGS WORK BEST WHEN EVERYONE'S PLAYING THEIR PART.

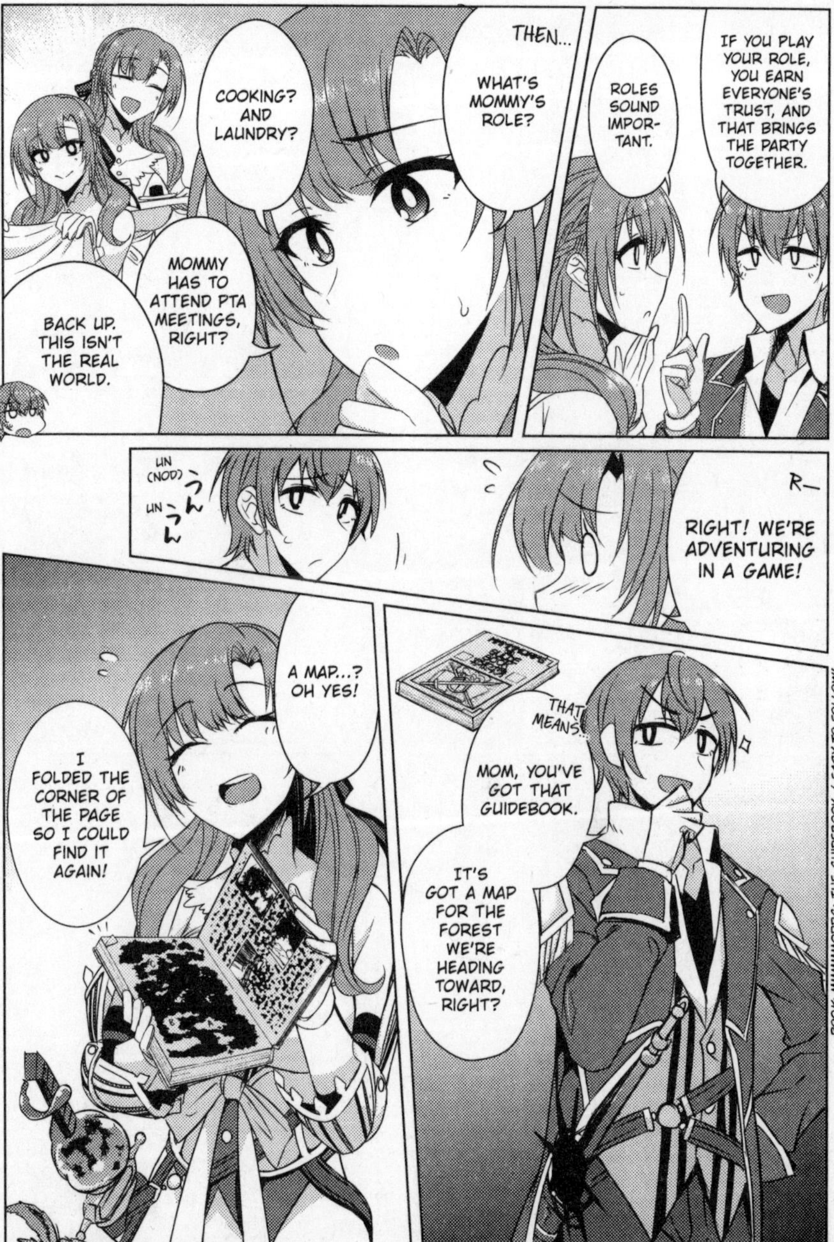
IF YOU PLAY YOUR ROLE, YOU EARN EVERYONE'S TRUST, AND THAT BRINGS THE PARTY TOGETHER.
ROLES SOUND IMPOR-TANT.
THEN...
WHAT'S MOMMY'S ROLE?
COOKING? AND LAUNDRY?
MOMMY HAS TO ATTEND PTA MEETINGS, RIGHT?
BACK UP. THIS ISN'T THE REAL WORLD.
R—
RIGHT! WE'RE ADVENTURING IN A GAME!
UN (NOD) うん
UN うん
THAT MEANS...
MOM, YOU'VE GOT THAT GUIDEBOOK.
IT'S GOT A MAP FOR THE FOREST WE'RE HEADING TOWARD, RIGHT?
A MAP...? OH YES!
I FOLDED THE CORNER OF THE PAGE SO I COULD FIND IT AGAIN!

BOOK: MMMMMORPG: THE GUIDEBOOK / EASY TO FOLLOW!

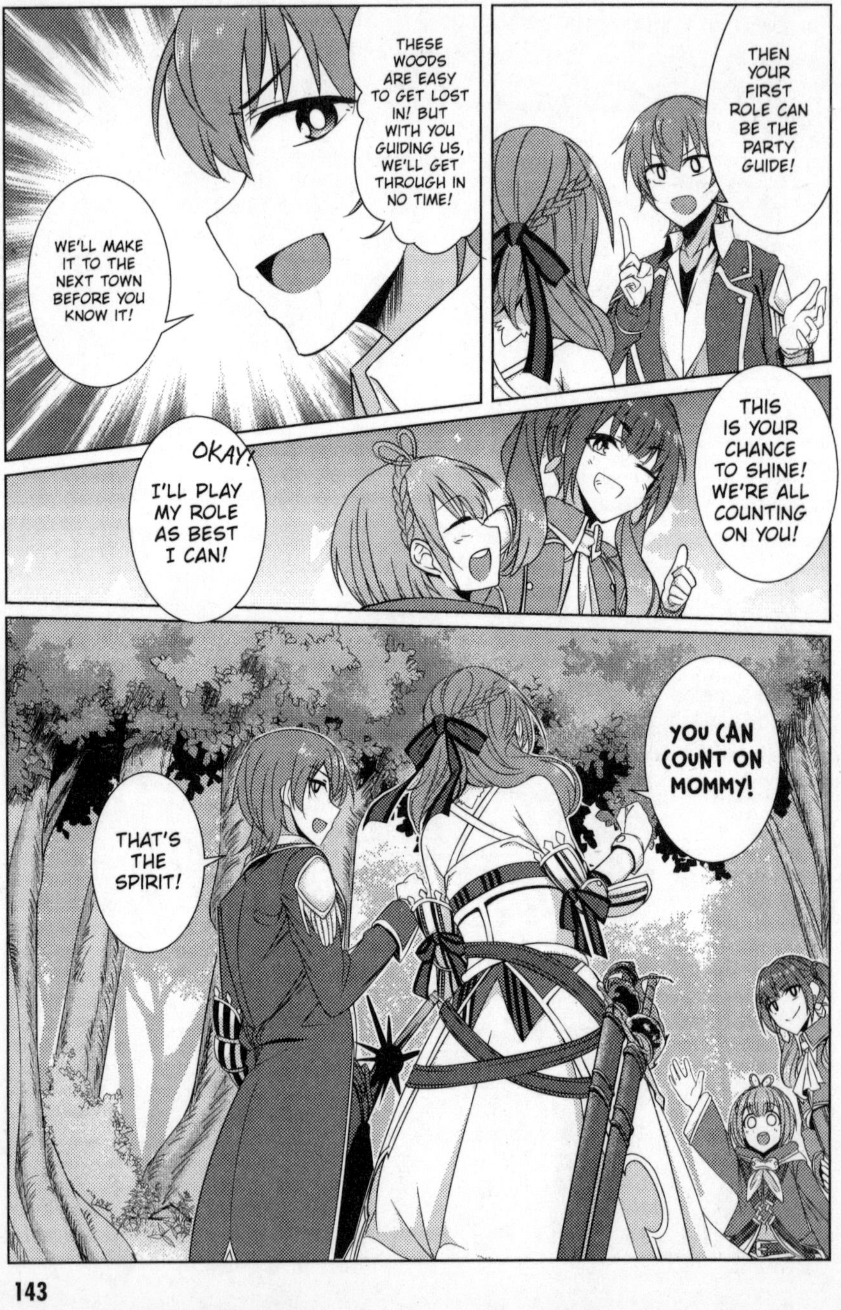
THEN YOUR FIRST ROLE CAN BE THE PARTY GUIDE!
THESE WOODS ARE EASY TO GET LOST IN! BUT WITH YOU GUIDING US, WE'LL GET THROUGH IN NO TIME!
WE'LL MAKE IT TO THE NEXT TOWN BEFORE YOU KNOW IT!
THIS IS YOUR CHANCE TO SHINE! WE'RE ALL COUNTING ON YOU!
OKAY!
I'LL PLAY MY ROLE AS BEST I CAN!
YOU CAN COUNT ON MOMMY!
THAT'S THE SPIRIT!

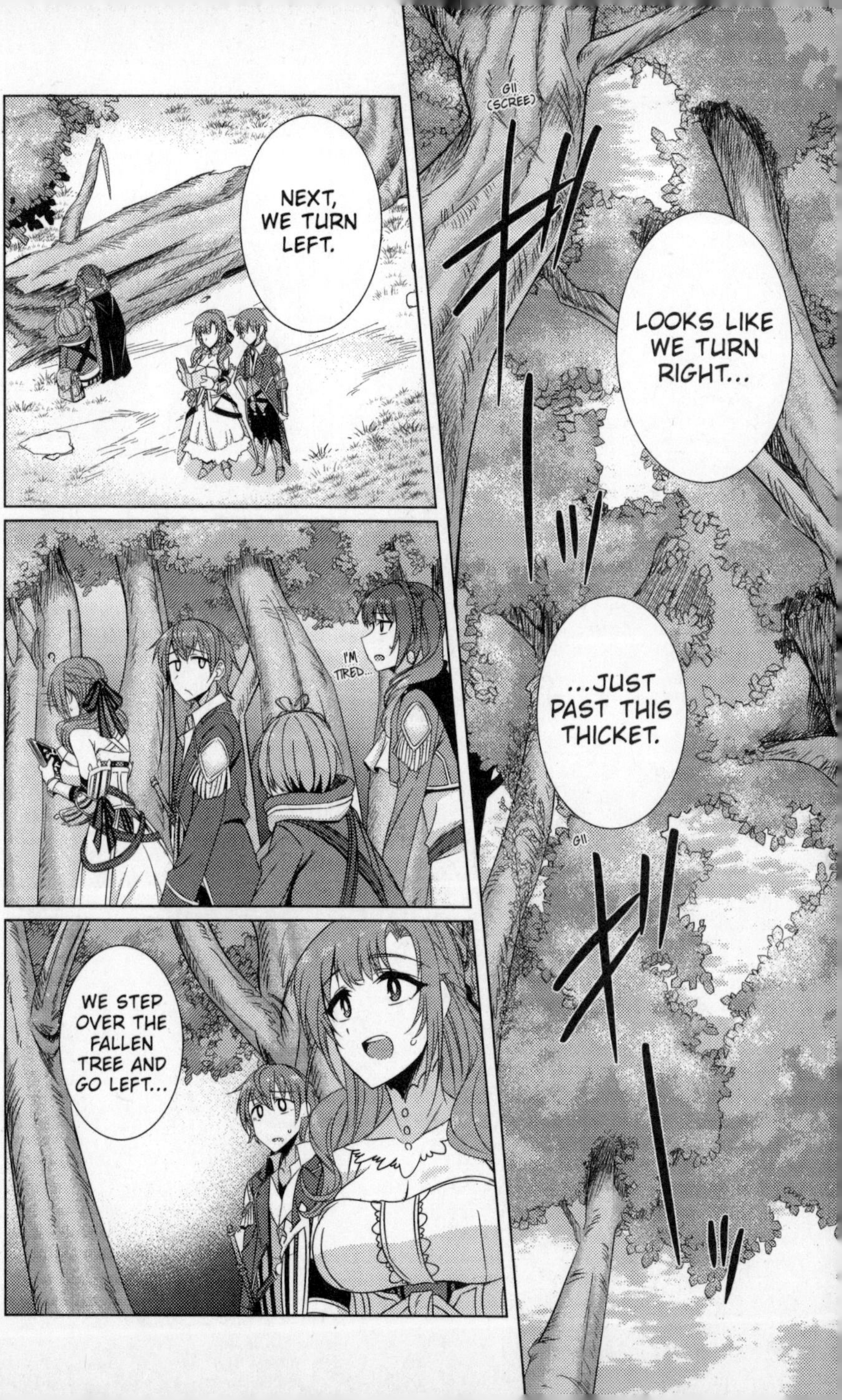
GII (SCREE)
LOOKS LIKE WE TURN RIGHT...
...JUST PAST THIS THICKET.
GII
NEXT, WE TURN LEFT.
I'M TIRED...
WE STEP OVER THE FALLEN TREE AND GO LEFT...

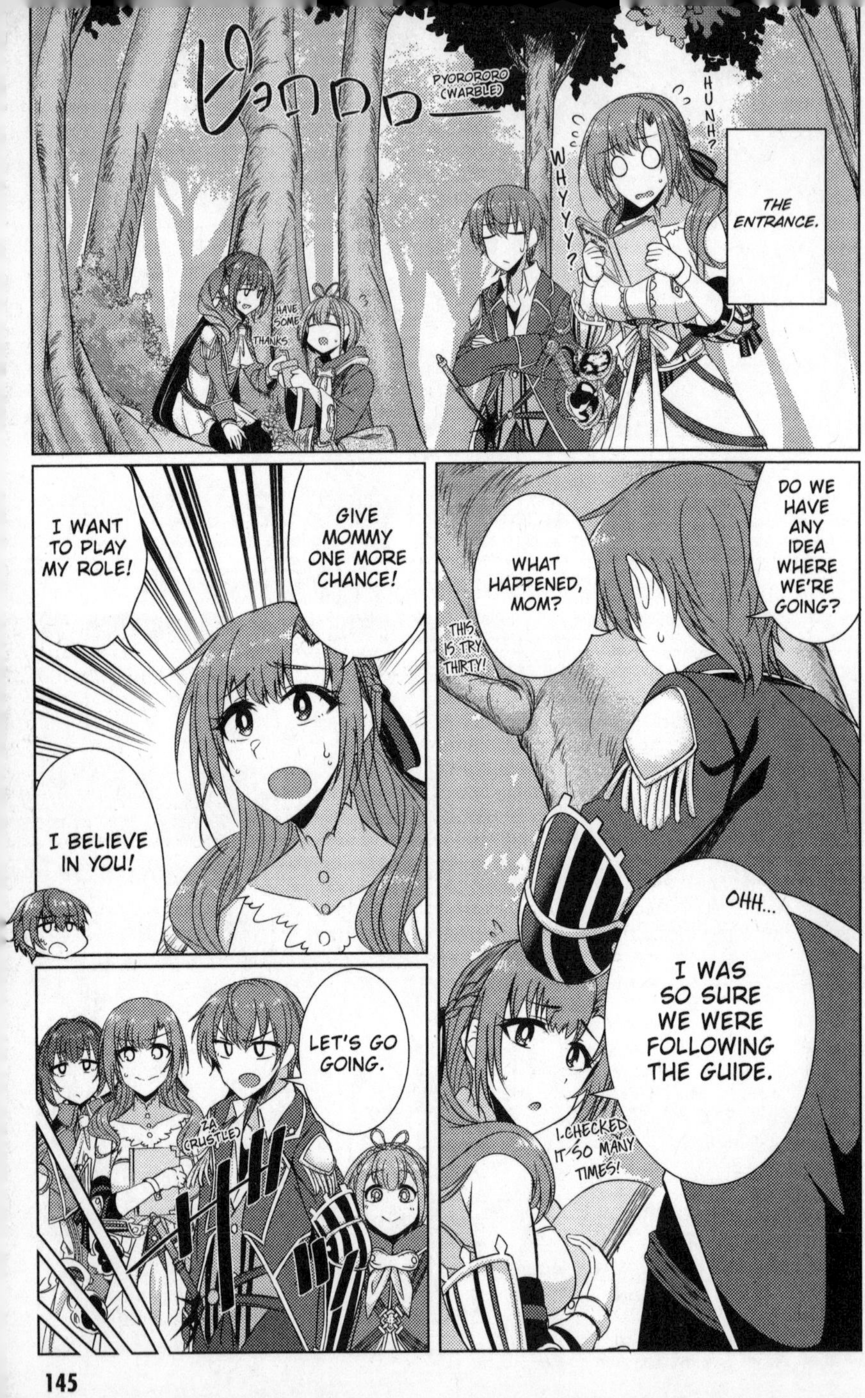
THE ENTRANCE.
HUNH?
WHYYY?
PYOROROROR (WARBLE)
HAVE SOME
THANKS
DO WE HAVE ANY IDEA WHERE WE'RE GOING?
WHAT HAPPENED, MOM?
THIS IS TRY THIRTY!
OHH...
I WAS SO SURE WE WERE FOLLOWING THE GUIDE.
I CHECKED IT SO MANY TIMES!
GIVE MOMMY ONE MORE CHANCE!
I WANT TO PLAY MY ROLE!
I BELIEVE IN YOU!
LET'S GO GOING.
ZA (RUSTLE)

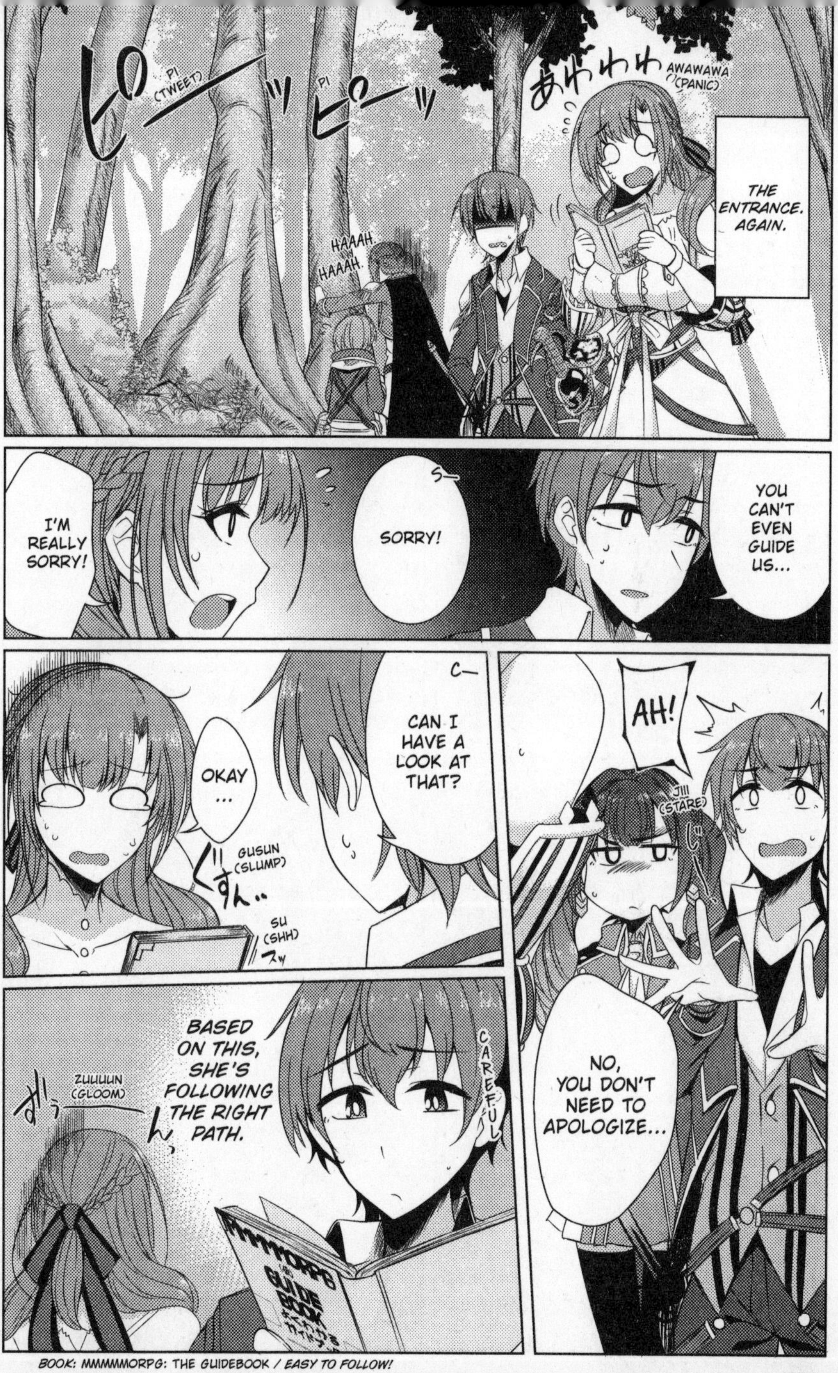
THE ENTRANCE. AGAIN.
あわわわ
AWAWAWA (PANIC)
ピーッ
PI
ピーッ
PI (TWEET)
HAAAH. HAAAH.
YOU CAN'T EVEN GUIDE US...
S— SORRY!
I'M REALLY SORRY!
AH!
JIII (STARE)
NO, YOU DON'T NEED TO APOLOGIZE...
C— CAN I HAVE A LOOK AT THAT?
OKAY ...
ぐすん..
GUSUN (SLUMP)
SU (SHH)
スッ
CAREFUL
BASED ON THIS, SHE'S FOLLOWING THE RIGHT PATH.
ずぅーん
ZUUUUN (GLOOM)

BOOK: MMMMMORPG: THE GUIDEBOOK / EASY TO FOLLOW!

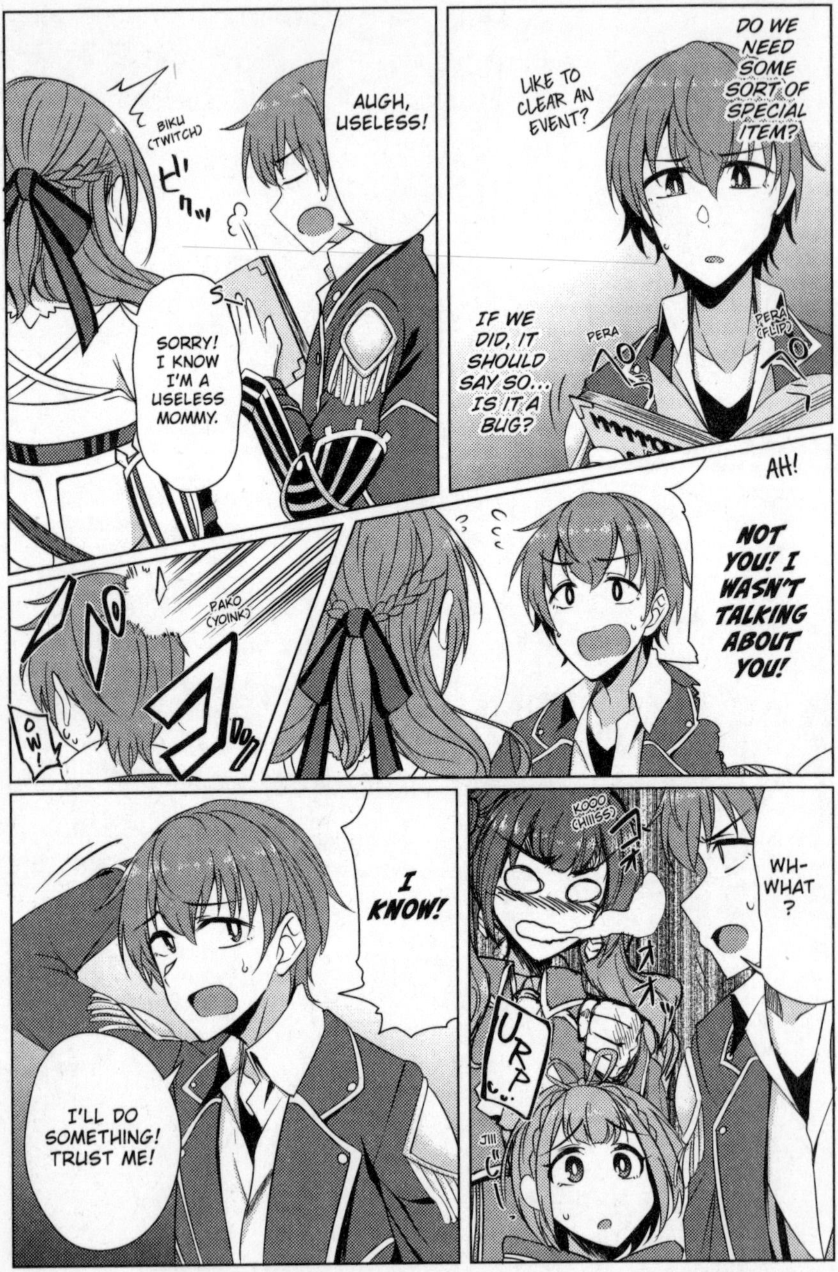
DO WE NEED SOME SORT OF SPECIAL ITEM?
LIKE TO CLEAR AN EVENT?
PERA
PERA (FLIP)
IF WE DID, IT SHOULD SAY SO... IS IT A BUG?
AUGH, USELESS!
BIKU (TWITCH)
SORRY! I KNOW I'M A USELESS MOMMY.
AH!
NOT YOU! I WASN'T TALKING ABOUT YOU!
PAKO (YOINK)
OW!
WH-WHAT?
KOOO (HIIISS)
URP
JIII
I KNOW!
I'LL DO SOMETHING! TRUST ME!

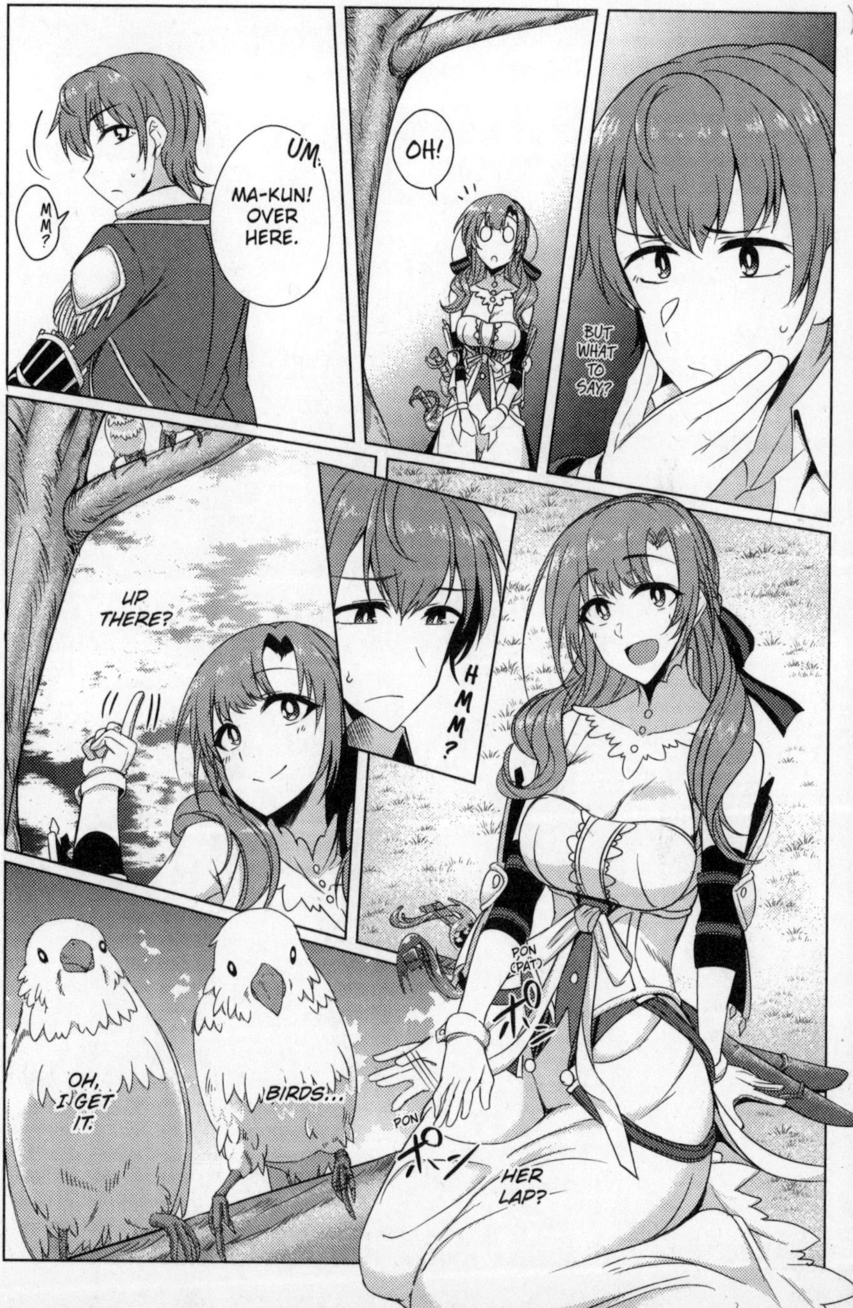
BUT WHAT TO SAY?
OH!
UM.
MA-KUN! OVER HERE.
MM?
PON (PAT)
PON
HER LAP?
HMM?
UP THERE?
BIRDS...
OH, I GET IT.

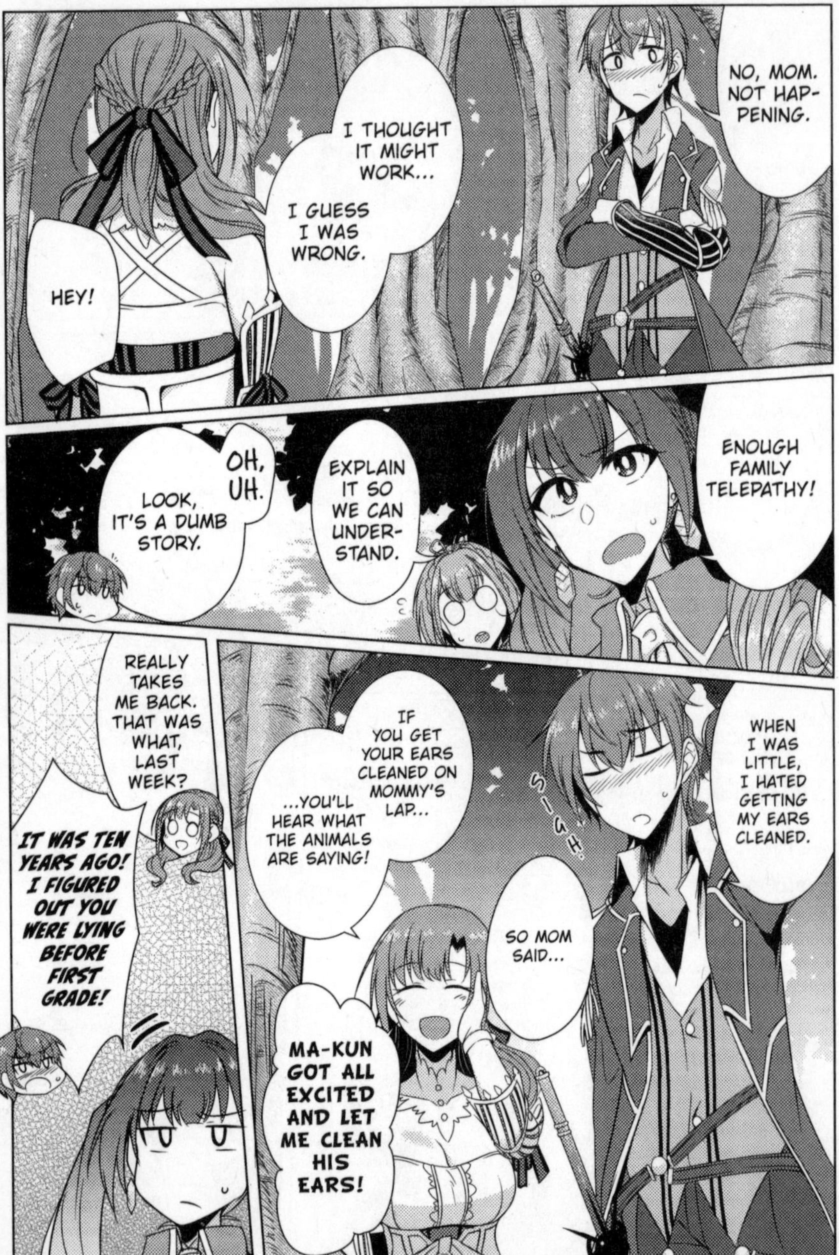
NO, MOM. NOT HAPPENING.
I THOUGHT IT MIGHT WORK...
I GUESS I WAS WRONG.
HEY!
ENOUGH FAMILY TELEPATHY!
EXPLAIN IT SO WE CAN UNDERSTAND.
OH, UH.
LOOK, IT'S A DUMB STORY.
WHEN I WAS LITTLE, I HATED GETTING MY EARS CLEANED.
SIGH
SO MOM SAID...
IF YOU GET YOUR EARS CLEANED ON MOMMY'S LAP...
...YOU'LL HEAR WHAT THE ANIMALS ARE SAYING!
MA-KUN GOT ALL EXCITED AND LET ME CLEAN HIS EARS!
REALLY TAKES ME BACK. THAT WAS WHAT, LAST WEEK?
IT WAS TEN YEARS AGO! I FIGURED OUT YOU WERE LYING BEFORE FIRST GRADE!

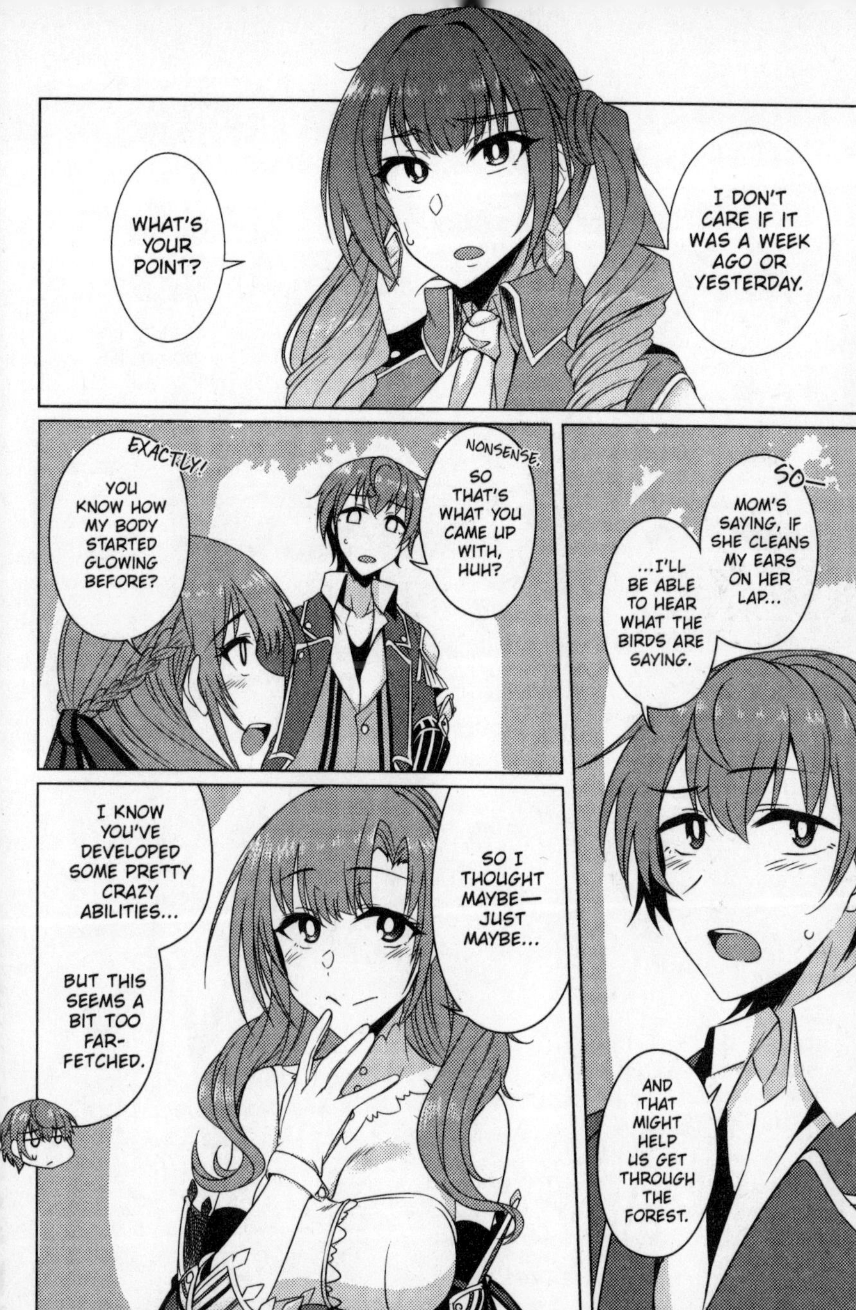
I DON'T CARE IF IT WAS A WEEK AGO OR YESTERDAY.
WHAT'S YOUR POINT?
SO—
MOM'S SAYING, IF SHE CLEANS MY EARS ON HER LAP...
...I'LL BE ABLE TO HEAR WHAT THE BIRDS ARE SAYING.
AND THAT MIGHT HELP US GET THROUGH THE FOREST.
NONSENSE.
SO THAT'S WHAT YOU CAME UP WITH, HUH?
EXACTLY!
YOU KNOW HOW MY BODY STARTED GLOWING BEFORE?
SO I THOUGHT MAYBE—JUST MAYBE...
I KNOW YOU'VE DEVELOPED SOME PRETTY CRAZY ABILITIES...
BUT THIS SEEMS A BIT TOO FAR-FETCHED.

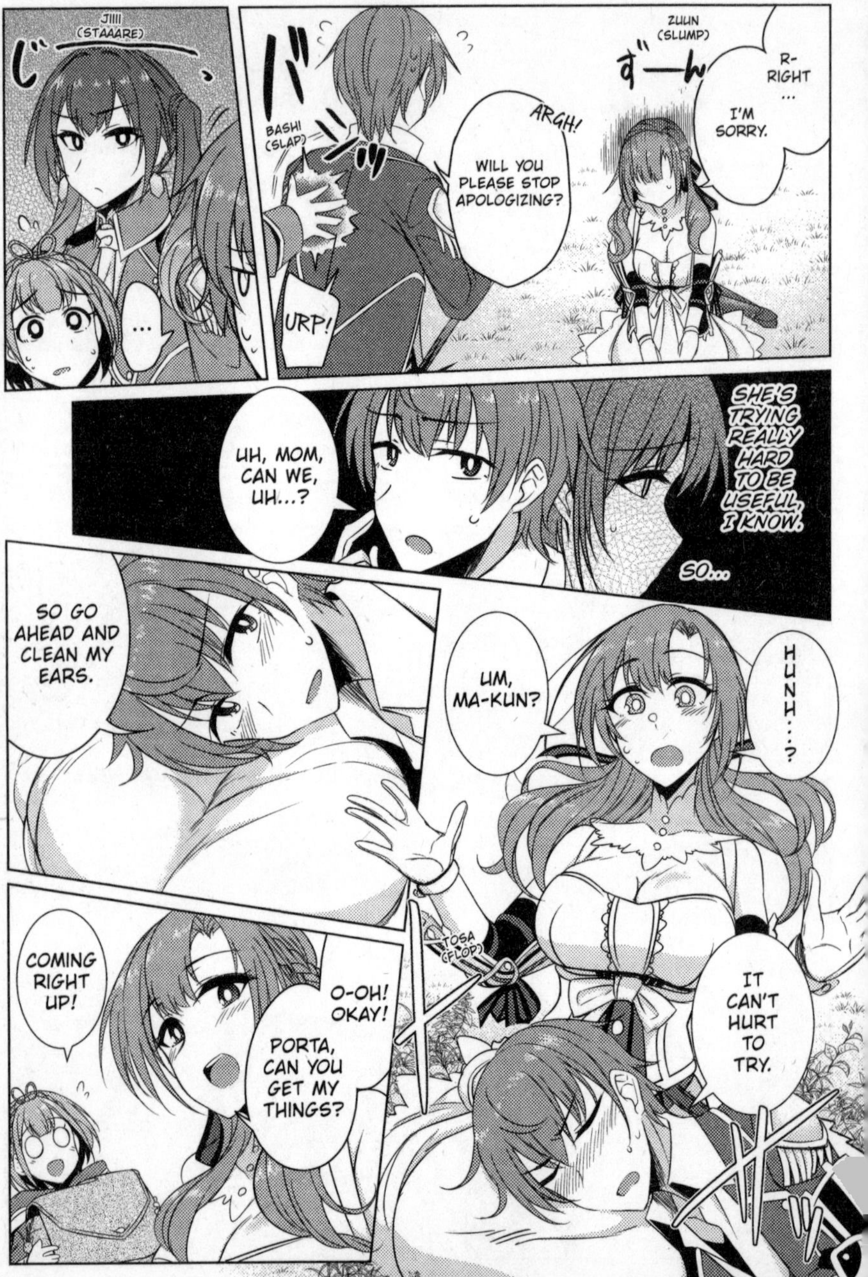
ZUUN (SLUMP)
ずーん
R-RIGHT ...
I'M SORRY.
BASHI (SLAP)
バ
ARGH!
WILL YOU PLEASE STOP APOLOGIZING?
URP!
JIIII (STAAARE)
じー
...
SHE'S TRYING REALLY HARD TO BE USEFUL, I KNOW.
SO...
UH, MOM, CAN WE, UH...?
HUNH...?
UM, MA-KUN?
SO GO AHEAD AND CLEAN MY EARS.
TOSA (FLOP)
IT CAN'T HURT TO TRY.
O-OH! OKAY!
PORTA, CAN YOU GET MY THINGS?
COMING RIGHT UP!

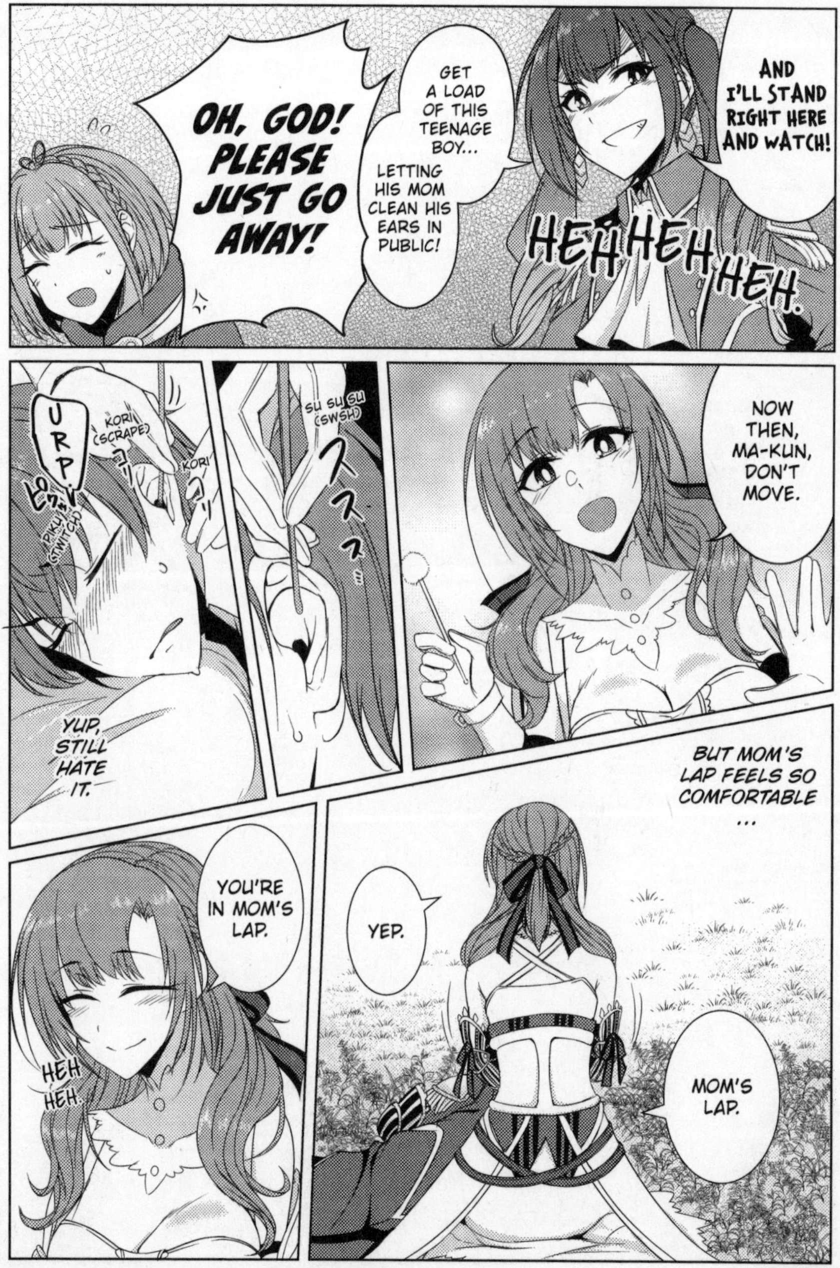
AND I'LL STAND RIGHT HERE AND WATCH!
HEH HEH HEH.
GET A LOAD OF THIS TEENAGE BOY...
LETTING HIS MOM CLEAN HIS EARS IN PUBLIC!
OH, GOD! PLEASE JUST GO AWAY!
NOW THEN, MA-KUN, DON'T MOVE.
SU SU SU (SWSH)
KORI
KORI (SCRAPE)
URP.
PIKU (TWITCH)
YUP, STILL HATE IT.
BUT MOM'S LAP FEELS SO COMFORTABLE ...
MOM'S LAP.
YEP.
YOU'RE IN MOM'S LAP.
HEH HEH.

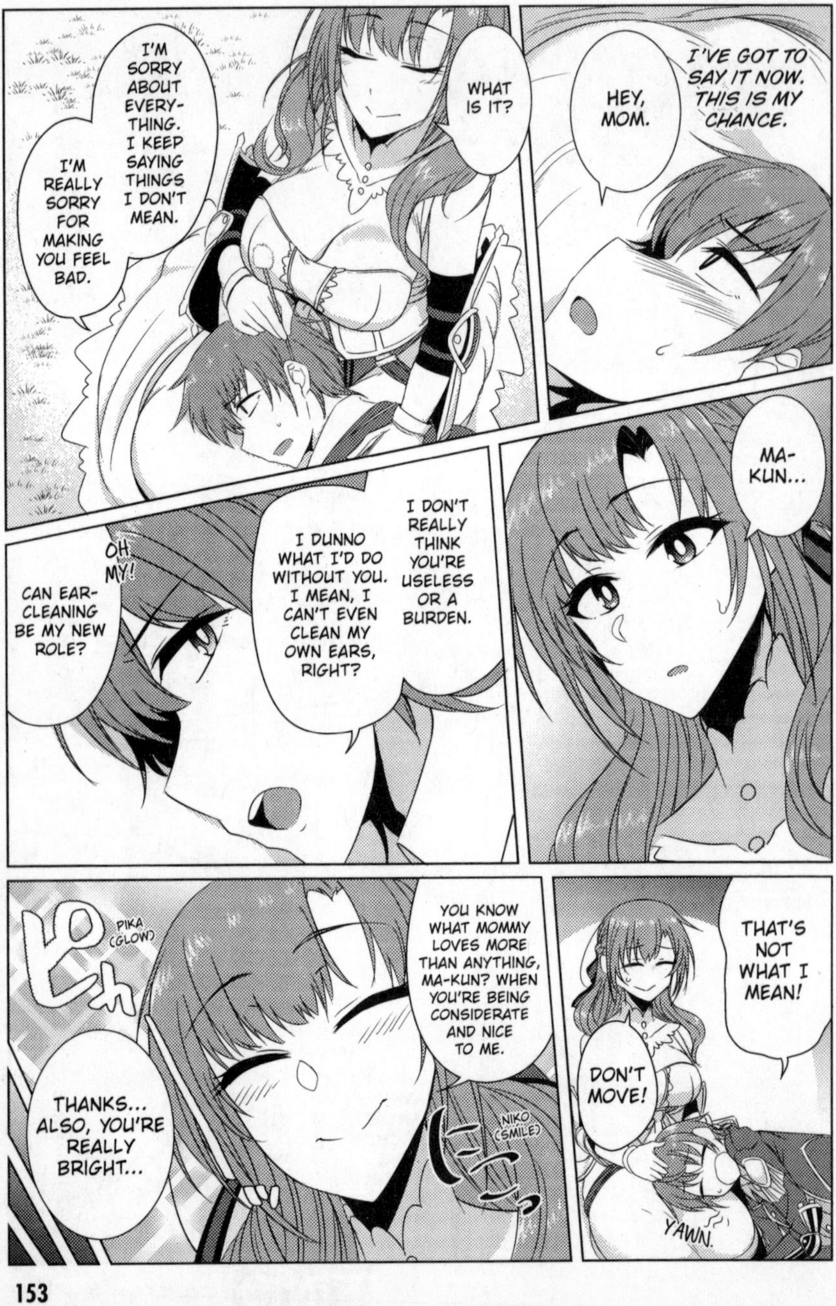
I'VE GOT TO SAY IT NOW. THIS IS MY CHANCE.
HEY, MOM.
WHAT IS IT?
I'M SORRY ABOUT EVERYTHING. I KEEP SAYING THINGS I DON'T MEAN.
I'M REALLY SORRY FOR MAKING YOU FEEL BAD.
MA-KUN...
I DON'T REALLY THINK YOU'RE USELESS OR A BURDEN.
I DUNNO WHAT I'D DO WITHOUT YOU. I MEAN, I CAN'T EVEN CLEAN MY OWN EARS, RIGHT?
OH MY!
CAN EAR-CLEANING BE MY NEW ROLE?
THAT'S NOT WHAT I MEAN!
DON'T MOVE!
YAWN.
PIKA (GLOW)
YOU KNOW WHAT MOMMY LOVES MORE THAN ANYTHING, MA-KUN? WHEN YOU'RE BEING CONSIDERATE AND NICE TO ME.
NIKO (SMILE)
THANKS... ALSO, YOU'RE REALLY BRIGHT...

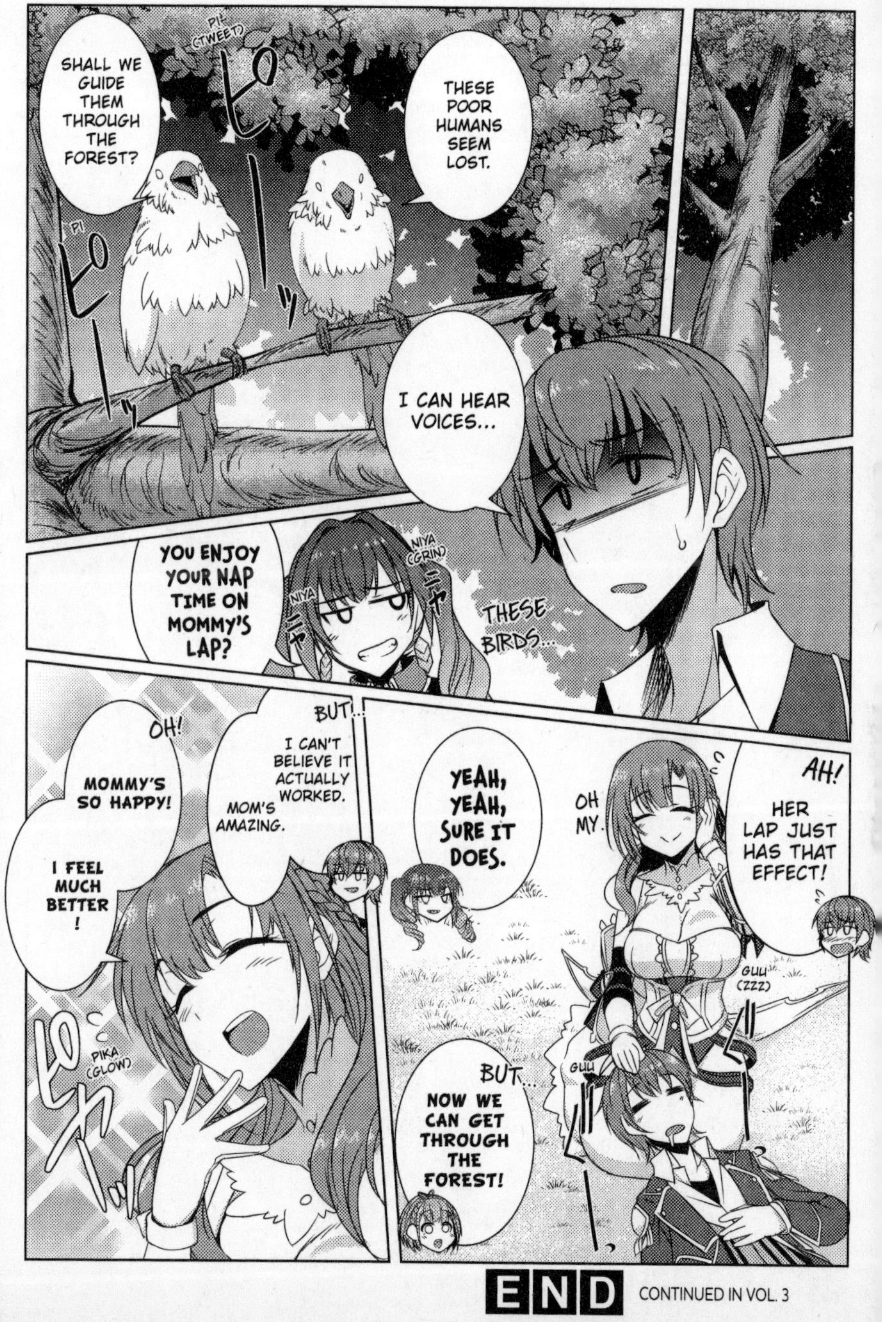
THESE POOR HUMANS SEEM LOST.
PI (TWEET)
SHALL WE GUIDE THEM THROUGH THE FOREST?
PI
I CAN HEAR VOICES...
THESE BIRDS...
NIYA (GRIN)
NIYA
YOU ENJOY YOUR NAP TIME ON MOMMY'S LAP?
AH! HER LAP JUST HAS THAT EFFECT!
OH MY.
GUU (ZZZ)
GUU
YEAH, YEAH, SURE IT DOES.
BUT... NOW WE CAN GET THROUGH THE FOREST!
BUT... I CAN'T BELIEVE IT ACTUALLY WORKED.
MOM'S AMAZING.
OH! MOMMY'S SO HAPPY!
I FEEL MUCH BETTER!
PIKA (GLOW)

END

CONTINUED IN VOL. 3

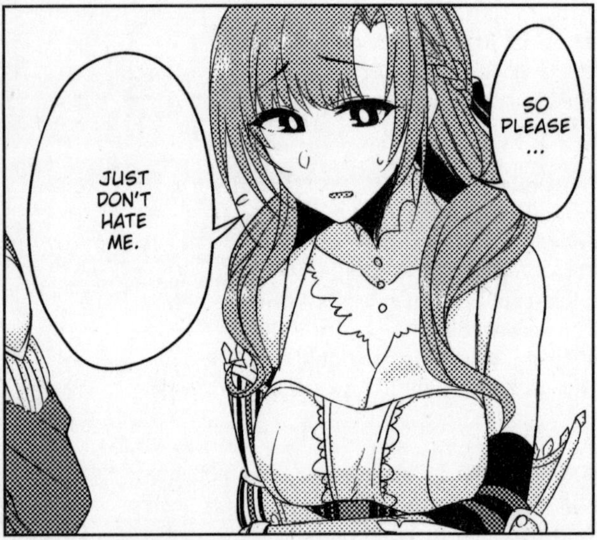
SO PLEASE ...
JUST DON'T HATE ME.

Wise slunk off and started helping Porta gather the gems that the monsters had dropped. Her shoulders were shaking; was she crying? Didn't matter.

While Masato fretted over how best to use his SP, Mamako stepped up next to him.

"If you're going to use your points, Mommy will, too!"

"We don't need to do this together! It's kinda personal. And if you get any stronger, I'll be in real trouble…"

"Oh, don't say that! Mommy really doesn't get these things, so she needs your help. Can you take a look, Makun? What should I raise?"

Mamako showed him her status screen.

Skin Tightness, Skin Glossiness, Hair Luster, Wrinkles (Reduction), Flab (Reduction), Makeup Techniques… The list went on and on.

"…Huh?"

Masato blinked in surprise and opened his own status screen.

HP, MP, STR, INT, MND, AGI, LUC… The standard, combat-focused stats of any RPG adventurer spread out before him.

"Yeah, that's it. Nothing wrong there. But…"

Masato looked back at Mamako's stat screen.

Cleaning Effectiveness, Laundry Water Conservation, Bathwater Conservation, Food-Prep Saltiness (Reduction), Cooking Preservation Time…an endless sea of options.

Distance from Child (Reduction), Time Spent with Child, Love for Child (Raises All Stats)… No matter how far he scrolled, more appeared.

"There's just too many! I can't decide…"

"Uh, yeah… That's a lot. But that's not the problem. Why are these stats so weird?"

"Well, if I'm raising anything, it should be my love for you! I don't really know what it means by *All Stats*, though. Hyah!"

"W-wait… Augh!?"

Mamako allotted all the SP she'd received to her love for her son—and got even stronger.

Mom's Stats Are All Kinds of Messed Up

Dachima Inaka

After clearing their first dungeon, the party was returning to Catharn to upgrade their equipment.

Porta was in the lead, but she suddenly stopped and stared into the forest.

"Oh! Something's coming out! Careful!"

"A monster!? All right, it's my time to shine! Leave this one to me!"

"No, it's mine! Just give me a second to chant!"

Masato glanced at Wise's fumbling and drew his sword, just as several mouse- and rabbit-type monsters came bursting out of the brush.

Begin combat! With his trusty sword in hand, the hero gallantly steps forward to slaughter the enemy…!

"Oh my! Monsters! Here goes! Hyah! Hyaaah!"

Mamako attacked; rock spikes shot out of the ground, and water bullets fired out of thin air with each swing of her holy swords, tearing all the monsters to shreds.

The monsters were defeated! Combat complete.

Masato's time to shine? Never came.

"Ma-kun, how was that? Mommy did her best! Eh-heh-heh!"

"Eh-heh-heh, my— I was all pumped, too! I wanted to attack!"

Unable to repress his growing irritation, Masato turned to give Mamako a lecture on fair play vis-à-vis her child.

But at that moment, a cheery sound effect played, and windows appeared in front of both of them, informing them that they'd leveled up.

"Oh my! A level up! Isn't that nice, Ma-kun?"

"Y-yeah…sure, that's great."

This good news helped Masato calm down a little. He decided to complain about Mamako later and began poking at the window.

When he switched to the status screen, he saw that his level had gone up by one and his HP, MP, Attack, and Defense had all been raised slightly.

He'd also received some SP, which could be spent to increase core stats or acquire new skills.

"Three more SP… Should I assign them to stats right away or bank them…? Hmm…"

"Couldn't hurt to boost your stats a bit. At this rate, you'll never catch up to Mamako. Pfft."

"Like you have, Wise?"

"Urk, that backfired…"

DO YOU LOVE YOUR MOM AND HER TWO-HIT, MULTI-TARGET ATTACKS?

COMIC: MEICHA
STORY: DACHIMA INAKA, ILLUST: IIDA POCHI.
VOLUME 2

Author: DACHIMA INAKA

Postscript

Inaka here! Thanks for reading.
Thanks to the efforts of Meicha, my editor, and all sorts of people involved in publication, the second volume of the *Mom* manga is now available. I'd like to wish them congratulations and offer my thanks.
The other day, I had a reminder of just how great manga is. *Mom* is being adapted into an anime. (I'm so grateful.)
Checking various minute details about the setting is part of that process. But I couldn't remember which page or line that information was on.
Then...manga to the rescue! It's so easy to find thanks to the pictures! Saves so much time.
I'm very grateful that even the smallest details of the setting have been carefully included here. Meicha, you really bailed me out!
This adventure with *Mom* will continue! I would love for it to keep going forever.
Thank you all again.

STAFF LIST

The author
Meicha

Assistant
Makoto Fujibayashi
Marugoshi

Design
Tsuyoshi Kusano Design